Civil War Q&A

Civil War Q&A
A Knowledge Challenge Handbook

LLOYD W. KLEIN *and*
ERIC J. WITTENBERG

McFarland & Company, Inc., Publishers
Jefferson, North Carolina

All photographs and other visual materials used in this book are believed to be in the public domain unless otherwise noted.

Library of Congress Cataloguing-in-Publication Data

Names: Klein, Lloyd W., author. | Wittenberg, Eric J., 1961– author.
Title: Civil War Q&A : a knowledge challenge handbook / Lloyd W. Klein and Eric J. Wittenberg.
Other titles: Civil War Q & A
Description: Jefferson, North Carolina : McFarland & Company, Inc., Publishers, 2023 | Includes bibliographical references and index.
Identifiers: LCCN 2023028807 | ISBN 9781476691237 (paperback : acid free paper) ∞
ISBN 9781476649559 (ebook)
Subjects: LCSH: United States—History—Civil War, 1861-1865—Miscellanea.
Classification: LCC E468 .K577 2023 | DDC 973.7—dc23/eng/20230705
LC record available at https://lccn.loc.gov/2023028807

British Library cataloguing data are available

ISBN (print) 978-1-4766-9123-7
ISBN (ebook) 978-1-4766-4955-9

© 2023 Lloyd W. Klein and Eric J. Wittenberg. All rights reserved

No part of this book may be reproduced or transmitted in any form or by any means, electronic or mechanical, including photocopying or recording, or by any information storage and retrieval system, without permission in writing from the publisher.

Front cover image: an engraving of Pickett's Charge at Gettysburg by Alfred Swinton (1826-1920) circa 1903 (Library of Congress)

Printed in the United States of America

McFarland & Company, Inc., Publishers
Box 611, Jefferson, North Carolina 28640
www.mcfarlandpub.com

To Barbara
Who possesses the perceptiveness of Mary Chesnut, the shrewdness of Elizabeth Van Lew, the organization skills of Clara Barton, and the business acumen of Mother Bickerdyke.
—Lloyd W. Klein

For Susan. None of this would be possible without your love and support.
—Eric J. Wittenberg

Table of Contents

Preface   1

Section	Topic		Pages
I	Prologue to the Civil War	Challenges Answers	3 17
II	Political Personalities	Challenges Answers	35 47
III	Lincoln's Speeches and Quotations	Challenges Answers	56 60
IV	Economic Issues of the War	Challenges Answers	66 72
V	Military Personalities	Challenges Answers	83 97
VI	1861 Battles and Campaigns	Challenges Answers	115 119
VII	1862 Battles and Campaigns	Challenges Answers	124 140
VIII	1863 Battles and Campaigns (Except Gettysburg)	Challenges Answers	157 166

Section	Topic		Pages
IX	Gettysburg	Challenges Answers	176 196
X	1864 Battles and Campaigns	Challenges Answers	217 235
XI	Spies and Secret Organizations	Challenges Answers	250 260
XII	Civil War Medicine	Challenges Answers	272 282
XIII	1865—The End of the War and the Lincoln Assassination	Challenges Answers	291 299

Essential Reading 312

Index 313

Preface

The profound lessons of the Civil War capture the imagination of tens of thousands who enjoy its meanings in many ways: as casual readers, students, tourists, reenactors, collectors, scholars of leadership and military thought, and as Americans who desire insights into our heritage. Those who study the Civil War recognize in the personalities of that time the same spectrum seen in every era: scoundrels, patriots, phony politicians, shrewd businessmen, tough women trailblazers, crooks, authentic geniuses, the courageous, and the unlucky. These imperfect people lived in an extraordinary time and made our country the nation it is.

To be a Civil War "buff" is a daunting prospect: it is impossible to read all of the estimated 60,000 books and thousands more articles. It's challenging to fully master even a single aspect, let alone the entire historical genre. Civil War aficionados take pride in their depth of knowledge of the personalities and events that led to the war, the political and economic issues that arose, and the battles and the campaigns. Everyone seeks ways to objectively evaluate and improve one's knowledge base and to self-assess areas in which further exploration would be beneficial.

The purpose of this book is to fill that void by challenging the reader to recall facts and details and to organize them to better understand the larger picture. Nearly 200 challenges covering the full range of the war were developed to stimulate a review of the critical moments. The "answers" given to the challenges posed are intrinsically incomplete and intended only as an introduction and invitation to the reader to further in-depth exploration. Sources for essential and further readings are suggested. It is anticipated that the reader will read and refer to sections of interest out of order; this book does not have to be experienced in a linear manner.

When we study history, we have an obligation to discover what really happened and why. Often in this quest, we discover that certain beliefs and facts we hold as truth aren't accurate; this can be distressing and disturbing. The single most important purpose of this book is to challenge you to reconsider what you think you know. If you come away recognizing that men considered great had flaws and those pronounced weak weren't that bad, then this book has fulfilled its mission.

Acknowledgments

Thanks to Edward Alexander who created all new battle maps to accompany this volume. Special thanks to our online friends who participate in the daily Coffee Cup Challenge Series; the concept of this book resulted from these stimulating and educational discussions.

—Lloyd W. Klein and Eric J. Wittenberg, September 2022

Section I

Prelude to the Civil War

Challenges

Challenge #I-1

Wars are the consequences of political calculations, cultural perceptions, and financial apprehensions. Considerations of power gradients, economic pressures, and social/political organization are critical influences. Wars represent the end result of diplomatic failures and are often an extreme extension of policy.

The Civil War occurred because citizens of both the North and the South perceived threats to their way of life and future prosperity. The South fought the war to preserve their social structure and expand slavery; the North fought to preserve the Union and prevent secession. Secession was the immediate cause of the war, and slavery was the primary cause of secession. There is no cogent analysis that does not recognize this foundation of the Civil War.

Challenge: What were the reasons for the Civil War? In what ways was slavery the root cause? Was the conflict necessary?

Challenge #I-2

In August 1619, the first recorded enslaved men carried from Africa to British North America arrived at the Jamestown colony of Virginia. They had been removed from a Portuguese slave ship and carried on the *White Lion*, an English privateer commanded by John Jope. The approximately 20 Africans on board were immediately sold as slave labor. With this event, 1619 is often identified as the origin of slavery in America, although captive Africans likely were present in the Americas as early as 1526. The first Africans brought to the colony of Virginia were Kimbundu-speaking peoples from the kingdom of Ndongo, located in present-day Angola. In the English colonies, slave status for Africans became hereditary with the adoption and application of civil law into colonial law.

The American Revolution generated widespread debate surrounding the morality of slavery and its consistency with the founding beliefs and doctrines of the nation. Both immediate and gradual emancipation in northern states resulted. Manumission also occurred, notably in Virginia. In 1782, the Virginia Assembly removed restrictions on masters to free their slaves, and in 1783, the assembly freed slaves who had fought on behalf of the Continental army. These new laws led to the rapid growth of Virginia's free black population. By 1810, there were 30,000 freed blacks in Virginia. However, South Carolina and Georgia remained committed to the African slave trade.

It is highly likely that unless the 1787 Constitutional Convention found a compromise over how to count slaves in determining a state's population, no alteration to the Articles of Confederation could have been ratified.

Challenges: (1) What was the compromise? (2) Why was it important?

Challenge #I-3

In 1820, the applications of Maine and Missouri for statehood further tested the enthusiasm of expanding slavery in the new nation. The Senate would lose its equal balance unless Missouri were admitted as a slave state. Henry Clay of Kentucky engineered a compromise in which Missouri would be admitted as a slave state, but slavery would be excluded from all remaining lands of the Louisiana Purchase north of the 36° 30' parallel.

The Mexican War (April 1846–February 1848) was the prelude to the expansion debate. It began after the annexation of Texas by the United States in 1845 and the subsequent dispute over its border (Nueces River, the Mexican claim versus the Rio Grande, the U.S. claim). The war resulted in the United States' acquisition of >500,000 square miles extending westward from the Rio Grande to the Pacific Ocean.

Support for the war divided by party lines: Democrats, particularly in the South, favored it, but Whigs questioned whether the Polk administration had created a war expressly to expand slavery by the acquisition of new territories below the Missouri Compromise line, designed to augment the South's political power. This question led to opposition to the war, especially among Whigs, including John Quincy Adams and first-term congressman Abraham Lincoln.

Emerging victorious, with the Treaty of Guadalupe Hidalgo, the United States did indeed expand its southern land holdings. Mexico relinquished the land now composing the states of New Mexico, Utah, Nevada, Arizona, California, Texas, and western Colorado for $15 million. These new land acquisitions intensified the debate over slavery. The South wanted all territories to be slave states, as stipulated in the Missouri Compromise. Such a decision would alter the balance of power and was opposed by the North. How many slave states would be admitted from this land mass?

President Polk submitted to Congress an appropriations bill for $2 million to settle the boundaries. Arrangements were made for the bill to be considered in a special session of the House in which the debate was to last two hours with no speech longer than 10 minutes. A congressman from Pennsylvania who strongly supported the Polk administration and was seen as a Southern sympathizer was recognized. His proposal forever changed the question of slavery in the territories.

Challenge: Who was he and what was his proposed amendment to the bill?

Challenge #I-4

Some have suggested that the origin of the Civil War began over a dispute over tariffs in 1828. What started as a debate over the rising tariff on foreign goods culminated in a crisis when the so-called Tariff of Abominations passed. Whether or not states in opposition to the tariff had to enforce it ("nullification") transformed into debates over state versus federal sovereignty. A crisis resulted when South Carolina threatened secession, an explicit threat of disunion.

The U.S. Constitution provided for tariffs as a means to produce revenue, and the concept of protective tariffs had been central to American economic policy since 1816. Tariffs were the major source of government revenue before the Civil War. Henry Clay of Kentucky adapted Alexander Hamilton's views to also protect American producers, which he titled the "American System." His concept was to incorporate high protective tariffs on imported manufactured goods to encourage the development of American industry. Initially, the added price that tariffs superimposed were relatively low but progressively increased annually. The 1828 tariff raised duties very high, as much as 30–50 percent on certain goods; these were intended to protect the mid-Atlantic and western states that produced them. Foreign markets blocked the sale of American cotton, the South's major export, in retaliation. Despite the South's objection, President Jackson maintained Southern support for his presidential campaign and, by backing the tariff, gained support from Northern and border states, which helped him win reelection.

Two years later, a debate in the U.S. Senate between South Carolina senator Robert Hayne and Massachusetts senator Daniel Webster reopened the argument. Hayne's position was that states were sovereign entities and hence permitted to nullify federal rulings when those rulings infringed on states' interests. He went so far as to argue that secession might be a remedy in order to preserve state and personal liberty.

Challenges: (1) What was Webster's famous response to Hayne and why was it important? (2) How was the nullification crisis and the concept of state's rights a forerunner of secession? (3) Did the imposition of tariffs cause the Civil War?

Challenge #I-5

One of the recurring myths of the prewar period is that slavery was dying and would have ended eventually without a war if only the North would have left it alone. In fact, the number of slaves was increasing throughout the antebellum period. Slavery had been present for 200 years before 1800 with relatively minimal increase in the slave population. In fact, accounts of plantation life before 1800 showed agricultural profitability to be low. But in the early 1800s, an exponential increase in the enslaved population and a massive increase in cotton production occurred.

Challenges: Describe the economics of slavery from a profit-cost perspective. Consider:

(1) if slavery was such a profitable labor management system, why was it failing before the founding of the United States? (2) What innovations changed this balance?

Challenge #I-6

The Underground Railroad was an association providing shelter to escaped enslaved people. It comprised a network of secret routes and safe houses used by enslaved African Americans to escape from the South into free states and Canada. Abolitionists and others sympathetic to the cause of freeing the slaves assisted. It was illegal to escape or to assist in the escape because of the Fugitive Slave Laws.

The "railroad" developed as a convergence of numerous separate clandestine efforts. Quaker abolitionist Isaac T. Hopper created an organization in Philadelphia early in the 19th century to assist escaped enslaved people. Quakers in North Carolina established abolitionist groups that also developed routes and shelters for escapees. The African Methodist Episcopal Church was another religious group that helped fugitive enslaved people.

For the most part, the Underground Railroad assisted escapees mainly from Kentucky, Virginia, and Maryland. But in the Deep South, the Fugitive Slave Acts made capturing escaped slaves a lucrative business; for that reason, it was a dangerous practice with fewer hiding places. Fugitive enslaved people were often on their own until they got farther north.

Challenges: (1) Who was the most celebrated conductor? (2) How did the railroad work?

Challenge #I-7

Senator Henry Clay of Kentucky was a secretary of state and speaker of the House, a founder of the Whig and Republican Parties, and renowned as "The Great Compromiser" for his work on the Missouri Compromise and as the primary creator of the compromise of 1850. Concerned over the growing anger in the rhetoric between North and South, he hoped to avoid civil war by enacting a long-term compromise over the issue of slavery. He succeeded in finding two critical supporters. Massachusetts senator Daniel Webster viewed the compromise of 1850 as a means of averting national conflict, but his support for the compromise disappointed his abolitionist supporters because it seemed to allow the extension of slavery. John C. Calhoun, a former vice president, now a senator from South Carolina, favored the expansion of slavery into new territories but agreed a compromise was the best solution.

When the full compromise failed to pass, Clay, facing health problems, grew too ill to argue his case further and withdrew. Stephen A. Douglas of Illinois saw an opportunity for both a compromise and personal advancement; he divided the omnibus bill into individual bills, which allowed a vote on each bill. The death of President Zachary Taylor and the subsequent promotion of pro-compromise Vice President Millard Fillmore contributed to facilitating the passage of each bill.

Challenges: (1) What did Webster and Clay say, and what were the implications for these men? (2) By dividing the compromise into five separate bills, Douglas was able to pass all even though bundled together it could not pass. That is highly unusual, as typically compromises pass as a group when separately they could not. Explain how Douglas managed this. (3) What were the five laws constituting the compromise of 1850?

Challenge #I-8

The Fugitive Slave Act of 1793 was a federal law that was written with the intent to enforce Article 4, Section 2, Clause 3 of the U.S. Constitution, which required the return of runaway enslaved people. The purpose of the law was to force free states to return fugitives of enslavement to their masters.

In response, Northern states passed "personal liberty laws," which required a jury trial before fugitive slaves could be returned. In some places, laws prohibited the use of jails or state officials to assist in the arrest or return of fugitive slaves. There were cases in which juries in state cases refused to convict individuals who had been indicted under the federal law. In fact, the Northern states practiced a form of nullification and argued for states' rights in this situation.

Challenge: What were the terms of the Fugitive Slave Act of 1850, and how did this contribute to causing the Civil War?

Challenge #I-9

Stephen Douglas's most significant contribution to the politics of the 1850s was to promote popular sovereignty as a middle position on the slavery issue. Under popular sovereignty, the people residing in a territory would decide whether or not their state would allow slavery. He said that residents of territories should be empowered to decide by voting whether or not slavery would be allowed in their territory. The federal government did not make the decision, and by appealing to democracy, Douglas hoped he could finesse the question of support for or opposed to slavery.

Mandated popular sovereignty was the underlying precept applied to Kansas in the Kansas-Nebraska Act, which passed Congress in 1854. The bill overturned the Missouri Compromise's use of latitude as the boundary between slave and free territory.

Douglas may have believed that slavery was already in a dying mode. It was widely thought that slavery would only be profitable where cotton and rice were grown; hence, slavery would not expand in unfavorable climatic conditions where the soil could not germinate these crops. In addition, Douglas also thought that the issue of slavery could be resolved if it were taken as a problem of the local community, not a constitutional one. These reasons led him to think that a compromise on the controversial question was the most politically expedient way to deal with them.

Douglas had initially sought to organize the territory of Nebraska for statehood. But Southern senators objected; the region lay north of latitude

36° 30' and so under the terms of the Missouri Compromise of 1820 would become a free state, affecting the delicate political balance in Congress. To gain the Southerners' support, Douglas proposed creating two territories in the area—Kansas and Nebraska—and repealing the Missouri Compromise. The question of whether the territories would be slave or free would be left to the settlers under the principle of popular sovereignty. Presumably, the more northern territory would oppose slavery while the more southern one would permit it, maintaining the political balance.

Challenge: Sounds like a great compromise in theory, but it backfired and ultimately led to Douglas losing support for his presidential ambitions. What went wrong?

Stephen Douglas by Julian Vannerson (Library of Congress).

Challenge #I-10

With the passage of the Kansas-Nebraska Act, a vote would inevitably be taken by both territories whether slavery would be allowed. Nebraska would easily vote free, but Kansas, bordering Missouri, was uncertain. Both sides attempted to rally supporters. Border state residents were encouraged to move into the territory to increase the voter rolls in their favor. "Bleeding Kansas" describes the repeated outbreaks of violent guerrilla warfare between pro-slavery and anti-slavery forces. About 55 people were killed between 1855 and 1859. The struggle intensified the ongoing debate over the future of slavery and was a violent precursor of what would follow.

In March 1855, elections took place for the first territorial legislature, and thousands of heavily armed "border ruffians" arrived to sway the elections. They ensured the election of a slate of pro-slavery legislators through illegal votes and voter intimidation. Northerners and other anti-slavery settlers ("jayhawkers") refused to accept this government and prepared for violence. In a sharp escalation, a pro-slavery group stormed the free state stronghold of Lawrence on May 21, 1856, destroying printing presses, looting homes and stores, and setting fire to a hotel.

In reaction, the abolitionist John Brown rode through Pottawatomie Valley in Kansas Territory on May 24, along with seven men, including four of his sons. The group dragged five pro-slavery men from their homes along Pottawatomie Creek and murdered them. The Battle of Osawatomie followed in which one of Brown's sons was killed.

In early 1857, in response to the violence surrounding Bleeding Kansas, President James Buchanan resolved to admit Kansas as a state as soon as possible. Buchanan persuaded Senator Robert Walker (Democrat-Mississippi) to serve as the territorial governor. Walker agreed on the condition that any constitution written must be voted on entirely by all the bona fide residents of Kansas, which Buchanan approved. Prior to Walker's arrival in Kansas, the pro-slavery territorial legislature called for a constitutional convention to be held in Lecompton, Kansas, in September 1857. Free-state men refused to participate in the June 1857 election for convention delegates, as they believed pro-slavery influences and fraud tainted the election. Consequently, pro-slavery delegates dominated the constitutional convention. Widespread voter fraud permeated this election; the main culprits of this fraud were ruffians who poured over the border from Missouri to stuff the ballot boxes. Without the authority to do so, Governor Walker rejected the fraudulent ballots, which gave anti-slavery forces control of the territorial legislature. Walker's intervention infuriated the pro-slavery settlers.

Challenges: (1) What were the terms of the Lecompton Constitution, and (2) what was the impact of these events?

Challenge #I-11

On May 22, 1856, in the U.S. Senate chamber, Representative Preston Brooks, a pro-slavery Democrat from South Carolina, used his walking cane to beat Senator Charles Sumner, an abolitionist Republican from Massachusetts. The attack was in retaliation for a speech given by Sumner two days earlier in which he fiercely criticized slaveholders, including a relative of Brooks, Andrew Butler. The beating nearly killed Sumner and contributed significantly to the country's polarization over the issue of slavery. His symptoms were consistent with what is now called traumatic brain injury, and he required three years' convalescing before returning to his Senate seat.

Challenge: What does a physical altercation in the U.S. Senate five years before the Civil War illustrate?

Challenge #I-12

A major contributing factor to the war was that the South wanted to expand slavery within the territories and even to expand the land holdings of the United States to create more slave states. A prime example was a memorandum written in 1854 by the U.S. ambassadors to Madrid, Paris, and London (the latter was to be the next U.S. president, James Buchanan) in which a land purchase was offered. It was stated that if not accepted, the United States would be "justified in wresting" the land for reasons of "national security." When the document's contents were leaked to the press by one of its authors, the Pierce administration tried to hide it; when it was released, its contents were highly embarrassing. Pierce had always been sympathetic to the Southern cause, but this incident suggested that the Democratic Party was ready to declare a war to further the interests of the slave holding states, which seemed to confirm the concerns expressed over the Mexican War. Northerners were outraged by what they considered a Southern attempt to extend slavery by starting a war. The controversy contributed to the divisions within the Democratic Party by presenting an obstacle between Northern and Southern Democrats.

Challenges: (1) What was the land in dispute, and (2) what was the name of this document?

Challenge #I-13

James Gadsden was a staunch secessionist and supporter of nullification from South Carolina. The Gadsden Purchase is named after him, pertaining to land that the United States bought from Mexico and that became the southern portions of Arizona and New Mexico. Gadsden considered slavery "a social blessing" and abolitionists "the greatest curse of the nation."

After graduating from Yale, he served directly under General Andrew Jackson. He served as U.S. minister to Mexico from 1853 to 1856, and it was in this role that the land of the Gadsden Purchase was negotiated and sold to the United States.

After the Mexican War, the Treaty of Guadalupe Hidalgo left much of the boundary between the United States and Mexico vague. In particular, the Mesilla Valley of New Mexico, north of El Paso, was an area of great conflict. President Pierce appointed Gadsden to purchase this land.

The land for southern New Mexico and Arizona was purchased for $10 million, and the boundary between the United States and Mexico was set as two long line segments between the Rio Grande at the western tip of Texas all the way to the River Colorado at the eastern boundary of California. The land bought by the Gadsden Purchase contains the site of Arizona's second largest city, Tucson, a one-time Spanish presidio town, as well as Las Cruces, New Mexico. Most of the land is an entirely uninhabitable part of the Sonoran Desert.

Challenges: (1) Why did President Pierce want to buy land that basically has no use, even to this day? (2) Why was Gadsden the right man for this job? So much so that the land purchase is named after him, not Pierce!

Challenge #I-14

The Dred Scott decision directly precipitated the war by tying the hands of Congress, preventing any compromise on the issues of fugitive slave laws and expansion of slavery into the territories. Dred Scott was an escaped slave who unsuccessfully sued for his freedom and that of his wife, Harriet, and their two daughters. Scott and his wife claimed their freedom because they had lived in Illinois and the Wisconsin Territory for four years as free blacks; in these states, slavery was illegal and the laws said that slaveholders gave up their rights if they stayed for an extended period. When his owners brought him back to Missouri, Scott sued for his freedom: first in Missouri state court, which ruled that he was still a slave under its law, and then in U.S. federal court, which ruled against him, deciding that it must apply Missouri law. He ultimately appealed these rulings to the U.S. Supreme Court.

In *Dred Scott v. Sandford* (1857), the U.S. Supreme Court decided 7–2 against Scott, finding that neither he nor any other person of African ancestry could claim citizenship in the United States, and therefore Scott could not legally bring suit in federal court. On behalf of the majority, Taney ruled that because Scott was considered the private property of his owners, he was subject to the Fifth Amendment, prohibiting the taking of property from its owner "without due process." Hence, Scott's temporary residence outside Missouri did not bring about his emancipation, as it would "improperly deprive Scott's owner of his legal property."

This ruling appeared to be in conflict with the provisions of the Missouri Compromise, passed in 1820, that admitted Missouri as a slave state in exchange for legislation that prohibited slavery north of the 36° 30' parallel except for Missouri. Taney noted that the compromise's legal provisions was intended to free slaves who were living north of this borderline in the western territories. Taney decided that this requirement constituted the government depriving slaveowners of their property. Therefore, the Missouri Compromise, which had kept the peace for 37 years, was ruled unconstitutional.

Challenges: (1) Why was the determination that the Missouri Compromise unconstitutional unnecessary? (2) Can a person be a citizen of a state but not of the country? (3) How was this aspect of the decision considered in legal parlance? (4) What was the political impact of the decision?

Challenge #I-15

The Lincoln-Douglas debates of 1858 was perhaps the most erudite discussion of slavery in the prewar period, particularly the issue of its expansion into the territories. Douglas's critical leadership in passing the compromise of 1850, including the Fugitive Slave Act, was a major topic. Moreover, his Kansas-Nebraska Act repealed the Missouri Compromise's ban on slavery in those territories and replaced it with the doctrine of popular sovereignty. Dred Scott made the status of fugitive slaves and the issue of territorial expansion other critical issues.

At the second debate, in Freeport, Illinois, Lincoln put Douglas in a position where he had to choose between two bad options; whichever response Douglas made would impact his chances of getting reelected. After Douglas indicated his respect for Supreme Court decisions, Lincoln requested that Douglas reconcile the concept of popular sovereignty with the Dred Scott decision. If states had to accept slavery because of the Constitution, how could territories decide by popular vote? Specifically, how can people choose to be free or slave if the Constitution precluded any restriction on slavery?

Challenge: What was Douglas's response, and why did it become a serious problem for Douglas?

Challenge #I-16

John J. Crittenden was a Kentuckian who served as congressman, senator, governor, and U.S. attorney general before the war. He is often remembered as Henry Clay's successor as a border state Whig and compromiser. He was frequently mentioned as a possible candidate for the presidency but always declined to run. He joined the Know-Nothing Party after the Whig Party collapse. In 1860, he organized and founded the Constitutional Union Party, though he refused the party's nomination for president in the 1860 election. After Lincoln's election, Crittenden proposed a series of resolutions and constitutional amendments to avert war.

Challenges: (1) What was the Crittenden Compromise? (2) How involved was his family during the war?

Challenge #I-17

The Corwin Amendment was proposed after the election of 1860 to reconcile the sectional differences on slavery and avoid the secession of the border states. Senator William H. Seward and Representative Thomas Corwin introduced the Corwin Amendment, which was endorsed by President James Buchanan. The amendment stated simply, "No amendment shall be made to the Constitution which will authorize or give to Congress the power to abolish or interfere, within any State, with the domestic institutions thereof, including that of persons held to labor or service by the laws of said State."

Challenges: (1) How would this amendment have prevented the Civil War? You will note that there is no mention of slavery! (2) What happened with it? (3) What was Lincoln's position? (4) The fact that the North proposed it is often interpreted as meaning that slavery wasn't the cause of the war. Is this accurate?

Challenge #I-18

The four border states were Kentucky, Missouri, Maryland, and Delaware. Also, the northwest rural area of Virginia remained Unionist; it later formed a new state, West Virginia, which became a fifth border state. Note that all are south of the Mason-Dixon line but north of the Missouri Compromise parallel.

Complementing their midway geographic location, these states also had an intermediate political identity. Slavery was legal in the border states, and they didn't support Lincoln in the 1860 election. However, there was strong pro–Unionist sentiment. For these reasons, the border states were crucial to the success of the Union. Besides being major agricultural areas of livestock and grain, these states contained transportation and communication lines that were vital to the war.

President Lincoln worked to maintain close relationships with these states. However, their political ideologies and economic realities generated divisions that had to be carefully negotiated, including slavery. Lincoln had to delicately balance the use of military force and political persuasion. How Lincoln kept these states in the Union was central to his success.

Section I. Prelude to the Civil War

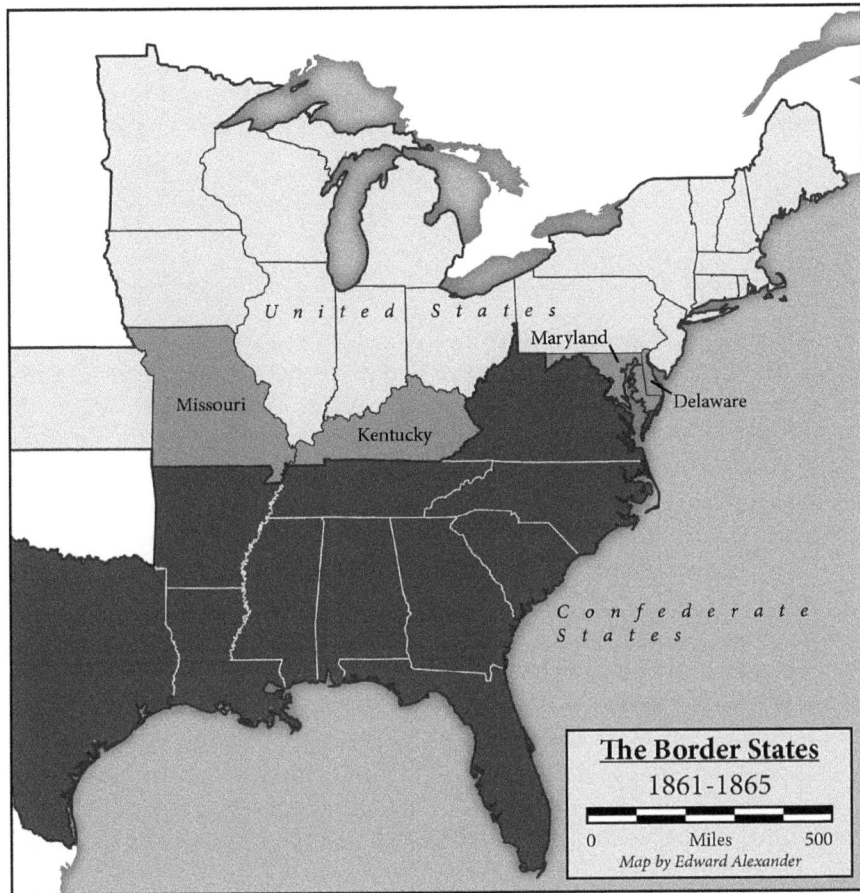

The Border States. Missouri, Kentucky, West Virginia, Maryland, and Delaware are depicted. West Virginia falls along the same geographic distribution: south of the Mason-Dixon Line but north of the agricultural South.

Challenges: (1) In which state did the following events occur?

(a) Lincoln suspended habeas corpus, jailed newspaper editors, arrested a congressman, most of the capital's local officials, and 27 state legislators prior to their meeting to consider secession.

(b) Despite wishing to remain neutral, a Confederate general occupied a city resulting in resignations of the governor and other state officials and ultimately leading to a military occupation and pro-Union sentiment.

(c) Was pro-Union because of its intensive integration into the Union economy and had minimal slavery despite widespread sympathy for the Confederate cause.

(d) A secession convention voted against secession; military action resulted in repeated Confederate defeats leading to a Union government recognized by Lincoln and a secessionist force in the southwest of the state, recognized by the Confederate Congress.

(2) Which of these states was considered the most crucial?

Challenge #I-19

Jefferson and Madison derived their ideas of government from John Locke, an English philosopher. Locke said that government is a social contract (from Rousseau and Hobbes). Governments are legitimate only with the consent of the governed. Power derives from the people (not divine rights as in medieval times), who agree to a contract: the royalty may govern on the people's behalf. In return, the people expect security, fairness, and a way to earn a living, which he articulated as "life, liberty and property." If the government doesn't do those things, then the people have the natural right to throw out the king and put in a different government. But before doing this, the people have to be sure that what the government has done is truly worthy of upheaval.

From this, Jefferson wrote the Declaration of Independence. He notes that men are born with the unalienable (meaning natural) rights to life, liberty, and the pursuit of happiness (changed from property in committee at Benjamin Franklin's suggestion). He then delineated the reasons why revolution was necessary. Twenty-three years later, Madison started with these ideas plus separation of powers (from Montesquieu) to write a constitution. Madison's problem was that he had to figure out a way to turn these philosophical principles into a politically palatable form of government. There were 13 states with many points of views and opinions, each with individual agendas like slavery and religion; there was a huge wealth difference between the affluent (who owned land) and the poor (who had no protections). To build a nation, they all had to compromise.

Challenges: (1) Why did Madison overlook the question of secession? (2) Whether a state could leave the union was a matter of intense discussion in the state ratifying conventions. Which important founding father debated on behalf of the right to leave and, when voted down, would not serve in Washington's cabinet? (3) When the Southern states seceded, did they argue secession was a legal remedy? (4) Was secession legal? Is the U.S. republic an agreement made in perpetuity? (5) What does the Constitution say? (6) What did the Supreme Court say before the war?

Section I. Prelude to the Civil War 17

Answers

Answer #I-1

Slavery was the structure underlying Southern culture, religion, and societal norms. "Slavery" in this context connotes a multitude of repercussions that were influential in causing the war. There were the moral aspects of "owning" humans: denying an entire race their humanity with social acceptance of their mistreatment. There were its economic features: slavery was a labor management strategy with added economic value as property. There were significant political implications: it was a multiplier of Southern votes in adding ⅗ vote for every male slave in the House of Representatives, provided sectional balance in the Senate, and amplified Southern influence over the presidency. There were its cultural properties: a sign of wealth, a floor of poverty, and a simulation of aristocracy. There was the class control of Southern society: the wealthy white, male planters became its leaders, controlling government, the judiciary, and the media. When "slavery" is discussed, all of these meanings are included.

The conflict between Southern agrarianism and Northern mercantilism was at the center of the slavery question because each had distinctive requirements of a labor force. As a moral issue, separate from its political and social implications, there was a wide spectrum of views in both sections of the country. Emancipation was an important motivator of the people of the Union. The North was not united behind the idea of ending slavery at the start of the war, but it was by its end. Conversely, slavery was the foundation of the Confederacy precisely because it was the basis of its economy and culture. The Confederate States of America encompassed a geographic region populated by 5.6 million free white people and 3.9 million enslaved black people.

The South was an agricultural economy; its wealth depended on slave labor (low overhead) to produce the raw materials (e.g., cotton, rice, sugar) that Northern industry turned into consumer products. Slaves had two critical economic functions: (1) slaves provided low overhead agricultural labor, keeping costs down and profits high, and (2) slaves were legally property, like horses or land, and their value was the central investment. The prosperity of planters depended on slaveholding, with a dollar value attached to each. Slave owners used their human property as collateral for bank loans for investment and debt payment. Selling and buying slaves was a lucrative business, and it is critical to understand that if slave commerce were limited, like any commodity, its value would decrease. An oligarchy of wealth and class was created by the ownership of people that depended on its expansion.

The most important political reasons for the South to defend slavery were (1) proportional representation in Congress that provided the South political power over the North for 75 years; (2) recognition that any limitation on slavery would diminish the value of their investments and shrink the geographic, economic, and political influences of the South; (3) fear of a slave revolt—for example, Nat Turner; and (4) insistence on states' rights, primarily to determine property rights—that is, slavery.

Answer #I-2

The Three-Fifths Compromise was an agreement as to how to count slaves to determine the number of seats in the House of Representatives and how much each state would pay in taxes. The compromise agreed on was that three-fifths of each state's slave population would be counted toward that state's total population for the purpose of apportioning the House of Representatives. Free Blacks were counted as one full person for representation. The Three-Fifths Compromise was part of Article 1, Section 2, Clause 3. Section 2 of the 14th Amendment (1868) superseded this clause and explicitly repealed the compromise.

The impact this agreement had is probably immeasurable. First, it resulted in the country having a roughly equal number of states that opposed and favored enslavement, a balance of power in the Senate of immense significance. Second, despite the denial of voting rights for slaves, Southern states received a third more Representatives and a third more presidential electoral votes than if slaves had not been counted. In 1793, Southern slave states had 47 out of 105 seats but would have had just 33 if based on free population; in 1833, 98 out of 240 seats instead of 73.

Another crucial aspect of the compromise is that although the word "slave" does not appear in the Constitution, the language included acknowledged that the institution had been formally endorsed and was a legal practice.

Further Reading

- Applestein, Donald. "The Three-Fifths Compromise: Rationalizing the Irrational." National Constitution Center, February 12, 2013.
- https://courses.lumenlearning.com/atd-fscj-africanamericanhistory/chapter/the-impact-of-the-revolution-on-slavery/
- The History of the Three-Fifths Compromise https://courses.

lumenlearning.com/atd-fscj-africanamericanhistory/chapter/the-impact-of-the-revolution-on-slavery/
- List of the Founding Fathers Who Owned Slaves https://slaveryadvocate.com/list-of-founding-fathers-who-owned-slaves/xhttps://www.thoughtco.com/three-fifths-compromise-4588466
- Wills, Garry. *Negro President: Jefferson and the Slave Power.* Houghton Mifflin, 2003.

Answer #I-3

Congressman David Wilmot of Pennsylvania presented a "proviso" on August 8, 1846. Had it been successful, the Wilmot Proviso would have effectively terminated the 1820 Missouri Compromise because it sought to prohibit slavery in an area below the parallel 36° 30' north. The proviso failed in the Senate where the South had equal representation. Although the Wilmot Proviso never became law, it was extremely important politically, as it essentially codified the position of the North until the compromise of 1850.

The Wilmot Proviso provided that the territories ceded from Mexico would not be slave states:

"Provided, That, as an express and fundamental condition to the acquisition of any territory from the Republic of Mexico by the United States, by virtue of any treaty which may be negotiated between them, and to the use by the Executive of the moneys herein appropriated, neither slavery nor involuntary servitude shall ever exist in any part of said territory, except for crime, whereof the party shall first be duly convicted."

FURTHER READING

- Impact of the Mexican-American War on Slavery
  https://globalpoliticstheory.wordpress.com/2016/12/14/impact-of-the-mexican-american-war-on-slavery/
  https://www.history.com/this-day-in-history/us-congress-declares-war-on-mexico

Answers #I-4

(1) Webster famously responded, "liberty and union, now and forever, one and inseparable." He also told Haynes, "It is, Sir, the people's Constitution, the people's government, made for the people, made by the people, and answerable to the people." Webster's point was that the people,

not the states, composed the union. If allowed, nullification would propagate secession, which in turn would destroy the union, the sole protector of liberty; thus, to protect liberty, one must preserve the union. Those who supported nullification argued that it was the states alone that protected individual freedoms from an overreaching federal government.

(2) President Jackson viewed threats of secession as a test of federal versus state powers. The nullification crisis was the first time states attempted to subvert the Supremacy Clause of the U.S. Constitution. Calhoun asserted that the tariff was "the occasion, rather than the real cause of the present unhappy state of things." The real fear was that the federal government might attack "the peculiar domestic institutions of the Southern States." In 1828, Calhoun secretly drafted the *South Carolina Exposition and Protest*, a pamphlet that laid out the doctrine of nullification. Subsequently, emphasis on states' rights and sectionalism became the norm.

Jackson planned for war and prepared to enter South Carolina to enforce the tariff. Jackson began a national campaign to discredit nullification among the American public, speaking out against nullification and promoting unionism. Jackson did not desire a civil war but hoped the nullifiers would back down. In response, South Carolina delayed the enactment of their ordinance. Jackson then supported Speaker of the House Henry Clay's efforts to lower the tariff. On March 2, 1833, Congress passed the tariff reduction; South Carolina then rescinded the Ordinance of Nullification. Although a compromise avoiding war was achieved, the crisis became the foundation for the secession arguments that reemerged in the 1850s.

(3) Tariffs were not a primary cause of secession. In 1860, when South Carolina seceded, tariffs were fairly low and friendly to the South. The tariffs in place had been set by the Tariff Act of 1857, which were historically at its lowest point in U.S. history. This bill was written by Robert M.T. Hunter, who was a U.S. senator from Virginia. The bill was widely supported in the Southern states, while those who opposed it were mainly from the Northern states. A Southern majority passed it; more Southerners voted in favor of the tariff than Northerners.

The Tariff of 1857 was 15–24 percent and was lower than it had been since before the Tariff of Abominations. Cotton exports were not subject to tariffs or duties of any kind, as articulated by the Export Clause in the U.S. Constitution.

The Morrill Tariff of 1861 is sometimes suggested as a cause of the war, but it passed after seven states seceded, with a vote of 25–14 with 12 abstaining in the Senate; so, without secession, it would not have passed. Confederate politicians made little mention of tariffs in their speeches and are hardly alluded to in the states' secession statements.

FURTHER READING
- https://www.battlefields.org/learn/articles/nullification-crisis
- https://www.essentialcivilwarcurriculum.com/tariffs-and-the-american-civil-war.html#:~:text=On%20the%20eve%20of%20the%20war%20in%201860%2C,mythology%2C%20tariffs%20did%20not%20%E2%80%9Ccause%E2%80%9D%20the%20Civil%20War

Answers #I-5

1. Agricultural production in the South was dependent on slave labor from the mid–1600s through the colonial period and up to 1860. Slave labor was the foundation of tobacco production in Virginia and the Carolinas, rice in South Carolina and Georgia, and sugar in the Caribbean. By the late 1700s, deteriorating tobacco lands and declining prices for Southern crops made slavery unprofitable. George Washington's diaries make clear that his plantation was dependent on continued crop production to pay his loans. The central problem was that the economic costs of slave labor were fixed and high; food, shelter, clothing, and so forth had to be supplied to each owned person, regardless of age, health, or production. Indeed, slave labor managed by threats of minor violence most assuredly could not be as productive as rewarded production or sharing in the profits.

2. Large plantations benefited the most: by having more workers, overall cost per worker decreased and were transformed to variable costs. Large businesses using slave labor could increase output and profit, which allowed them to buy more and better land and more enslaved workers to increase production even further.

Slavery became enormously profitable. Cotton exports alone constituted 50–60 percent of the value of the nation's total exports by 1860. Slave labor provided the raw material for New England's textile mills, stimulating industrialization. Slave-produced commercial crops also required the development of "middlemen," a new occupation, to sell and transport the crops to markets.

FURTHER READING
- Chernow, Ron. *Washington*. Penguin Books, 2011.
- https://www.history.com/news/slavery-profitable-southern-economy
- https://hti.osu.edu/history-lesson-plans/united-states-history/cotton-gin

- https://www.sutori.com/story/eli-whitney-s-cotton-gin—bbUzHn8VKpy5Gy9wtxS32HLf
- https://wps.ablongman.com/wps/media/objects/244/250679/carnesmg/G237A.gif

Answers #I-6

1. Perhaps the most famous conductor was Harriet Tubman. Tubman herself escaped slavery and then organized 19 missions, rescuing around 70 enslaved people, including family and friends. She also led soldiers on missions during the war; after the war, Tubman became an activist in the women's suffrage movement.

2. "Conductors" led the fugitives from station to station at huge personal risk. Sometimes conductors pretended to be one of the enslaved to gain entrance into a plantation. Then the conductor would arrange the escape and lead the runaways to the North. Enslaved people traveled at night, about 10–20 miles between each station. They would stop at the "stations" or "depots" during the day and rest. When the roads seemed clear, a message was sent to the next station to let the "station master" know that new escapees were on their way. The stations were located in basements, barns, churches, caves, hollowed-out riverbanks, and schoolhouses. There were routes that traveled west through Ohio to Indiana and Iowa. An eastern route brought people through Pennsylvania into New England or through Detroit, and sometimes to Canada. Traditional northern "terminals" have traditionally been home to African Americans in communities near Chicago, Detroit, Cleveland, Cincinnati, and other cities.

Further Reading
- https://www.battlefields.org/learn/biographies/harriet-tubman
- http://www.harriet-tubman.org/
- https://www.history.com/topics/black-history/harriet-tubman

Answers #I-7

1. Clay in his speech to the Senate said, "I have, Senators, believed from the first that the agitation of the subject of slavery would, if not prevented by some timely and effective measure, end in disunion." He died several weeks later. Webster lost Northern support

as a presidential candidate. Many believe that Clay, Webster, and Calhoun were among the greatest American politicians never to be elected president.

    2. Douglas recognized that there was a small bipartisan coalition of Whigs and Democrats from both sections who wanted to avoid war. Thus, for each law, he could count on a majority from sectional voting plus this coalition. Three bills won a bipartisan coalition of Whigs and Democrats from both geographic regions, while its opposition arose from the South. The other two bills had the opposite support.

    3. These five laws were the following:

        i. A law allowing slavery in Washington, D.C., but outlawing slave auctions

        ii. A law that added California to the Union as a "free state"

        iii. A law that recognized the Utah and New Mexico territories and provided that they could decide via popular sovereignty if they would permit slavery

        iv. A law that defined boundaries for Texas following the Mexican-American War, removing its claims to parts of New Mexico but awarding the state $10 million in compensation

        v. The Fugitive Slave Act of 1850, which required citizens in every state to apprehend runaway slaves and denied enslaved people a right to trial by jury.

FURTHER READING

- https://www.history.com/topics/abolitionist-movement/compromise-of-1850
- https://www.senate.gov/artandhistory/history/minute/Clays_Last_Compromise.htm

Answer #I-8

The Fugitive Slave Act of 1850 compelled the assistance of every citizen, regardless of local law, in the capture of runaway slaves and, moreover, denied the right to a jury trial. It placed the determination of individual cases under the control of federal commissioners, who were paid more for returning a suspected slave than for freeing them, an obvious bias in favor of Southern slaveholders.

In response to state laws in Pennsylvania and Missouri weakening the original Fugitive Slave Act, the Fugitive Slave Act of 1850 penalized officials who did not arrest runaway slaves. Habeas corpus was declared immaterial. The commissioner before whom the fugitive slave was brought for a hearing—no jury was permitted and the alleged fugitive slave could not testify—was compensated $10 if he found that the individual was a fugitive and only $5 if he determined the proof to be insufficient.

The impact of the new law led to increased traffic in the Underground Railroad during the 1850s. Northern states avoided enforcing the law, and by 1860, the number of runaways successfully returned to slaveholders remained quite low (around 330).

The Fugitive Slave Law of 1850 mobilized Northern anti-slavery citizens who were outraged that despite their moral and legal positions, they and their institutions were responsible for enforcing slavery, including states that had outlawed slavery. Where before, many in the North had little or no opinions or feelings on slavery, this law demanded their direct assent to the practice of human bondage, and it galvanized Northern sentiments against slavery. Abolitionists were confronted with choosing to defy what they believed to be unjust law or ignoring their conscience and following federal law. Harriet Beecher Stowe wrote *Uncle Tom's Cabin* (1852) in partial response to the law.

FURTHER READING

- https://www.history.com/topics/abolitionist-movement/compromise-of-1850

Answers #I-9

The Kansas-Nebraska Act had two unexpected consequences:

1. Dropping the Missouri Compromise of 1820 (which prevented slavery from being allowed in Kansas) became a major boost for the expansion of slavery. Overnight, outrage united anti-slavery forces across the North into an "anti–Nebraska" movement that soon was organized as the Republican Party, with its firm commitment to stop the expansion of slavery.

2. Then, pro- and anti-slavery elements moved into Kansas with the intention of voting slavery up or down, rather than leaving the decision to its long-term inhabitants, leading to a raging state-level civil war, called Bleeding Kansas.

Answers #I-10

From October 19 to November 8, 1857, the pro-slavery convention wrote the Lecompton Constitution, prohibiting any amendment for a period of seven years, required governors to be citizens for at least 20 years, and prohibited free blacks from entering the state. The constitution guaranteed slaveholders their property rights for them and their descendants. The constitution left the question if new slaves could be brought into the territory to the voters. Voters were to have only the options of this constitution with slavery or without slavery. There was no option to reject the constitution entirely, which would have represented the true anti-slavery choice.

Senator Stephen Douglas vehemently opposed the Lecompton Constitution because it lacked true popular sovereignty. Buchanan's support for the Lecompton Constitution never wavered, and it became increasingly clear that he would stake his administration on the passage of a Kansas statehood bill.

Douglas broke with Buchanan and joined with the Republicans trying to block the Kansas statehood bill, but it passed the Senate by a vote of 33–25; Northern anti–Lecompton Democrats and Republicans in the House blocked the passage of the bill by a vote of 120–112. On March 29, 1858, the anti–Lecompton Democrats offered Buchanan a compromise to break the stalemate—they would vote in favor of the statehood bill on the condition that Kansans could amend their constitution at any time and not wait the seven years stipulated. For some reason that perplexes everyone to this day, Buchanan rejected this deal. A joint House-Senate Committee broke the stalemate when they adopted a compromise that the Lecompton Constitution should be sent back to Kansas to be voted on expressly. On August 2, 1858, Kansans overwhelmingly rejected the Lecompton Constitution 11,300–1,788. Kansas was admitted as a free state in 1861 after four more years of conflict.

Stephen Douglas's principle of popular sovereignty lost support in both the North and the South as a possible solution. James Buchanan would not be renominated by the Democrats, and the party would splinter. John Brown would go on to foment violence at Harpers Ferry in 1860.

Further Reading

- https://www.battlefields.org/learn/articles/lecompton-constitution
- https://www.history.com/topics/19th-century/bleeding-kansas
- https://www.nps.gov/articles/bleeding-kansas.htm

Answer #I-11

The threat of violence had actually become real. It has been considered symbolic of the "breakdown of reasoned discourse" and the use of violence that eventually led to the Civil War. The episode revealed the polarization in America, which had now reached the floor of the Senate. Sumner became a martyr in the North and Brooks a hero in the South. Northerners were outraged. The *Cincinnati Gazette* said, "The South cannot tolerate free speech anywhere, and would stifle it in Washington with the bludgeon and the bowie-knife, as they are now trying to stifle it in Kansas by massacre, rapine, and murder." More than a million copies of Sumner's speech were distributed. Two weeks after the caning, Ralph Waldo Emerson described the divide the incident represented: "I do not see how a barbarous community and a civilized community can constitute one state. I think we must get rid of slavery, or we must get rid of freedom."

Answers #I-12

(1) Cuba; (2) The Ostend Manifesto.

The Ostend Manifesto (October 18, 1854) was a communication from three U.S. diplomats to Secretary of State William L. Marcy, advocating U.S. seizure of Cuba from Spain. It stated undiplomatically why the United States should purchase Cuba from Spain and suggested that the United States should declare war if Spain refused.

After Pierre Soulé, the U.S. minister to Spain, was unable to arrange the purchase of Cuba, Marcy requested James Buchanan, minister to Great Britain, and John Y. Mason, minister to France, to meet with Soulé at Ostend, Belgium. He likely expected Buchanan to control the meeting, and it remains a matter of debate as to why Soulé did instead. Soulé leaked the manifesto to the press, precipitating an international scandal. The Whigs insisted on its public release, which was blocked by Pierce for four months.

The Ostend Manifesto called for the United States to exert all possible efforts to annex Cuba, including war. It represents perhaps the most extreme written expression of a Southern dream to export slavery. Cuba's annexation was a known long-term goal of U.S. slaveholding expansionists, so the manifesto appeared to tilt foreign policy toward the interests of one region. Southerners generally favored the idea because of the belief that Cuba would become an independent black republic like Haiti. Northerners were opposed to the manifesto as a clear attempt by Southerners to spread slavery and increase their power in Congress.

The damage to the Pierce administration was irreparable. Pierce was known to be highly sympathetic to the Southern cause, but the controversy over the Ostend Manifesto made clear the depth of his views. It further convinced Whigs and Republicans that a Democrat-controlled "slave power" controlled the country. It was quickly denounced by the national governments in Madrid, London, and Paris, effectively ending any possibility of Cuba's annexation. To preserve international relations, Soulé was ordered to cease discussion of Cuba; he promptly resigned.

The incident contributed significantly to the rise of the Republican Party, and the manifesto was specifically criticized in its first platform in 1856. The Democratic Party began to splinter into Northern and Southern factions. Buchanan was elected president two years later in 1856. Buchanan may have signed the manifesto knowing it would embarrass Secretary Marcy, his main rival for the Democratic nomination, more than it would himself.

FURTHER READING

- Ostend Manifesto https://www.u-s-history.com/pages/h147.html http://dictionary.sensagent.com/Ostend%20Manifesto/en-en/
- *Ostend Manifesto, Controversial Proposal for the United States to Acquire Cuba* https://www.thoughtco.com/ostend-manifesto-4590301

Answer #I-13

Gadsden had served as the president of the South Carolina Railroad Company from 1840 to 1850. This railroad was the longest in the world under one management at one time.

Gadsden was a friend of Jefferson Davis and a sincere believer in slavery. He wanted this land purchase so that a transcontinental railroad using a Southern route—the future Confederacy—could run west across the area. He also wanted California to break up into two parts, with the southern part being pro slavery. Gadsden and his associates promoted the construction of a Southern transcontinental railroad from the Atlantic to the Pacific Oceans as early as 1846. The idea, which Pierce may well have bought into, was that a Confederate independent country would have this route, leading to empire and expansion.

The Southern railroad idea failed because Stephen Douglas wanted the railroad routed through the states that he had a financial interest in, Illinois and Nebraska.

The importance of this event in American history, taken along with the Ostend Manifesto, is its suggestion that the South was thinking of annexation and empire well before secession. The purchase was named for Gadsden since it was his idea from its conception.

FURTHER READING
- https://centrepoints.org/en/Gadsden_Purchase-6206004626

Answers #1-14

Perhaps the most terrible Supreme Court decision of all time, the determination that slaves were property and could never be U.S. citizens, even if freed, is not based on the Constitution. The decision stated that a man could be a citizen of a state but not a citizen of the country. Moreover, slavery could not legally be excluded from U.S. territories or states because it is recognized in the Constitution.

1. If Scott wasn't a citizen, and that precluded his bringing suit in the first place, that should have been the end of the decision. Moreover, there was another reason the court need not consider the Missouri Compromise—it had been repealed in effect by the Kansas-Nebraska Act.

2. Both Justice Benjamin R. Curtis and Justice John McLean wrote dissenting opinions of great value.

Justice Curtis objected to the accuracy of the majority's historical data, noting that black men were allowed to vote in five of the thirteen states of the Union at the time of the ratification of the Constitution. He viewed the right to vote as evidence that black men were already citizens of both their states and of the United States. To argue that Scott was not an American citizen, Curtis wrote, was "more a matter of taste than of law."

"The citizens of each State shall be entitled to all privileges and immunities of citizens in the several States" (Article IV, section 2). Another thing Taney directly contradicted in his ruling by denying that state citizenship accorded African Americans the rights of national citizenship.

Free blacks were given full citizenship and voted in some states—but not allowed on juries. There is no precedent to be a state citizen and not a U.S. citizen.

3. Justice McLean argued that by ruling that Scott was not a citizen, the court had also ruled that it did not have jurisdiction to hear his case. Consequently, McLean contended that the court should have simply dismissed the case without further judgment. McLean's dissent famously stated that the argument that black people could not be citizens "more a matter of taste than of law." He attacked much of the court's decision as obiter dicta (literally, by the way) and thus an opinion that is not legally binding.

4. No question the Constitution at the time protected slavery

in the states; the Three-Fifths Compromise made that clear. But the political effect of the Dred Scott decision was that Congress was also powerless to regulate slavery in the territories because laws like the Missouri Compromise could no longer occur and had no power to prevent its spread. Furthermore, it meant that slavery had to be recognized even in states in which slavery was illegal.

Practically, Taney's ruling threw judicial support to slave power and threatened freesoilers' efforts to restrict slavery's spread. Abraham Lincoln in the House Divided speech illustrated how Taney effectively threatened the power of the free states to ban slavery within their own jurisdiction: "We shall lie down pleasantly dreaming that the people of Missouri are on the verge of making their State free; and we shall awake to the reality, instead, that the Supreme Court has made Illinois a slave State."

FURTHER READING

- Fehenbacher, Don E. *The Dred Scott Case: Its Significance in American Law and Politics*. Oxford University Press, 1978.
- Wallance, Gregory J. *Dred Scott Decision: The Lawsuit That Started the Civil War*. HistoryNet, 2006.
- https://web.archive.org/web/20070930201342/http://www.historynet.com/magazines/civil_war_times/3037746.html

Answers #I-15

Douglas responded with what has since been known as the Freeport Doctrine: that the people of a territory could vote to keep slavery out, despite the Supreme Court decision that the federal government had no authority to exclude slavery, by not passing a slave code and other legislation needed to protect slavery. In other words, it was up to the state to decide on enforcement. This is nullification in its essence and would ordinarily not be considered constitutional. Lincoln's retort was that Douglas was insufficiently convinced of the humanity of the slave. Voting to maintain slavery was beyond self-determination: it was wrong.

Lincoln had taken the moral high ground and articulated the logical and political problem with popular sovereignty. Nevertheless, it was not a strong political response at that time and led to his being on the defensive at Alton. At that debate, his weakest, he was forced to deflect supporting full rights to free blacks. The Freeport Doctrine was also satisfactory to the legislators of Illinois, who reelected Douglas to the Senate.

However, Freeport left Douglas in a position that alienated Southern pro-slavery Democrats who thought he was too weak in his support of slavery. Southern Democrats were demanding protection for slavery, not a shrewd work-around. The Southern Democrats broke off and ran their own candidate against Lincoln and Douglas in 1860. Douglas ultimately became the victim of the very politics he sought to remove from territorial policy by advancing the idea of popular sovereignty. His efforts were not judged in terms of their intent but rather appraised by their actual impact on the power struggle between the North and the South and to the issue of expansion of slavery in the territories. Despite Douglas's intentions, the territories continued to be pawns in the larger political controversy.

Answers #I-16

1. In December 1860, Crittenden proposed a compromise to resolve the secession crisis. The "Crittenden Compromise" was composed of six proposed constitutional amendments and four proposed congressional resolutions that would have guaranteed the permanent existence of slavery by reestablishing the free-slave demarcation line drawn by the 1820 Missouri Compromise. One amendment guaranteed that future constitutional amendments could not change the other five amendments or the three-fifths and fugitive slave clauses of the Constitution. In essence, in return for not seceding, slavery would forever be protected by the Constitution and unconstitutional for future congresses to end slavery.

2. Despite popular support for Crittenden's compromise, Congress failed to enact it. Incoming Secretary of State William Seward backed the plan, but most Republicans agreed with President-Elect Abraham Lincoln, who opposed it; his opposition was determinative.

3. One of his sons was a Union general, another was a Confederate general, and a grandson was killed at the Battle of the Little Bighorn. His son Thomas was a corps commander in the Army of the Cumberland, relieved in the post–Chickamauga housecleaning, and his son George was a Confederate commander early in the war, commanding a division until relieved and court-martialed for drunkenness. Thomas Crittenden was returned to active duty, though at a lower level—he commanded a division in Burnside's Ninth Corps for part of the Overland Campaign.

FURTHER READING

- https://www.history.com/topics/american-civil-war/crittenden-compromise

- https://www.battlefields.org/learn/primary-sources/crittenden-compromise

Answers #I-17

1. The text refers to slavery with terms such as "domestic institutions" and "persons held to labor or service" and avoids using the word "slavery," following the example set by the Constitution. The idea was that slavery in those states that already had it would be protected forever by an amendment, and states that had abolished it would not have to recognize it—an antidote to Dred Scott.

2. The House and Senate both voted in favor of it. Buchanan endorsed it, although the president has no formal role in a constitutional amendment. The amendment was sent to the states for approval and five states ratified it. In theory, it is still a "live" proposal. However, its obvious conflict with the 13th, 14th and 15th Amendments and the question of whether an amendment can be irrevocable pose interesting but abstract questions of constitutional law and enforcement.

3. Lincoln said of it in his first inaugural address: "I understand a proposed amendment to the Constitution—which amendment, however, I have not seen—has passed Congress, to the effect that the Federal Government shall never interfere with the domestic institutions of the States, including that of persons held to service.... Holding such a provision to now be implied constitutional law, I have no objection to its being made express and irrevocable."

4. Actually, it shows that Lincoln had no intention of eliminating slavery in the near term and also that the South wasn't completely honest that fear of Lincoln abolishing slavery was why they seceded. Both sides accepted that slavery in the states was protected constitutionally. What it does demonstrate is that expansion of slavery into the territories was precisely the foundation of the conflict.

Answers #I-18

1. (a) Maryland, (b) Kentucky, (c) Delaware, (d) Missouri

2. Kentucky was strategically crucial to Union victory in the Civil War. Lincoln once said, "I think to lose Kentucky is nearly the same as to lose the whole game." Lincoln reportedly also declared, "I hope to have God on my side, but I must have Kentucky."

On September 3, 1861, Confederate general (and bishop) Leonidas Polk violated Kentucky's neutrality by sending General Pillow to occupy Columbus, Kentucky. Columbus was of strategic importance to both armies because the Mobile and Ohio Railroad terminated there and because of its position along the Mississippi River. Union general Grant responded by entering Paducah on September 6, 1861, which gave the Union control of the mouth of the Tennessee River.

Governor Beriah Magoffin rebuked both sides for violating Kentucky's neutrality and he called for both sides to withdraw. But the next day, the General Assembly passed a resolution ordering the withdrawal of only Confederate forces. Magoffin vetoed it, but both houses voted to override, and Magoffin issued the proclamation, later resigning.

The state's neutrality formally ended on September 18, 1861, when the General Assembly ordered the U.S. flag to be raised over the Kentucky state capitol in Frankfort. Kentucky remained with the Union, which was solidified by the Confederate defeat at Mill Creek in January 1862.

FURTHER READING

- https://www.thegreatcoursesdaily.com/the-american-civil-war-question-of-border-states-loyalty/

Answers #1-19

1. Because a state is part of the government, it has no right to leave it. Like the king can't secede from his government, a state can't secede from the republic. The Constitution is all about regulating the powers of the states and the federal government. The people always have the natural right of revolution—they put in the government and they can change it—but that's not a legal remedy; it's an inherent right of humankind. There is also the reality that every government is self-sustaining and makes no allowances for leaving it.

Madison chose the first words to be "We the People"; that is saying that this document is a social contract made by the people. The people are creating a representative democracy. This agreement lays out which powers are the government's and which are the people's. There is nothing about the states being part of this agreement except they are part of the government. So the Constitution doesn't say anything about states seceding because that makes no sense; they are part of the government, not part of the people. This was debated both at the Constitutional Convention and each state ratification convention. It was not a secret, and it was ratified.

Section I. Prelude to the Civil War

2. Patrick Henry. He became governor of Virginia and would not participate in the U.S. federal government.

3. No, that only came after the war. They left but expected a war and knew a rebellion was treasonous. People can leave the country and rebel (note: that's what they called themselves), but it's not legal to do so.

4. The Union was declared to be perpetual by the "Articles of Confederation and Perpetual Union" (note the title) and subsequently expressed to be made "more perfect" by the Preamble to the Constitution. The Constitution's purpose was to strengthen the weak central government of the Articles of the Confederation. It certainly doesn't follow that strengthening the central government would somehow make the Union nonperpetual. It's very hard to see how a perpetual union writing a document to make itself more perfect could be so if it can be destroyed by any state at will. This was Justice Story's argument well before the war. There is plenty of judicial authority from before 1861 leading to the conclusion that secession was illegal and that the Union was perpetual and in law indestructible.

The words "in order to form a more perfect union" can mean a lot of things. But it can't mean that we aren't perpetual or else it isn't more perfect. Lincoln goes into this in the First Inaugural Address in extraordinary detail. He makes the point, also Justice Story's idea, that even if there were a contract with the states, that there is no contract that only one party can abrogate. Both parties have to agree to end a contract.

5. The Supremacy Clause of the Constitution states that the federal government is the supreme power of the land (Article VI, clause 2), the states notwithstanding.

The Constitution has a specific mechanism for adding states. No such mechanism has ever existed for removing states. One key aspect that would have needed addressing was the disposition of federal land and property in departing states, and the Constitution has no such content. Seceded states seized U.S. property soon after secession (or had it traitorously surrendered) because there was no provision for disposition of federal property, or attacked it directly—for example, Fort Sumter.

One often sees the 9th and 10th Amendments misquoted to say that secession was legal. Neither amendment is to be construed as creating new rights; rather, it protects those not enumerated in the Constitution for the states and the people. Specifically, the states are given benefit of the doubt over federal government. Since secession isn't a right, then it's not a protected right to anyone.

6. The formal legal issue with secession rests on whether the union exists in perpetuity. If it does, then a right to secession can't exist. Justices Story and Marshall decided well before the war that the perpetual guarantee is part of the Constitution. Since there's no right to or power of secession, neither amendment applies here.

It was not the state legislatures that created the Constitution but "We the People of the United States." The arbiter of the Constitution is the Supreme Court, not the courts or legislatures of the individual states. Consequently, individual state governments possess no legitimate authority to declare a severance of the Union. If it were to be severed, that would be a decision for the whole people of the United States. Recognizing this legal problem, the Confederate States of America Constitution clarifies that this agreement—or contract—is with the states.

There were decades of Supreme Court opinions—before the war—saying that the union is absolute. Chief Justice Marshall, a member of the Virginia Ratifying Convention, wrote, "The constitution, when thus adopted, was of complete obligation, and bound the state sovereignties" (17 U.S. 316, 404) and "The people made the constitution, and the people can unmake it. It is the creature of their will, and lives only by their will. But this supreme and irresistible power to make or to unmake, resides only in the whole body of the people, not in any sub-division of them. The attempt of any of the parts to exercise it is usurpation, and ought to be repelled by those to whom the people have delegated their power of repelling it" (19 US 264, 389).

Other antebellum decisions upholding federal supremacy and perpetuity of the nation include *Cohens v. Virginia*, *Fletcher v. Peck*, *McCullough v. Maryland*, *Gibbons v. Ogden*, and *Dodge v. Woolsey*.

Further Reading

- https://studycivilwar.wordpress.com/unilateral-secession-is-illegal/?fbclid=IwAR33J4l5vIN2iNi_4pq79iP-QRq-91M_bgvpNvYhkMfUhuPz_y2UFXJVkA0

Section II

Political Personalities

Challenges

A. **Confederate Politicians**

Challenge #II-1a–c

#II-1a

Jefferson Davis had an impressive political career before he became president of the Confederacy. He served as U.S. congressman, U.S. senator from Mississippi twice, and secretary of war. But he was appointed, not popularly elected, to many of these offices. His limited experience with electoral politics was a handicap to his presidency, including his lack of personal qualities that made Abraham Lincoln a successful president. He didn't listen to the advice of others, chose those who agreed with him for responsible office and eschewed those who didn't, and tended toward dictatorship in his dealings with his Congress.

Challenge: Name the single office to which Jefferson Davis was actually elected by popular vote.

#II-1b

Being secretary of war under Franklin Pierce gave Jefferson Davis quite a few advantages in planning a future country. He knew the nation's military strengths and weaknesses. Most presume that he was thinking ahead, and he was in the perfect position to assure that his future army would have the most experienced officers.

Challenge: Name at least three officers in the old army Davis promoted to privileged command who ultimately became Confederate officers.

#II-1c

Davis was dignified, possessed a distinguished military record, and had extensive experience in political affairs. The fact is that he was not a good choice for this position as history has shown. He really had the wrong personality: he was impatient with others, especially those who disagreed with him. He did not seem to understand people; he chose favorites, and these men seemed to be the least capable. He expected full loyalty from those around him.

Davis's presidency showed him to have a limited knowledge of economics, practical politics, and military strategy. He was a highly manipulative person. He had clearly planned for a Southern nation years in advance, which made him desirable to all sides.

Challenge: Nevertheless, from a political perspective, Davis was the ideal choice of the Confederate Congress. Explain.

Challenge #II-2

Alexander Stephens was a Georgia lawyer and congressman before the war, known for his pro-slavery sentiments. He was a delegate to the Georgia Secession Convention and elected to the Confederate Congress. He became vice president of the Confederacy and gave the Cornerstone Speech. He was one of the three Confederate representatives at the Hampton Road Conference.

Challenges: (1) What was his original position concerning secession at the Georgia state convention and why? (2) What was the purpose of the Cornerstone Speech? (3) What was his

Jefferson Davis by Mathew Brady (Library of Congress).

Section II. Political Personalities   37

relationship with President Jefferson Davis? (4) Why was he one of the commissioners to the Hampton Road Conference?

Challenge #II-3a-e The Confederate Cabinet

#II-3a

Robert Toombs was a lawyer, planter, and politician from Georgia who was one of the primary organizers of the Confederacy. He served as its first secretary of state in Jefferson Davis's cabinet. He later became one of Davis's most outspoken critics.

He had ambitions to be the president of the Confederacy. However, public drunkenness and rumors of a severe drinking problem prevented his gaining support at the Montgomery Convention.

Challenge: What important advice did he give Jefferson Davis as his secretary of state that was ignored, leading to their rupture?

#II-3b

Challenge: How many Confederate secretaries of war were there in the four years of its existence?
Name them.

#II-3c

The first Treasury secretary was a hard currency man, but as the war turned against them, he was forced to institute income taxes and produce national currency, which are antithetical to a nation built on states' rights. He put his own portrait on the Confederate $5 bill.

He was also the primary author of the Provisional Confederate Constitution. He moved during the convention to have a committee to draft a constitution of which he had already written a first draft.

Challenges: (1) Who was he? (2) In what crucial ways did the Confederate States of America (CSA) Constitution differ from the U.S. Constitution?

#II-3d

Scarlett: I simply couldn't sleep for thinking. It's not true they're going to hang you? Would you be sorry? Oh, Rhett! **Rhett Butler:** Well, don't worry yet. They have plotted some charge against me, but they're really after my money. They think I made off with the Confederate Treasury. **Scarlett:** Well, did you? **Rhett Butler:** What a leading question.

He was the real-life inspiration for Rhett Butler. A South Carolina plantation owner, businessman, and politician, he was born into a wealthy plantation family. He became director of a large cotton merchant business in the 1850s. During the war, he made millions blockade running and eventually became secretary of the Confederate Treasury. His exploits were as exciting as the character Clark Gable portrayed. He was tall, handsome, fearless, shrewd, highly intelligent, and very rich. Except there was no Scarlett; unlike Rhett, he married at age 21, and he and his wife had 13 children (her name was Anna, FYI).

He was one of the richest men in the South before the war. His grandfather was a huge slave owner in Haiti before the slave revolution. He inherited large holdings of land and slaves. At age 16, he joined a cotton brokerage based in Charleston, South Carolina, called John Fraser and Co. By 1853, he rose to partner and became its managing partner when Fraser died. He was one of the wealthiest men in the United States, owning ships, hotels, docks, plantations, and cotton.

A shipping and banking magnate, he masterminded and amassed an even greater fortune during the war. His business was a commercial firm based in Charleston that shipped cotton to Great Britain, among other ventures. He headed the company starting in 1853. Starting with a cotton export business, the firm diversified to become an international bank representing the CSA and then built and operated ships to run the blockade. The firm served as the overseas banker of the CSA, financing the supply of weaponry and essential goods in exchange for cotton, tobacco, and turpentine.

When secession was declared, he moved his firm's headquarters from New York City to the West Indies and built an ironclad and 12 ships for the Confederacy. He eventually owned 60 commercial ships running the blockade and he became even wealthier. He worked directly with the Confederate government to supply their military needs. He paid for building of ships called blockade runners in England. His firm diversified to become an international bank representing the CSA and then built and operated ships to run the blockade.

He served as Secretary of the Treasury of the Confederacy during the last year of the Civil War and was in charge of the Confederate gold when Richmond fell. It would not be surprising if whatever Confederate gold there was found its way into his pockets.

He never faced legal actions for treason despite the fact that in essence, he bankrolled the Confederate war machine. There is no doubt that he hid his money overseas, in the Caribbean and London, and that his agent, Charles Prioleau, funneled the money here and there. He died a very wealthy man at age 69.

Challenges: (1) Who was he and what was the name of his business? (2) How did he get out of taking responsibility for these obviously treasonous acts?

#II-3e

Judah Philip Benjamin had an amazing career; if Shelby Foote had named a third authentic genius of the war, it should have been Benjamin. A graduate of Yale, he moved to Louisiana to study law. He became a highly successful lawyer, sugar plantation owner, and politician. Benjamin was the first Jewish American to be elected to the U.S. Senate. He was also the first to hold a cabinet position in an American government, including attorney general, secretary of war, and secretary of state in the CSA.

He escaped Richmond with Jefferson Davis at the end of the war, avoided capture, and sailed to England. There, he created a new career as a distinguished barrister and Queen's Counsel. He notably established himself as a distinguished lawyer and public servant in two countries.

Challenges: (1) What was the environment regarding Jews in the Confederacy? (2) What were President Davis's views on Benjamin? (3) How was it possible for him to succeed in a legal career in Britain?

Challenge #II-4a–e The Fire-Eaters and Southern Nationalists

A quotation and a very brief biographical vignette are provided. Your challenge is to identify the person described.

#II-4a

He was a Low Country aristocrat and South Carolina "fire-eater" who campaigned for secession as early as 1844, when he called for his state to stand for nullification or else declare secession. He opposed the compromise of 1850. He became U.S. senator after Calhoun's death. He resigned when his state refused to secede in 1852. He served in the Confederate House of Representatives but never rose beyond, as he was a critic of President Davis.

"Terrors of Submission: If the South once submits to the rule of abolitionists by the general government there is probably an end of all peaceful separation of the Union. We can only escape the ruin they meditate for the South by war. The ruin of the South by the emancipation of her slaves is not like the ruin of any other people. It is not a mere loss of liberty, but it is a loss of liberty, property, home, country, everything that makes life worth living."—From the *Charleston Mercury*

Challenge: Who was he?

#II-4b

This man probably qualifies to be on a short list of the most immoral politicians in American history, and his racial views are just the tip of the iceberg. He owned two plantations and 190 slaves. This South Carolina planter obstructed every attempt to resolve the impending crisis peacefully and then, after secession, resisted providing assistance to the Confederate government.

He wasn't bothered by the morality of slavery:

"The means therefore, whatever they may have been, by which the African race, now in this county, have been reduced to slavery, cannot affect us since they are our property, as your land is your property, by inheritance or purchase and prescriptive right. You will say that man cannot hold property in man. The answer is that he can, and actually does, hold property in his fellow, all over the world, in a variety of forms, and has always done so."

He also famously expressed this view in the Senate on March 4, 1858: "No, you dare not make war on cotton. No power on earth dares to make war upon it. Cotton is king."

Challenge: Who was this reprehensible man and American politician?

#II-4c

This man promoted Southern business development and railroads early in the 1840s and 1850s with an eye to secession. He published a very important Southern magazine in New Orleans with a vision of an independent Southern nation way before anyone else. He was probably the greatest propaganda artist of the Southern antebellum.

"The non-slaveholder of the South preserves the status of the white man, and is not regarded as an inferior or a dependent. He is not told that the Declaration of Independence, when it says that all men are born free and equal, refers to the negro equally with himself.... No white man at the South serves another as a body-servant, to clean his boots, wait on his table, and perform the menial services of his household!"

Challenge: Who was this highly influential man?

#II-4d

This hero of the old South, called "The Prince of the Fire-Eaters," served as U.S. congressman and member of the Confederate Senate from Alabama. He was famous for speaking for hours at a time, completely holding his audience's attention, and was sometimes referred to as the "Orator of Secession." He favored slavery so strongly that he opposed even giving an opportunity for public expression. He was Stephen Douglas's main opponent on the question of popular sovereignty, coining the phrase "squatter sovereignty" as its counterpoint.

From the Charleston Convention, 1860, regarding expansion of slavery into the territories:

"We shall go to the wall upon this issue if events shall demand it, and accept defeat upon it. Let the threatened thunders roll and the lightning flash through the sky, and let the dark cloud now resting on the Southern horizon be pointed out by you. Let the world know that our people are in earnest. In accepting defeat upon that issue, my countrymen, we are bound to rise, if there is virtue in the Constitution. But if we accept your policy, where shall we be?"

Challenge: Who was this highly respected orator?

#II-4e

When you think of a fire-eater, this man comes to mind for his advocacy of states' rights, slavery, and secession. He was elected mayor of Charleston in 1855 and served in the U.S. House of Representatives from 1857 until South Carolina seceded. He participated in the South Carolina state secession convention. He was also a representative from his state at the Confederate convention in Montgomery, which established the provisional government and constitution for the Confederate states. He was later elected to the Confederate House of Representatives.

"They are not contending for an abstract principle—they are not influenced by a mere spirit of fanatical opposition to slavery.... They are deliberately, intentionally, and advisedly aiming a deadly blow at the South. It is intended as a blow. It is intended to repress her energies—to check her development—to diminish and eventually destroy her political weight and influence in this confederacy."

Challenge: (1) Who was he? (2) What is his most famous claim to Confederate fame?

B. Union Political Personalities

Challenge #II-5

Andrew Johnson was selected by Lincoln to be his running mate in 1864. His only qualification was that he was a Democrat who was the only U.S. senator from a Confederate state who did not resign upon his state's secession. Lincoln wanted a war Democrat as his vice president to show national unity. He sent General Daniel Sickles to Tennessee to interview the governor for this post.

Challenge: Johnson's demeanor at his vice presidential inauguration was described by the newspapers as "solemn and dignified." Can you give a better, more accurate description?

Challenge #II-6a–c The Union Cabinet

#II-6a

William Seward was a prominent New York politician who had been elected both governor and senator. He was outspoken in his opposition to the spread of slavery. He had been a Whig who was a founder of the Republican Party.

At the start of the 1860 presidential election, he was the leading candidate for the Republican presidential nomination. However, his opposition to slavery, his support for immigrants and Catholics, and his association with political boss Thurlow Weed provided his opposition with sufficient votes to prevent his gaining the nomination. Despite being devastated by his loss, he nevertheless worked hard and campaigned for Lincoln. He was appointed secretary of state after Lincoln won.

But Seward became Lincoln's closest confidant. Seward worked hard to prevent secession but then became completely devoted to winning the war. His transformation from defeated rival to closest ally was a major reason the Union won. His efforts to prevent foreign intervention in the war were highly effective. He was a target of the Booth assassination plot but remained secretary of state in the Johnson administration.

Challenges: (1) In 1858 in Rochester, New York, Seward made a speech in which he made a highly controversial statement that was so divisive that it may well have led to his defeat for the nomination. What did he say? (2) What national holiday did Seward support and convince Lincoln to declare? (3) Which of the conspirators was responsible for assassinating him? (4) What was his position regarding the impeachment of Andrew Johnson? (5) What state did Seward bring into the Union?

#II-6b

"No President ever had a Cabinet of which the members were so independent, had so large individual followings, and were so inharmonious," noted New York politician Chancey Depew. Doris Kearns Goodwin's *Team of Rivals* explains in great detail that Lincoln believed in keeping one's friends close and one's enemies closer. He also relied on his own judgment in making tough decisions. Despite inherent conflicts of interest, many of his appointees were brilliant administrators who made excellent decisions.

One of them was a ruthless, manipulative politician whose ambition to be president was no secret to anyone. He had run against Lincoln in 1860 and had ongoing impaired relations with the president. His outstanding work as Secretary of the Treasury will be discussed in the Economics section. In order to get him out of the cabinet, Lincoln nominated him to replace Roger Taney as chief justice of the Supreme Court on his death. Nevertheless, he tried and failed to get the Republican nomination for president in 1868 and the Democratic nomination in 1872.

Challenge: Who was he?

#II-6c

Edwin Stanton was a legal rival of Lincoln's before the war in the McCormick reaper patent case, asking Lincoln not to participate out of contempt. He also invented the temporary insanity defense when he became Daniel Sickles's lawyer. He was a pro–Breckinridge Democrat who served as attorney general under Buchanan. He became secretary of war when Simon Cameron was forced to resign. He bristled at the president's directions and occasionally refused to obey them. He often conspired with Salmon Chase behind the president's back. Lincoln respected his resolve and organizational skills and put up with his conceit and treachery. His stealthy capabilities and rumored participation in clandestine and borderline legal conspiracies is one of the recurring themes of the Lincoln administration.

Stanton was a sharp and abusive critic of Lincoln at the beginning of the war.

Challenge: What interesting description did he give to Mr. Lincoln?

Challenge #II-7

Britain proclaimed neutrality at the beginning of the Civil War. The Confederacy was recognized as a belligerent, but it was too premature to recognize it as a sovereign state. The Secretary of State, William Seward, threatened to treat as hostile any country that recognized the Confederacy.

The Trent Affair in November 1861 produced a diplomatic crisis. The British threatened a war and Seward seemed willing to fight. Only Abraham Lincoln kept the crisis in check. Ambassador Charles Francis Adams played a crucial role in resolving it, but for a time, things looked bleak.

Challenges: (1) What was the Trent Affair about? (2) What did Lincoln tell Seward that prevented a war with Britain? (3) How was the crisis averted?

Challenge #II-8a–e The Abolitionists

Two quotes and a brief biographical vignette are provided. Your challenge is to identify the person described.

#II-8a

- "You can not possibly have a broader basis for government than that which includes all the people, with all their rights in their hands, and with an equal power to maintain their rights."
- "The Declaration of Independence had declared 'that all men are created equal....' It is not a declaration of equality of property, bodily strength or beauty, intellectually or moral development, industrial or inventive powers, but equality of RIGHTS—not of one race, but of all races."

He founded the widely read anti-slavery newspaper *The Liberator* in 1831. It was published until slavery was abolished in 1865. He was one of the founders of the American Anti-Slavery Society and promoted immediate and uncompensated, as opposed to gradual and compensated, emancipation of slaves in the United States.

Challenge: Who was he?

#II-8b

- "I believe that no poet in this age can write much that is good unless he gives himself up to [the radical] tendency.... The proof of poetry is, in my mind, that it reduces to the essence of a single line the vague philosophy which is floating in all men's minds, and so render it portable and useful, and ready to the hand."
- "Once to every person and nation come the moment to decide. In the conflict of truth with falsehood, for the good or evil side."

An authentic genius, he was a famous poet, graduate of Harvard College and Harvard Law School, and later professor of languages at Harvard.

He was editor of the *Atlantic Monthly* before becoming the ambassador to Great Britain and the minister to Spain. He believed that poets were prophets and valuable as critics of society. He employed poetry as a mechanism to produce reform, especially regarding abolitionism.
Challenge: Who was he?

#II-8c

- "To be yourself in a world that is constantly trying to make you something else is the greatest accomplishment."
- "A foolish consistency is the hobgoblin of little minds, adored by little statesmen and philosophers and divines."

He was the central figure in American literary romanticism, transcendentalism, and naturalism in the prewar era. He was staunchly opposed to slavery. He gave a number of speeches and lectures favoring abolition and welcomed John Brown to his home. He supported Abraham Lincoln for president. However, he became disappointed that Lincoln was more focused on preserving the Union than eliminating slavery. Once the American Civil War broke out, he made it clear that he believed in immediate emancipation of the slaves.
Challenge: Who was he? Bonus: What is a hobgoblin?

#II-8d

These quotes were said *about* the person in question:

- "What ought to be done with them. We would say: Send them back to the place from whence they came, and if any of their authors, or the agents of them, should be found here, lynch them."—*The Cincinnati Daily Post*, August 1835
- "We have little doubt that his office will be torn down, but we trust that Mr. xxx will receive no personal harm. Notwithstanding his mad notions, we consider him an honest and benevolent man. He is resolute, too. Not having been permitted to open his battery in this State, he is determined to cannonade us from across the river. Isn't it rather too long a shot for execution, Mr. xxx?"—*Louisville Journal*, January 1836

This was one tough man whom others came to hate and threaten violence. He was a member of the American Colonization Society, which advocated for the migration of African Americans to the continent of Africa. In 1833, he rejected its precepts and began to advocate for the immediate abolition of slavery. He subsequently freed his slaves and declared as an abolitionist. In 1835, he moved to Cincinnati and became editor of the *Philanthropist*, which first appeared in January 1836. Although his office was looted three times and he himself narrowly escaped injury at the hands of a mob, he made the paper one of the most influential abolitionist newspapers in the west. He was the two-time presidential nominee of the Liberty Party, a forerunner of the Free-Soil Party.

Challenge: Who was he? Hint: Two of his sons were Union generals.

#II-8e

Challenge: Identify from only two statements.

- "Once you learn to read, you will be forever free."
- "If there is no struggle, there is no progress. Those who profess to favor freedom, and yet depreciate agitation, are men who want crops without plowing up the ground. They want rain without thunder and lightning. They want the ocean without the awful roar of its many waters. This struggle may be a moral one; or it may be a physical one; or it may be both moral and physical; but it must be a struggle. Power concedes nothing without a demand. It never did and it never will."

Answers

Answers #II-1

#II-1a

The only election Davis ever won was an election in 1845 to Congress. All of the other offices he held were either by appointment or votes taken in state legislatures by men of his own economic and social class.

#II-1b

Davis created two new cavalry regiments, and he especially favored the Second Cavalry. He made certain that it had the best weapons, equipment, and horses. The men received new, state-of-the-art rifles and equipped with Colt revolvers. The regiment's elite status is clear by the quality of its officers that Davis hand selected. Most of these officers were from the South. Colonel Albert Sidney Johnston was the commander of the regiment, and the second-in-command was Robert E. Lee. The senior major was William J. Hardee, George Thomas was also a major, and the captains included Earl Van Dorn, Edmund Kirby Smith, and George Stoneman. All of these officers rose to high command and, except Thomas and Stoneman, led the Confederate army.

#II-1c

He was the best choice because although he was not a fire-eater, there was no doubt of his political views: he spoke out strongly for states' rights and favored secession. In fact, like Lincoln, Davis was a compromise candidate. He was the man best positioned to appease both the moderate and radical factions in the Congress. It was known that he would not negotiate on independence.

Why not John Breckinridge who had just carried the South in the election? He was from Kentucky which had not seceded. He remained U.S. vice president under Buchanan and would be named U.S. senator from Kentucky until he resigned. What that Congress wanted was a man of their class and background. Toombs of South Carolina wanted the job, but his drinking problem was on display at the convention. This is why you need elections. Committee appointments don't bring out the executive functions in action needed to lead. These deficits would have been obvious in a campaign.

Further Reading

- Davis, William C. *Jefferson Davis: The Man and His Hour.* Louisiana State University Press, 1996.

Answers #II-2

1. He voted against secession at the Georgia Secession Convention in 1861 and opposed it during the 1860 presidential campaign, arguing that it would take decades to reverse Dred Scott. In fact, there were many Southern Unionists before and during the war. Most, like Stephens, converted to secessionism as its popularity increased after Lincoln's election and especially after South Carolina formally seceded.

2. On March 21, 1861, Stephens gave the Cornerstone Speech in Savannah, Georgia. The purpose was for the new vice president of the new Confederate States of America to articulate the reasons for secession. Here are two brief excerpts:

"The new Constitution has put at rest forever all the agitating questions relating to our peculiar institution—African slavery as it exists among us—the proper status of the Negro in our form of civilization. This was the immediate cause of the late rupture and present revolution."

"Our new government is founded upon exactly the opposite ideas; its foundations are laid, its cornerstone rests, upon the great truth that the negro is not equal to the white man; that slavery, subordination to the superior race, is his natural and normal condition. This, our new government, is the first, in the history of the world, based upon this great physical, philosophical, and moral truth."

3. He became increasingly critical of President Davis's policies as the war progressed. He was especially vocal concerning Confederate conscription and the suspension of habeas corpus.

4. Stephens was a friend of Lincoln when they were both in Congress. It is believed that Davis selected him and the others, who were not his allies, recognizing that it would fail.

Further Reading

- https://www.history.com/topics/american-civil-war/alexander-h-stephens

Answers #II-3

#II-3a

He advised Mr. Davis not to attack Fort Sumter—it would bring on a war. He was advocating for a policy to wait until the Confederacy had a more established military and economic foundation.

#II-3b

Five: Leroy Pope Walker, Judah P. Benjamin, George W. Randolph, James Seddon, and John C. Breckinridge

#II-3c

1. Christopher Memminger
2. At least 18 differences are often cited. Among them:
   - The Preamble was amended so that the Constitution made the states party to the agreement, not the people directly: "We, the people of the Confederate States, each state acting in its sovereign and independent character, in order to form a permanent federal government, establish justice, insure domestic tranquility, and secure the blessings of liberty to ourselves and our posterity—invoking the favor and guidance of Almighty God—do ordain and establish this Constitution for the Confederate States of America."
   - The president was to be elected to a single six-year term. There was no party system.

   It also added two critical sections concerning slavery:
   - Article I, Section 9, Paragraph 4: "No bill of attainder, ex post facto law, or law denying or impairing the right of property in negro slaves shall be passed."
   - Article IV, Section 3, Paragraph 3: "The Confederate States may acquire new territory.... In all such territory, the institution of negro slavery, as it now exists in the Confederate States, shall be recognized and protected by Congress and the territorial government."

To be admitted as a state in the Confederate States of America, a state had to make slavery legal. *https://www.libs.uga.edu/hargrett/selections/confed/trans.html*

#II-3d

1. George Alfred Trenholm; Fraser, Trenholm, & Company
2. Trenholm, just like Rhett Butler, was imprisoned for treason. Just like Rhett, he was believed to have possession of the Confederate gold. Just like Rhett, he used his charm and influence, which extended into the U.S. Army and the White House, and likely his substantial fortune, to get out of prison and secure a pardon. The granting of the pardon was especially clever because he never officially asked for it, nor did he admit that he had done anything wrong.

After his release, Trenholm fought the federal government in lengthy lawsuits. The government claimed Trenholm and his partners had illegally converted today's equivalent of billions of dollars in Confederate assets. He disingenuously claimed he was bankrupt, saying he had lost everything in the war. And just like Rhett, he was cleared and then lived a lavish life until his death. Tomorrow is another day.

#II-3e

1. Anti–Semitic sentiment existed throughout America in the mid–1800s. Jews in the Confederacy were more often accorded equal opportunity than in the North. A substantial amount of money for the Confederate cause came from Jewish philanthropists and businesses. However, as secretary of war, the Southern newspapers unfairly smeared Benjamin when the war went badly. Many people blamed him when the war didn't go well in large part due to anti–Semitism. The word "Judas" was used in print.
2. He escaped Richmond with Davis but separated right before capture. Davis said he thought Benjamin was brilliant. He was Davis's closest confidant and friend.
3. Born in the British West Indies, he was a citizen of Britain, so moving there when the Confederate States of America collapsed was straightforward. His book *Sales and Secured Transactions* remains a standard in English law to this day.

FURTHER READING

- https://bonniekgoodman.medium.com/mysterious-prince-of-the-confederacy-judah-p-benjamin-and-the-jewish-goal-of-whiteness-in-the-65aadc2ba377#:~:text=On%20November%2021%2C%201861%2C%20former%20Senator%20Judah%20P.,states%2C%20and%20the%20rise%20of%20anti-Semitism%20in%20America

- Brook, Daniel. "The Forgotten Confederate Jew. How History Lost Judah P. Benjamin, the Most Prominent American Jew of the 19th Century." *Tablet Magazine*, July 17, 2012. https://www.tabletmag.com/jewish-arts-and-culture/books/106227/the-forgotten-confederate-jew
- Evans, Eli N. *Judah P. Benjamin, the Jewish Confederate*. Free Press, 1989.

Answers #II-4

#II-4a

Robert Barnwell Rhett, editor, *Charleston Mercury* (born Robert Barnwell Smith). He was a congressman and U.S. senator from South Carolina. He was one of the Democratic Party Southern delegates who walked out of the 1860 convention because the platform wasn't sufficiently pro-slavery. It has been said that the resulting presidential election was therefore guaranteed to elect a Republican and that Rhett and others knew this would be the result.

Rhett was elected to the South Carolina Secession Convention, which was the first state to declare secession in December 1860. He was then chosen as a deputy to the Provisional Confederate States Congress in Montgomery. He was the chairman of the committee that reported the Confederate States Constitution. He was a member of the Confederate House of Representatives.

#II-4b

James Henry Hammond. He also had a number of mixed-race children and he was the subject of a scandal of sexual abuse involving at least two of his slaves and perhaps his own illegitimate children. This publicity put his political career on temporary hold but didn't prevent him from being elected to the U.S. Senate.

#II-4c

James Dunwoody Brownson De Bow, editor of *De Bow's Review*. The impact of this journal on antebellum Southern thought was profound.

#II-4d

William Lowndes Yancey. He was really an exciting speaker. Out of context, one might certainly read this speech and find oneself in agreement. That's why it helps knowing exactly what he was referring to. And that was precisely part of his appeal: unless you know he is talking about owning people, you couldn't look at these words and be offended.

#II-4e

(1) William Porcher Miles. (2) He is notable for having designed the most popular version of the Confederate flag. Although it was rejected as the national flag in 1861, the Army of Northern Virginia later adopted it as the battle flag.

Answer #II-5

Drunk or intoxicated would be a place to start. When Andrew Johnson was inaugurated as vice president, he was appreciably inebriated. Michigan senator Zachariah Chandler later wrote, "The inauguration went off very well except that the Vice President Elect was too drunk to perform his duties." As a baseline personality trait, Johnson was an outspoken, cantankerous man. When drunk, he was downright belligerent. One wonders if Sickles, who was no stranger to liquor, sealed the deal over a drink or three.

Johnson had arrived in Washington perhaps suffering from typhoid fever. He seems to have relied on drinking whiskey for a cure. On the evening before his inauguration, Johnson attended a party in his honor and drank heavily. Hungover the following morning at the Capitol, he asked Vice President Hamlin for some whiskey. Hamlin produced a flask and Johnson had two large drinks, stating, "I need all the strength for the occasion I can have."

In the Senate chamber, Johnson delivered a rambling address as Lincoln, the Congress, and numerous dignitaries looked on. The result was one of the most bizarre political speeches ever delivered.

One highlight of this infamous speech was when he called out cabinet members by name and demanded they never forget that power came from the people. Hamlin, sensing what was happening, actually yanked on Johnson's coat to get him to stop, but Johnson kept talking.

Incredibly, things got worse. As he exhorted each member of the cabinet, Johnson forgot a name. David O. Stewart writes in his book *Impeached* that this led Johnson to call out in a "stage whisper" loud enough to be heard by everyone present, "What is the name of the Secretary of the Navy?"

Essentially incomprehensible, he finally stopped to catch his breath. Hamlin hastily swore him in as vice president. Lincoln watched sadly, then went to his own swearing-in outside the Capitol and delivered his acclaimed Second Inaugural Address.

There was still one final embarrassment. Although Johnson attempted to perform his duty of swearing in the new senators, he had to be relieved of the task. He was not seen in Washington again until he was sworn in as president the morning of Lincoln's death.

Answers #II-6

#II-6a

1. Seward said that the United States had two "antagonistic systems [that] are continually coming into closer contact, and collision results…. It is an irrepressible conflict between opposing and enduring forces, and it means that the United States must and will, sooner or later, become entirely either a slave-holding nation, or entirely a free-labor nation." The phrase "irrepressible conflict" was interpreted as a declaration of war by white Southerners. He was therefore seen as radical and ahead of public opinion; Lincoln cultivated a position as middle of the road and flexible, which played much better in New Jersey, Pennsylvania, and Illinois. William Seward was not nominated for president in 1860 because he was considered too anti-slavery. One of the reasons Lincoln was the nominee was that he was seen as acceptable to "moderates" on slavery and thought able to win swing states such as Pennsylvania.

2. He proposed to Lincoln that he proclaim a day of "national thanksgiving," which has been a continuous annual tradition by presidential proclamation since 1863.

3. He was seriously wounded by Lewis Powell, being stabbed in the face and neck five times. Powell also wounded four other members of Seward's household.

4. He opposed impeachment and supported Johnson.

5. He negotiated the purchase of Alaska from Russia for $7 million. The press labeled it "Seward's Folly." Seward also seriously considered purchasing Iceland and Greenland.

#II-6b

Salmon P. Chase

Further Reading

- Semi-fictional: Vidal, Gore. *Lincoln: A Novel*. Vintage, 2000.

#II-6c

Stanton called Lincoln "the original gorilla."

Answers #II-7

1. On November 8, 1861, the USS *San Jacinto*, commanded by Union captain Charles Wilkes, intercepted the British mail packet RMS *Trent*. Two Confederate envoys, James Murray Mason and John Slidell, were made prisoners as contraband of war. The envoys were traveling to Britain and France to make the case for diplomatic recognition and to lobby for financial and military support.

The popular U.S. sentiment was to celebrate the capture and rally against Britain. In the Confederacy, there was hope that the incident would lead to diplomatic recognition by Britain. The Confederates realized their independence potentially depended on foreign intervention.

In Britain, there was widespread disapproval of what was interpreted as a violation of neutral rights. The British government demanded an apology. Palmerston called the action "a declared and gross insult" and demanded the release of the two diplomats. He also ordered 3,000 troops to Canada. In a letter to Queen Victoria on December 5, 1861, he said that if his demands were not met, "Great Britain is in a better state than at any former time to inflict a severe blow upon and to read a lesson to the United States which will not soon be forgotten." In another letter to his foreign secretary, he forecast the possibility of war between Britain and the Union.

2. President Abraham Lincoln did not want to risk war with Britain over this issue. "One war at a time," Lincoln told Seward.

3. The crisis was resolved when the Lincoln administration quietly released the envoys. Officially, the United States disavowed Captain Wilkes's actions but gave no formal apology. Diplomats Mason and Slidell resumed their mission.

The peaceful resolution of the Trent Affair was a serious blow to Confederate diplomacy. Great Britain recognized that the United States was prepared to defend itself when necessary but recognized its responsibility to comply with international law. Moreover, Great Britain and France realized that peace could be preserved as long as the Europeans maintained strict neutrality.

FURTHER READING

- https://www.history.com/topics/american-civil-war/trent-affair

Answers #II-8

#II-8a

William Lloyd Garrison

#II-8b

James Russell Lowell. True Boston blueblood. A quotation from a toast given in 1910 at a Holy Cross alumni dinner: "Here's to dear old Boston, The home of the bean and the cod, Where Lowells speak only to Cabots, and Cabots speak only to God."

#II-8c

Ralph Waldo Emerson
Bonus: An ethereal spirit haunting in nature but crucially, an imaginary one.

#II-8d

James G. Birney. His sons were General David Birney and General William Birney.

#II-8e

Frederick Douglass

FURTHER READING

- Blight, David W. *Frederick Douglass: Prophet of Freedom*. Simon & Schuster, 2018.
- Douglass, Frederick. *Narrative of the Life of Frederick Douglass*. Blackstone, 2019.

SECTION III

Lincoln's Speeches and Quotations

Challenges

Challenge #III-1

A house divided against itself cannot stand. I believe this government cannot endure permanently half slave and half free. I do not expect the Union to be dissolved—I do not expect the house to fall—but I do expect it will cease to be divided. It will become all one thing, or all the other.

Challenges: What does this phrase mean? How was it misinterpreted (intentionally) by Stephen Douglas?

Challenge #III-2

Lincoln did say something like:

The ballot is stronger than the bullet.

And he said it several times. But not exactly that.
Challenge: What did Lincoln actually say? Bonus if you know when and where.

Challenge #III-3

One of his most famous aphorisms was:

You can fool some of the people all of the time, and all of the people some of the time, but you cannot fool all of the people all of the time.

Section III. Lincoln's Speeches and Quotations

Challenge: Did Lincoln really say it? What did he say exactly?

Bonus if you know when and where.

Challenge #III-4

In the Gettysburg Address, Lincoln articulates why the war is being fought and young men are dying. It famously and brilliantly ends with his conclusion,

> that government of the people, by the people, for the people, shall not perish from the earth.

Challenge: Who actually said it first? There are actually four answers.

Abraham Lincoln by Mathew Brady (Library of Congress).

Challenge #III-5

Lincoln once wrote that his primary goal as president was to save the Union and that ending slavery was important to him only as it influenced saving the Union. He then concluded,

> I have here stated my purpose according to my view of official duty; and I intend no modification of my oft-expressed personal wish that all men everywhere could be free.

Challenges: (1) To whom did Lincoln express these words? (2) What does it mean?

Challenge #III-6

> The mystic chords of memory, stretching from every battlefield, and patriot grave, to every living heart and hearthstone, all over this broad land, will yet swell the chorus of the Union, when again touched, as surely they will be, by the better angels of our nature.

In his First Inaugural Address, given before the war had started, Lincoln brilliantly lays out his positions about slavery and where common ground with the secessionists might be found in legal terms. The above quote is his conclusion, calling on the Southern states to reconsider their actions lest war result.

The speech has several points of note. This sentence, though, is the most memorable. Its appeal to "the better angels of our nature" has become widely recognizable. But the reference to the "mystic chords of memory" is often overlooked.

Challenges: (1) Why is memory structured as "mystic chords"? (2) Who first used the phrase "better angels"?

Challenge #III-7

> I defy any man to show that any one of them [the founding fathers] ever, in his whole life, declared that, in his understanding, any proper division of local from federal authority, or any part of the Constitution, forbade the Federal Government to control as to slavery in the federal territories.

Challenges: (1) Where did Mr. Lincoln utter these words, which although not as famous as so many other things he said, actually directly demonstrates the political master he was? (2) Why was this such a virtuoso statement?

Challenge #III-8

> America will never be destroyed from the outside. If we falter and lose our freedoms, it will be because we destroyed ourselves.

This quote has been repurposed a number of times in recent history, including by several U.S. senators and a president's daughter. It certainly seems as if Lincoln's wisdom of 160 years ago remains applicable today. But he never actually said exactly that.

Challenge: What did he say and when did he say it?

Challenge #III-9

> With malice toward none, with charity for all, with firmness in the right as God gives us to see the right.

Only 703 words long, Lincoln's Second Inaugural Address took less than seven minutes to deliver yet contains many of the most memorable phrases

Section III. Lincoln's Speeches and Quotations

in American political oratory. So many book titles emanate from this speech that perhaps every phrase has been usurped. Despite the imminent end of the war in victory, the speech eschewed gloating and rejoicing. Rather, it offered Lincoln's most philosophical reflections on the meaning of the war. The above quote is its best line, widely admired and rightly so; it is at once poetic, reflective, understanding, and prospective. It encapsulates political genius.

But the two sentences that comes just before are deeply intriguing:

> Fondly do we hope, fervently do we pray, that this mighty scourge of war may speedily pass away. Yet, if God wills that it continue until all the wealth piled by the bondsman's two hundred and fifty years of unrequited toil shall be sunk and until every drop of blood drawn with the lash shall be paid by another drawn with the sword as was said three thousand years ago so still it must be said "the judgments of the Lord are true and righteous altogether."

Let's be frank, this is not how politicians speak, not then and not now. This was coming from his heart; this was the lesson that he personally drew from four years of war. The first sentence is an intentionally rhyming couplet, not a device typically used in a political speech. And the second? It's hard to imagine a modern president saying anything like this.

Challenge: What does this passage mean? From where is it derived?

Answers

Answer #III-1

Lincoln's "House Divided" speech was his acceptance of the nomination as the Republican candidate for the U.S. Senate by the Illinois State Convention in Springfield. It derives from Mark 3:24-25: "And if a kingdom be divided against itself, that kingdom cannot stand. And if a house be divided against itself, that house cannot stand."

Stephen Douglas interpreted it during their debates to be an abolitionist declaration. But Lincoln's point was that popular sovereignty, in which each state decided, was not the solution to the slavery question and that a deliberate national choice would need to be made.

Answers #III-2

The ballots versus bullets distinction seems to have been a theme for Lincoln, who used the rhetorical device several times.

1. "To give the victory to the right, not bloody bullets, but peaceful ballots only, are necessary." Republican County Convention at Edwardsville, Illinois, on May 18, 1858. c. May 18, 1858.—*Collected Works of Abraham Lincoln*, ed. Roy P. Basler, vol. 2, p. 454 (1953).

2. His message to Congress of July 4, 1861: "That ballots are the rightful, and peaceful, successors of bullets; and that when ballots have fairly, and constitutionally, decided, there can be no successful appeal, back to bullets" (vol. 4, p. 439); and in a letter to James C. Conkling, August 26, 1863: "There can be no successful appeal from the ballot to the bullet" (vol. 6, p. 410).

3. In *The Writings of Abraham Lincoln*, ed. Arthur Brooks Lapsley (1905), there is a reconstruction, 40 years later, of a speech to the first Republican state convention of Illinois, Bloomington, Illinois, May 29, 1856, in which this sentence appears: "Do not mistake that the ballot is stronger than the bullet" (vol. 2, p. 269).

Answer #III-3

He probably did not ever say this precisely. But maybe he said something like this on September 2, 1858, during his debate with Stephen

Douglas at Clinton, Illinois. The quote first appeared in 1904 by E.E. Pierson, who recalled Lewis Campbell, a respected citizen of DeWitt County, telling him of the 1858 speeches that Lincoln and Douglas delivered in Clinton. According to Campbell, Lincoln said, "Judge Douglas cannot fool the people: you may fool people for a time; you can fool a part of the people all the time; but you can't fool all the people all the time."

Further Reading

- https://historynewsnetwork.org/article/161924

Answers #III-4

1. Theodore Parker was a preacher who gave a speech to an antislavery convention and used this phraseology in Boston's Music Hall on July 4, 1858. Lincoln's law partner, William H. Herndon, visited Boston and returned to Springfield with some of Parker's sermons and addresses. Herndon wrote that Lincoln marked with pencil the portion of the Music Hall address: "There is what I call the American idea.... This idea demands, as the proximate organization thereof, a democracy, that is, a government of all the people, by all the people, for all the people; of course, a government after the principles of eternal justice, the unchanging law of God; for shortness' sake, I will call it the idea of Freedom."

2. Daniel Webster from 1830: "It is, Sir, the people's government, made for the people, made by the people, and answerable to the people. The people of the United States have declared that this Constitution shall be the supreme law." This comment was made while discussing the limitations of states' rights and the supremacy of federal law in his "Second Speech on Foote's Resolution" in the U.S. Senate on January 26, 1830. Garry Wills quotes these two men and gives huge credit to Parker. Wills gives Parker credit for other aspects of the Gettysburg Address as well.

3. Parker may have himself read this as written by British politician Benjamin Disraeli, who expressed the sentiment in his novel *Vivian Grey* (1826): "All power is a trust; that we are accountable for its exercise; that from the people and for the people all springs, and all must exist."

4. In 1384, John Wycliffe wrote in the prologue to his translation of the Bible, "The Bible is for the Government of the People, by the People, and for the People." That's the earliest reference found.

None of this is plagiarism. Lincoln borrowed the phrase and he used it to a new and practical political purpose, not a philosophical or religious one. He was arguing why these young men were dying and why the long war was necessary. In that context, Lincoln's use of an obscure phrase is rightly seen as a mark of genius and political wisdom.

FURTHER READING
- Wills, Garry. *Lincoln at Gettysburg: The Words That Remade America.* Simon & Schuster, 1992.

Answer #III-5

This sentence composes the often-overlooked final paragraph in his letter to Horace Greeley in 1862. He is reiterating that his primary war goal, in his official role as president, was to save the Union, not to free the slaves, although he personally wanted to see them free.

Often, this letter is quoted out of context to suggest that Lincoln didn't really care about slavery. In fact, its intent is to say that while Lincoln the man and citizen hated slavery, his role as president meant he had to do what his job responsibilities required.

One month later, he released the preliminary Emancipation Proclamation having determined that freeing the slaves was a necessary goal of the war, which the majority in the Union now supported.

Answers #III-6

1. Collective memory is essential for patriotism because it reinforces national pride in a country's history. Remembering our traditions and history, cultural ideologies can endure the troubles and difficulties that arise. As long as everyone takes pride in shared values and trials that made our country what it is, we can overcome those obstacles.

A chord refers to a musical term for a harmonic set of multiple notes that are heard simultaneously in a pleasing manner, even though they are different. Each individual has their own memories and reasons to be patriotic, and together we are in perfect harmony. The word "mystic" is used because it's hard to define or understand the origin of a common memory; although it is obscure as to how such bonds develop, they are necessary to feel a shared identity. Lincoln is invoking a spiritual connection among Americans.

2. Shakespeare's *Sonnet 144* (1599):

> The *better angel* is a man right fair,
> The worser spirit a woman colored ill.

The phrase also appears in Shakespeare's *Othello* (1603):

> Did he live now,
> This sight would make him do a desperate turn,
> Yea, curse his *better angel* from his side.

The phrase "our better angels" was from Dickens's novel *Barnaby Rudge* (1841):

> So do the shadows of our own desires stand between us and *our better angels*, and thus their brightness is eclipsed.

Secretary of State William Seward is often given credit for suggesting this phrase to Lincoln.

Answers #III-7

1. New York City 1860; the Cooper Union speech.
2. Lincoln was questioning the Dred Scott decision which held that the constitution didn't allow the federal government to control expansion of slavery, protected slavery forever, and made slaves property without chance of citizenship. This is the position that won him the presidency.

Lincoln's Cooper Union speech lifted him above that of a prairie politician to a serious candidate for the presidency because he alone staked out a principled argument against the spread of slavery and the fugitive slave laws that had a legal context and was politically centrist for its time.

Stephen Douglas was likely going to be the Democratic candidate that year. He was a masterful politician who had led the Fugitive Slave Act of 1850 through Congress when Henry Clay had failed. He became the chief proponent of popular sovereignty and used it to get the Kansas-Nebraska Act passed. Dred Scott had made both of these positions illegal.

Lincoln saw that these two ideas were in conflict. He realized that the Freeport Doctrine was nothing more than a political "shell game" and that what he needed to do was to show that Douglas was not taking the moral position for political purposes. And he needed a response to Dred Scott.

Lincoln was able to show that the founding fathers had actually intended Congress to regulate enslavement. He specifically cited those signers of the Constitution who had later voted, while in Congress, to regulate enslavement. He also demonstrated that George Washington himself, as president, had signed a bill into law that regulated enslavement despite owning slaves himself.

Douglas had now been flanked politically. In the South, he argued that popular sovereignty was in their favor. And in the North, he argued for anti-slavery positions while having been the architect of pro-slavery legislation. Douglas was thus shown to be saying one thing in one place and another in another place, and neither was principled. Abraham Lincoln at Cooper Union appeared to be the solution to many Northerners.

Further Reading

- https://www.history.com/topics/19th-century/lincoln-douglas-debates
- https://www.thoughtco.com/lincolns-cooper-union-address-1773575

Answer #III-8

The quote is a distortion of a phrase from Lincoln's address on January 27, 1838, to the Young Men's Lyceum in Springfield, Illinois, in what is often considered Lincoln's first great speech:

> At what point then is the approach of danger to be expected? I answer, if it ever reach us, it must spring up amongst us. It cannot come from abroad. If destruction be our lot, we must ourselves be its author and finisher. As a nation of freemen, we must live through all time, or die by suicide.

Further Reading

- https://quod.lib.umich.edu/l/lincoln/lincoln1/1:130?rgn=div1;singlegenre=All;sort=occur;subview=detail;type=simple;view=fulltext;q1=by+suicide
- https://www.reuters.com/article/uk-factcheck-lincoln-quote-fake-idUSKBN29V2HH

Answers #III-9

The biblical origin of this passage, and indeed the entire speech, is remarkable given that Lincoln was not a religious man. It is truly extraordinary for a politician to refer to God multiple (seven) times and quote directly from the Bible (three times) in an inaugural address.

Lincoln was addressing the meaning of a nation divided by slavery which required a war of enormous destruction and considerable death to resolve. He was drawing a parallel to a divine adjudication and suggesting that the war was retribution and a sign of God's judgment on the United States.

- The "scourge of war" is divine punishment for the sin of slavery, a sin in which all Americans, North as well as South, were complicit. The use of the word "scourge" has biblical roots, implying punishment by a divine power.
- "Two hundred and fifty years of unrequited toil" refers to the labors of the African slaves from 1619 to 1864. It's phrasing recalls Exodus 12–40: "Now the sojourning of the children of Israel, who dwelt in Egypt, was four hundred and thirty years."
- The treasure expended in the war is not enough to atone for our sins, and our collective punishment must continue until "every drop of blood drawn with the lash shall be paid by another drawn with the sword." This is an allusion to the crucifixion of Christ and rebirth, where the old country had to be destroyed to be reborn free of sin.
- "The fear of the Lord is clean, enduring forever; the judgments of the Lord are true and righteous altogether" (Psalm 19:9).

Lincoln had concluded that God's will was unknowable, and that was the deep lesson he drew from the war. His statement to Thurlow Weed about this speech is itself insightful: "I believe it is not immediately popular. Men are not flattered by being shown that there has been a difference of purpose between the Almighty and them."

Further Reading

- https://www.nps.gov/linc/learn/historyculture/lincoln-second-inaugural.htm
- Slagell, Amy R. "Anatomy of a Masterpiece: A Close Textual Analysis of Abraham Lincoln's Second Inaugural Address." *Communication Studies* 42, no. 2 (1991): 155–171.
- White, Ronald C. *Lincoln's Greatest Speech: The Second Inaugural.* Simon & Schuster, 2006.

Section IV

Economic Issues of the War

Challenges

Challenge #IV-1

The cost of the Civil War has been estimated at $5.5 billion ($1.5 billion to the North and $4 billion to the South), which is $68.17 billion in 2019 dollars. The South's higher cost is ascribed to its severe inflation, which was over 9,000 percent by the war's end.

In the 1850s, U.S. federal expenditures had averaged roughly $1 million a week. Once the war started, the government was spending $1.5 million a day and at the end of the war, $3.5 million a day. During the war, the U.S. annual budget skyrocketed to become the first national economy to exceed $1 billion in expenditures. Where was the government to find this amount of revenue?

In the summer of 1861, Salmon P. Chase, the secretary of the Treasury, reported to Congress that he would need $320 million over the next fiscal year to finance the war. He could raise $300 million by borrowing some of it, increasing existing taxes, and by the sale of public lands. Congress was tasked with finding a way to raise the remaining $20 million.

Challenge: Name and describe two highly innovative ways Lincoln and the U.S. Congress developed to finance the war that remain foundations of our economic system today.

Challenge #IV-2

Financing the war was also a critical problem for Jefferson Davis. Although the Confederate government initially issued bonds, investment from the Confederate public fell far short of demands. Taxes were lower in the Confederate States of America than in the Union and were collected less efficiently. European investment was also insufficient. A growing deficit and hyperinflation made it difficult to sell bonds and support the war effort.

The Confederacy also authorized a national income tax in 1863. A graduated income tax passed after great debate. Confederate financial efforts failed as the war turned against them. As wages decreased, so did the tax base. Confederate paper currency depreciated rapidly because it was printed without gold reserves to back its value. Eventually, the inflation in the Confederacy currency led to food riots. It was said that using Confederate currency, you could "use a wheelbarrow to take your money to market and only a basket to bring your purchases home."

As the war proceeded and debts piled up, both the Confederate government and the individual states comprising the Confederacy printed more and more paper money to pay the bills. But the Confederate government did not stop either national or states from printing currency because President Davis believed that under states' rights, he had no authority to limit the states in producing currency.

Challenges: (1) What was the impact of printing paper money without gold reserves in the Treasury to back it? (Hint: Economists call this "expansion of the money supply.") (2) In 1864, the Confederate Congress made a move that helped. What did it do?

Challenge #IV-3

Would slavery have eventually disappeared on its own without a war? The strongest argument against this assertion is the economic fact that owning human slaves was highly profitable. It is sad to say, but slaveholding was a fantastic financial investment in the Deep South.

Southern Planters were highly optimistic about their investment in human property; the rise in value of these assets had grown exponentially. In 1805, there were just over 1 million slaves worth about $300 million; in 1860, just 55 years later, there were 4 million slaves worth $2.7–$3.0 billion.

Challenges: (1) What factors were involved in the rise in economic value over this time frame? (2) What economic impact would Lincoln's opposition to the expansion of slavery to the territories have on the planters' investment? (3) Why did the South secede in winter 1860—spring 1861?

Challenge IV-4

Class distinctions in the Old South played a critical role in precipitating and conducting the war. The planter class was determined to preserve its financial advantages, which allowed them to dictate political and cultural norms. The Confederate States of America encompassed a geographic region populated by 5.6 million white people and 3.6 million enslaved people. The Confederacy was a "minority republic," since the power of voting and legal recognition was reserved for the fewer than 3 million white men, constituting less than a third of its population. The oligarchy of those white men who wielded political power was defined by land ownership descending through family connections and with it, the enslaved who worked the fields.

Several hundred political leaders in the southeastern part of the country fomented secession. They were greatly similar in their social and cultural beliefs, financial holdings, and dependence on agriculture. After Lincoln's election, they attended each other's conventions and lobbied in speeches to make slavery their main issue. The Confederacy's 11 states had 316,632 slave owners in a free population of 5.6 million. Thus, about 5.7 percent of the free population of the Confederacy were slave owners in 1860. Since a legal slave owner was just the person in a family who legally owned them, usually the patriarch, this underestimates the practice. The census of 1860 documented that 30.3 percent of the free families in the Confederacy owned at least one slave. Moreover, of these, 12 percent of slaveholders (about 37,000) owned 20 or more enslaved individuals, or 3.6 percent of the population. This oligarchy essentially controlled the Confederate economy and political system; this was the group from whom political leaders, newspaper publishers, and judges were drawn.

Poor whites therefore constituted a large percentage of the population but had minimal voice in their society. In fact, the slave system had negative effects on white people, including lower wages and fewer jobs, resulting from competition with forced labor. To move toward secession meant convincing the working class that slavery was also beneficial to them. Thus, the narrative had to be created that slave labor was the core of the Southern culture: religion, social strata, and worker. These economic differences among the classes were used to manipulate public opinion and were central to the origin of secession and the Civil War.

Challenges: (1) What were the benefits of owning slaves to the wealthy landowner? (2) How does one go about convincing the middle and working classes that investing their money, lives, and futures in a war in which the odds of victory are small will be beneficial to them even if they don't themselves own slaves? (3) How did the Industrial Revolution in the North, which was nonexistent in the South, play into these class conflicts?

Challenge #IV-5

Jefferson Davis had very complex economic challenges, which were made almost insolvable by the states' rights tradition. Developing a

Section IV. Economic Issues of the War

centralized nation-state with an independent economy required doing all the things that the states' rights tradition said he should not. The difficulty put him in conflict with the state governors and planters, precisely those whose support he most depended on.

One of his biggest mistakes was the cotton embargo. Jefferson Davis's decision to engage in a cotton embargo (to take cotton off the world market) was an attempt at economic blackmail. At the beginning of the Civil War, cotton had become the most valuable crop of the South; it composed 59 percent of the exports from the United States. The strength of the Confederate economy depended on brisk sales and cheap production. Accordingly, the cotton commodity played a crucial role: cotton growth and export would have to continue despite a war in progress. However, for Southern producers, the war disrupted both the producing and the marketing of the financial basis of their new nation.

Consequently, the production of cotton in the Confederate states diminished from 5 million bales in 1860 to about one-quarter million in 1865. Considering that cotton was the South's major cash crop, you have to wonder what Mr. Davis was thinking to engage in this risky gamble.

Challenges: (1) What was Mr. Davis thinking? (2) Why didn't it work out?

Challenge #IV-6

For independence to succeed, the Confederacy needed to import food, not just money and weapons. The Union blockade of Confederate ports succeeded for the most part in preventing the arrival of food from other countries. Moreover, the food that was being produced domestically was diverted to feed the Confederate troops. Additionally, with the onset of war, less food was being grown both because the men were in the military and because fighting had destroyed farmlands, as the war was mainly fought in the South. As the supply of food became scarcer, the continuing demand increased prices as much as 10 times prewar levels.

In 1862, the Confederate Congress attempted to restrict and, in some cases, prohibit cotton production to promote growing food crops on plantations. State governments insisted that corn, wheat, potatoes, and hogs replace cotton production. Southern newspapers promoted the idea of self-subsistence, but the planters continued to produce their cash crop. Each planter thought that they didn't need to forgo their profits and weren't patriotic in their outlook.

The deteriorating economic situation in Richmond in the spring of 1863 was precipitated in part by hoarding and speculation stimulated by spiraling inflation, diminishing morale, and ineffective government actions. The Impressment Act allowed the government to seize food, slaves, and any other materials it deemed necessary for the war effort. A subsequent law allowed the government to impress crops.

After a winter of 20 snow days, a massive snowstorm struck Richmond in March. The melting snow turned roads into muddy paths, complicating transportation into the city of food being grown locally. In addition, the proximity of Richmond to the fighting and the continued influx of wounded soldiers, civil servants, and government staff increased the city's population, stressing an already overburdened system. Rents had skyrocketed, living conditions were overcrowded, and costs of living were exorbitant.

Challenges: (1) What was Mr. Davis's response to the crisis? (2) What transpired then?

Challenge #IV-7

An estimated 450 million pounds of salt was consumed annually in the South before the war began. There was almost none produced in the antebellum South; most was imported from Wales; ships carried salt as ballast when they sailed to Southern ports to load the bales of cotton.

Salt had numerous commercial uses in the 19th century. These included, for example, tanning leather for use in making harnesses and shoes. Salt's most important use was as a preservative: before refrigeration, all pork and beef that was not cooked and served immediately had to be preserved in brine.

Once the blockade of Southern ports took place, salt could no longer be imported. At first, New Orleans had large stockpiles of salt, but this accumulation had quickly diminished by the fall of 1861. The price for salt surged; farmers who raised hogs were unable to preserve the meat. The salt famine became severe by 1862. Facing striking shortages, Southern leaders attempted to encourage domestic salt production. The government actually took control of the salt industry, a form of socialization.

It was apparent from the start that blocking salt production and trade in the South could win the war. Union leadership designed entire military campaigns to do so.

Challenges: (1) Why was salt such a crucial commodity to the Confederacy? (2) What battles and campaigns had this goal in mind? (3) Few people today realize that Jefferson Davis socialized the salt industry. In many ways, the Davis government's nationalization of the salt industry predates how leaders in Eastern Europe and Soviet Russia tried to solve their production problem in industries post–World War II. What are the similarities and differences?

Challenge #IV-8

A strong economic argument can be made that there was a missed opportunity to negotiate a settlement that would have freed the slaves without resorting to secession and war, with its attendant adverse consequences. The term that has been used for this suggestion is "compensated emancipation"—that is, the federal government would pay the slave owner market price for the person, then legally make the person a freedman. The argument continues: perhaps had planters been more willing to negotiate and abolitionists been less righteous, cooler heads might have prevailed and a well-considered plan implemented to free the slaves and integrate them into society.

Challenges: (1) Why didn't Lincoln offer to pay for freeing the slaves, thus obviating the need for a war? (2) Why didn't the federal government pay the slave owners for their property, free them, and save all the blood and treasure of a huge civil war? Was this a feasible solution? (3) In fact, Lincoln signed two compensated emancipation laws for D.C. slaves in 1862. What was the bargain price for these 3,185 people, which was set by a federal commission (i.e., not negotiated)?

Challenge #IV-9

Tanks—motorized vehicles with heavy shielding—move faster than cavalry. Despite requiring gasoline and maintenance, the upkeep is much less than of a horse. Finding a strong animal and supplying sufficient water, fodder, saddles, shoes, and so forth was a nontrivial logistics problem. Horses don't perform at top levels without being well cared for.

Challenges: (1) What did a horse cost at the time of the war? (2) What was the cost of annual upkeep of a cavalry regiment? (3) What is the amount of feed necessary to maintain one horse for one day?

Answers

Answers #IV-1

1. Paper Currency

In 1862, the federal government created the "greenback dollar," or paper currency. Previous brief trials with paper money had been unsuccessful because U.S. citizens didn't trust the stability of these paper notes and preferred gold and silver coin. The greenback was a necessity for the U.S. government to raise the cash to continue the war effort. The "greenback" was federally issued paper currency guaranteed for trade in coin or specie. In essence, it was a promissory note of the U.S. government. Its success led to the nationalization of paper money, which had previously been issued by states, municipalities, and banks.

The first paper money was printed in $5, $10, and $20 denominations. They were called "demand notes" because they were redeemable in coin "on demand" and were also called "greenbacks," a colloquialism still in use today to refer to U.S. currency because they were printed in green ink.

The first $1 bill was issued in 1862, showing a portrait of Salmon P. Chase. The photo (see next page) shows the bill, today worth close to $1,000. It was called a legal tender note, meaning that the law required banks or citizens to recognize them as valid payment for any debt when offered ("tendered").

These paper bills did lead to some inflation (federal paper currency bottomed out at around 40 percent of its nominal value), but the value of currency improved with Union military fortunes.

2. Personal Income Tax

An income tax had been previously considered to finance the War of 1812, but opposition to the concept had led to its stalling in Congress. The enormous cost of the war caused the idea to resurface.

Congress drafted the Revenue Act of 1861, with provisions to increase import tariffs, property taxes, and a flat-rate income tax: this was the first income tax in the United States. The original tax rate was 3 percent on those making above $800. The problem with this legislation was that it lacked a comprehensive enforcement mechanism.

In 1862, a "progressive" income tax was passed. The law imposed a 3 percent tax on incomes between $600 and $10,000 and a 5 percent tax on higher incomes. The law was amended in 1864 to levy a tax of 5 percent

Section IV. Economic Issues of the War

U.S. $1 bill. The Greenback. First U.S. Paper Currency. Note likeness of Secretary of the Treasury Salmon Chase on front.

on incomes between $600 and $5,000, a 7.5 percent tax on incomes in the $5,000–$10,000 range, and a 10 percent tax on everything higher.

Further Reading

- https://www.americanheritage.com/content/funding-civil-war
- https://www.battlefields.org/learn/articles/first-income-tax
- Klein, L.W. "U.S. Government Financing of the Civil War." https://emergingcivilwar.com/2021/07/27/us-government-financing-of-the-civil-war
- https://www.moaf.org/exhibits/checks_balances/abraham-lincoln/greenback
- https://www.thoughtco.com/greenbacks-definition-1773325

Answers #IV-2

(1) Mr. Davis failed to raise the finances necessary to carry out the war, and his powerlessness to control the value of his nation's currency must be considered a central cause of the loss of the war. It is not known if he actually understood the implications of printing paper with no gold reserve to back it.

According to inflationdata.com, "Inflation increased from 60% in 1861 to 300% in 1863 and 600% in 1864. From October 1861 to March 1864 the commodity price index rose an average rate of 10 percent per month." By the end of the war in April 1865, the cost of living in the South was 92 times what it had been before the war started.

Further, at the beginning of the war, $1 Confederate would purchase $1 U.S. gold dollar. By May, it took $1.05 Confederate, or 5 percent inflation in four months. In February 1862, it took $1.25 Confederate dollars, or 25 percent inflation. By February 1863, it required $3.00 Confederate, or 200 percent inflation since 1861. Because inflation is measured annually, comparing the price to one year earlier, from $1.25 to $3.00, is 140 percent annual inflation.

(2) The Confederate Congress passed the Currency Reform Act, which decreased the Southern money supply by one-third. In February 1864, the Confederate Congress decreed a currency reform. All bills greater than $5 were to be converted into bonds paying 4 percent interest. All bills not converted by April 1 would be exchanged for a new issue at a ratio of two for three. The reform was completed by May 1864, with the stock of money reduced by one-third. The general price index declined. In spite of invading Union armies, the impending military defeat, the reduction of foreign trade, the disorganized government, and the low morale of the Confederate army, the value of the Confederate dollar stabilized. Reducing the amount of circulating money had a more significant effect on prices than these powerful forces.

Further Reading

- Klein, L.W. "The Economic Challenges of the Confederacy." https://emergingcivilwar.com/2021/07/29/the-economic-challenges-of-the-confederacy/
- McMahon, Tim. "Confederate Inflation during the Civil War." https://inflationdata.com/articles/confederate-inflation/
- Ransom, Roger L. "The Economics of the Civil War." https://eh.net/encyclopedia/the-economics-of-the-civil-war/

Answers #IV-3

(1) The economic prosperity of the South was dependent on the valuation of slaves as property. The ownership of slaves was the foundation of Southern economic prosperity. The value of $3 billion compares to the 1860 per capita income in the South of $3,978 and in the North of $2,040. Another way to look at this is that $1,500 in 1861 is worth $56,109 in today's currency.

In the 11 states that formed the Confederacy, 40 percent of the people were enslaved in 1860, accounting for more than half the agricultural labor. The practice of slavery was heavily concentrated in agricultural areas but was not limited there. There was no prolonged time period during which the value of the slaves did not increase markedly.

Part of the explanation was the closing of the international slave trade in 1808 as mandated by the Constitution. Another factor was that the enslaved people were reproducing, creating more enslaved.

(2) The value of every commodity depends on the balance of supply and demand. For the value invested into slave ownership to continue to increase, more markets would have to open. By closing territories to slave ownership, the value of slaves would depreciate rapidly, especially as the population continued to increase.

(3) Lincoln's election was the proximate cause of secession and hence the war. The election of a Northern Republican without a single Southern vote (he wasn't on the ballot) meant that the South was losing its political clout due to demographics, and that eventually, even if Lincoln didn't do it, the free-soilers would win and hence these economic concerns would come to pass.

FURTHER READING

- Carlton, Genevieve. "The Map That Helped Convince Lincoln Slavery Had to End." https://www.ranker.com/list/map-that-convinced-lincoln-to-end-slavery/genevieve-carlton
- Dattel, Eugene. "Cotton and the Civil War." http://www.mshistorynow.mdah.ms.gov/articles/291/cotton-and-the-civil-war
- Williamson, S.H., and Cain, L.P. "Measuring Slavery in 2020 Dollars." https://www.measuringworth.com/slavery.php

Answers #IV-4

(1) Indisputably, the political views of the Southern upper class were determined by the economic forces that afforded status, power, prestige,

and clout in their society. An aristocratic class of means and position was defined by the ownership of people and land. The labor management benefit of slavery to the owners in agricultural environments that is often emphasized in historical accounts was only one facet of its practice: slavery was the underpinning of Southern culture, religion, and social norms.

Slaves had three critical economic functions to Southern society:

(a) They were property and thus their value was the central part of the prosperity of planters.
(b) As property, they were collateral for investment and paying off debts.
(c) The value of their labor was not paid.

Class in the aristocratic South was centered on capital, which was unequally distributed. The richest 10 percent of Southern families controlled 75 percent of the wealth, demonstrating a very large skew of who possessed substantial wealth in the antebellum South. Although the mean per capita worth in Southern states was significantly higher than in the North, much of the wealth attributed to the South was a consequence of the value of enslaved individuals, rather than actual savings, volume of commerce, or worth of land.

So any threat that might devalue slave property was basically a threat to the planters' status in society, their wealth, and their identity. Naturally, they fought very hard to maintain their privileges. In the lead-up to the war, they pressured and bought politicians, newspaper editors, and judges in an effort to keep their wealth. If slavery can be exported to the western territories, or if new areas can be added to the U.S. map south of the Missouri Compromise line, then their slave holdings will increase in value.

(2) But once Lincoln was elected, without any support from the South, then the Southern elite recognized that this portended a loss of power on a national level and a bad sign for their future. Lincoln's political platform threatened to limit the source of their economic prosperity: the value of their property would plummet. The politicians—many of whom were in the planter class themselves—could not compromise further. The fire-eaters told the public and carried in the newspapers, we are going to secede and fight, appealing to patriotism and sectional identity.

They used all of these levers of power to convince the other 70 percent that it was their fight. They manipulated the issues at hand to suggest that the Northerners threatened homes and communities. In particular, white supremacy was a critical point to maintain the social and cultural status quo. Thus, although 70 percent of white Southern families did not own slaves, secession and independence centered on the interests of the upper class.

Section IV. Economic Issues of the War

The political focus in 1860 was on fugitive slave laws and the rights of territories and states to regulate slavery. But the "Declaration of the Immediate Causes Which Induce and Justify the Secession of South Carolina from the Federal Union," the Cornerstone Speech of Alexander Stephens, and the secession statements of the states in the Deep South make clear that the very existence of slavery was at stake. And from an economic viewpoint, it was.

(3) The industrial economy of Northern that educated workers, with shared economic and political power, was antithetical to the hierarchical system of human enslavement. Southern states, whose agricultural economy rested on the production of raw materials by enslaved workers, opposed equality. Industrialization alone would not have made slavery obsolete or changed these cultural differences. There remained ample opportunity for the enslaved to be used in menial labor. The postwar experience with sharecropping demonstrates that Southern farmers growing tobacco and cotton needed large amounts of cheap labor. The modern labor structure of immigrants who do field work is predicated on these experiences and their 20th-century struggle for fair labor practices.

Further Reading

- https://www.battlefields.org/learn/articles/why-non-slaveholding-southerners-fought
- https://www.essentialcivilwarcurriculum.com/class-conflict-in-the-union-and-the-confederacy.html

Answers #IV-5

(1) Confederate foreign relations relied on what has been termed "cotton diplomacy." Planters and the Confederate leaders believed that international cotton shortages would secure full diplomatic recognition and possibly aid from European consumers of their produce. Foremost was Great Britain, which manufactured most of the material into clothes and other goods in their textile mills. In order to decrease the amount of cotton on the world market, the Confederates placed an embargo on cotton exports in the summer of 1861.

Basically, the idea was that Davis was trying to blackmail Britain to recognize the Confederacy. By drastically cutting back on the raw material, the idea was to force the world to demand it, create an economic crisis, and maybe the British mediate to make the war stop. Cotton factors and Southern planters assumed that Europe could not do without American cotton, and Confederate political leaders believed that this was the route to diplomatic recognition.

(2) The strategy backfired entirely and was a total economic disaster for the South. Cotton traders in Liverpool held hundreds of thousands of bales of American cotton at the start of the war. In January 1862, there were a quarter million bales being held in warehouses. Since the war was expected to be brief, there seemed to be little need for more cotton. Meanwhile, the Confederacy's shrinking territory as the war continued and the loss of its ports and markets made them unreliable suppliers. The British began producing cotton in Egypt and India instead.

The impact on the Southern economy was catastrophic. There was no significant import revenue, cotton bales that were produced couldn't be sold domestically, and meanwhile the costs of slave labor and field maintenance continued.

Answers #IV-6

(1) In response to these severe economic problems, President Davis called for a day of fasting and prayer. He designated March 27, 1863, for prayer. As you would imagine, the working class, on whom these burdens fell especially hard, did not consider this an adequate solution.

(2) An uprising in the streets of Richmond followed to protest this development. On April 2, 1863, riots spawned by food deprivation erupted. The Richmond Bread Riot was the largest but not the only civil disturbance in the Confederacy.

On April 1, a group of women consisting of Confederate ordnance workers and the wives of the Tredegar ironworkers met at the Belvidere Hill Baptist Church to discuss what to do about the severe food shortage. They decided to march on Governor John Letcher's office to demand action.

More than 100 women arrived to meet the governor armed with axes, knives, and other weapons on April 2. Letcher listened, but his response did not mollify their concerns, and he did not guarantee any near-term relief. The women continued their march, crying, "Bread! Bread!" and "Bread or blood!" As the march continued, more Richmond residents carrying weapons joined the march. The group increased in size to hundreds, perhaps thousands, of rioters. Violence commenced on commercial businesses. The governor called out the public guard, but it was unable to quell the crowd. The rioters then broke into government food storehouses and nearby businesses, taking food and supplies intended for the war effort.

The bread riot was subdued only when Jefferson Davis himself climbed atop a wagon to talk to the crowd. He threatened to have Confederate troops, who had been called out to support the public guard, open fire on the crowd to maintain order. He is said to have pulled out his pocket watch and given the rioters five minutes to disperse and return home. At the last minute, they dispersed. Over 60 people were arrested and faced charges; those who appeared at trial better dressed reportedly received lighter punishments.

Additional riots took place in Atlanta, Augusta, Columbus, and Macon, Georgia; Salisbury and High Point, North Carolina; and Mobile, Alabama.

FURTHER READING

- Dattel, Eugene. "Cotton and the Civil War." *http://www.mshistorynow.mdah.ms.gov/articles/291/cotton-and-the-civil-war*
- https://emergingcivilwar.com/2021/07/29/the-economic-challenges-of-the-confederacy/
- https://encyclopediavirginia.org/entries/bread-riot-richmond/
- https://encyclopediavirginia.org/entries/confederate-impressment-during-the-civil-war/

Answers #IV-7

(1)"What good could it do to destroy salt?" the U.S. Navy admiral David Dixon Porter asked rhetorically, 20 years after the war. "It was the life of the Confederate army.... They could not pack their meats without it." A soldier with a small piece of boiled beef, six ounces of corn meal, and four ounces of salt was provisioned for a three-day march.

Preserving meat was the critical problem. Salted beef and pork were dietary staples for both soldiers and civilians. The situation quickly became dire, given the widespread practice of hog farming in the agricultural South, The Commissary General of the Confederacy, Lucius B. Northrup, noted in 1862 that "in consequence of the insufficient quantity and inferior quality of salt among the inhabitants, much of their meat is spoiling." Speculation and shipping delays further compounded the problem, and prices rose markedly, along with inflation. A 200-pound sack of salt in New Orleans before the war cost 50 cents, but by 1862, the price had increased 50 times to $25.

(2)The salt manufacturing areas around Kanawha Valley in Virginia and Goose Creek in Kentucky were captured or destroyed by the North early in the war. Union forces seized New Iberia, Louisiana, and captured Avery Island in 1863.

Often, the downfall of Southern saltworks was due to the bravery of the enslaved, who gave vital information on their location and defenses. One example was an offshore mining camp. A group of enslaved men escaped and boarded the U.S. naval ship *Kingfisher*. They informed the captain of a half-finished saltworks in Saint Joseph's Bay. The ship sailed to the mining area and "sent a flag of truce, and politely informed them they must stop, or we should destroy them." When the saltworks refused to respond, the *Kingfisher* fired two shells into the building. After it was vacated, the entire building was demolished. The Confederate government had planned to obtain an entire winter's worth of salt for Florida and Georgia from the destroyed site and experienced the loss as a serious setback.

For the rest of the war, several offensives were undertaken in the South with this goal in mind. Enslaved men and women who had been forced to work at salt production often led Union forces to salt-making cauldrons hidden in swamps. Skyrocketing salt prices and what was labeled a "salt famine" resulted.

The Union's strategy culminated with repeated attacks on the aptly named Saltville, Virginia, which was finally captured in December 1864. This ended most salt production in the South.

(3) Although the production facilities in Saltville allowed Virginia to have reasonable salt supplies most of the war, there was a real famine elsewhere. Georgia and Florida asked their governors to take control, leading to the interesting economic condition of socialism in a society founded on principles of states' rights and capitalism. The Confederate government panicked and started giving out rewards for domestic salt production. But as soon as a business to process it was formed, the Union would target and destroy these salt production facilities.

The Southern government underwent great economic stress by the demands of total war. As it suffered from limited finances and the lack of an industrial base, decisions and arrangements were made with cotton, rail, manufacturing, and salt industries that went well beyond states' rights theory. As the war proceeded and events rendered the economic news bleaker and bleaker, the Confederate government transformed into a centralized nationalist state. The Confederate States of America (CSA) essentially nationalized the Southern economy. For example, the CSA government established the Cotton Bureau, a cartel to regulate every aspect of the production, sale, and distribution of the South's major commodity.

Further Reading

- Thomas, Emory M. *The Confederacy as a Revolutionary Experience*. University of South Carolina Press, 1992

- https://www.atlasobscura.com/articles/civil-war-salt
- http://usslave.blogspot.com/2013/04/the-confederacys-salt-famine-by-andrew.html

Answers #IV-8

(1) He did; that is the key point. In November 1861, President Lincoln drafted an act to be introduced before the legislature of Delaware for compensated emancipation, but it was narrowly defeated. Lincoln was also behind national legislation toward the same end, but the Southern states, which regarded themselves as having seceded from the Union, ignored the proposals.

(2) The concept of compensated emancipation, or a "buy out" of the economic interest of Southern slaveholders, was discussed in its time. The major problem was that the costs of such a scheme would have been enormous. The cost in 1860 would have been about $2.7 billion ($4 million at $675 per person). Perhaps a plan of gradual emancipation over several generations to spread out the debt might have succeeded. Most modern economists do not think this was ever a viable solution.

- https://www.google.com/amp/s/amp.theatlantic.com/amp/article/277073/

Although this might have cost about the same as fighting the war with fewer deaths, such a large sum could not be paid all at once. Even if the payments were spread over 25 years, the annual costs of such a scheme would involve a *tripling* of federal government outlays of the time. The costs could be reduced substantially if instead of freeing all the slaves at once, children were left in bondage until the age of 18 or 21.

Needless to say, a whole bunch of even more complicated moral, political, and economic problems would surely follow. It raises obvious moral issues of paying vast sums to a few already wealthy people who would earn a windfall for a highly unethical practice and the fact that slavery would still be legal. Where would the money come from to educate, house, and maintain the formerly enslaved now released into society? Where would they live? What would they do to earn a living?

(3) Lincoln signed two compensated emancipation laws for D.C. slaves in 1862. To free 3,185 people cost about $1 million. Even at this bargain price of $314 per person, which was set by a federally appointed board, the cost for 4 million people would exceed $1.25 billion.

Answers #IV-9

(1) The cost of a horse was $119 at the start of the war and increased to $190 by the end of the war. For comparison, the average lieutenant's monthly salary was about $100/month. With the inflation in the Confederacy, the price was close to $3,000.

(2) About $100,000.

(3) The daily feed ration for Union cavalry horses was 10 pounds of hay and 14 pounds of grain.

Section V

Military Personalities of the Civil War

Challenges

1. Union Army

Challenge #V-1

The perception of Grant as a drunkard originated in the aftermath of the horrific losses suffered at the Battle of Shiloh in April 1862 by officers jealous of Grant's rapid rise. Newspaper reports critical of Grant's command were intended to increase sales, if not influence the political debate. These articles reported that Grant, who many believed had been forced from the army because of an alcohol problem, was drunk at the moment of Albert Sydney Johnston's surprise attack. Whitelaw Reid of the *Cincinnati Gazette* reported the events of the battle incorrectly, stating that Grant had been taken by surprise at Shiloh and that soldiers had been bayonetted in their tents. This myth persists to this day. The high casualty rate at Shiloh was related to the intensity of the battle, not the nature of Grant's problems with liquor, but rumors of his drinking nevertheless followed.

Challenge: Name the specific dates during the war when Grant was indisputably inebriated.

Challenge #V-2a,b

#V-2a

In November 1859, William Tecumseh Sherman was appointed superintendent of Louisiana's new military academy, which later became

Louisiana State University. He enjoyed the position and the people he met in the South. But he was disturbed at the talk of secession and the glibness of the residents about the possibility of war.

Sherman famously suggested that if war came, the North would win after a long struggle. He said another time that it would take 200,000 soldiers to win the war. The latter statement resulted in his being declared insane and relieved from duty. Both statements turned out to be astoundingly accurate.

Challenge: What exactly did he say and to whom about (1) the South starting a war and (2) how many soldiers be required to win the war?

#V-2b

On November 15, 1864, 62,000 men under the command of General Sherman departed Atlanta and commenced the March to the Sea. "Behind us lay Atlanta, smoldering and in ruins; the black smoke arising high in the air, and hanging over the ruined city." A regimental band struck up the strains of "John Brown's Body" and the entire corps began to sing. "Never before or since" had Sherman heard it "done with more spirit or in better harmony of time and place."

Challenges: What did Sherman himself say about (1) the romance of war, (2) his army's actions during the March to the Sea, and (3) his lack of popularity?

General Ulysses S. Grant (Library of Congress).

Challenge #V-3

Major General Henry Jackson Hunt was acknowledged by his contemporaries as the greatest artillery tactician and strategist of the war. He was a master of the science of artillery and rewrote the manual on the organization and use of artillery in early modern armies. His courage and tactics influenced the outcome of some of the most significant battles in the war, including Malvern Hill, Antietam, Fredericksburg, and most notably at Gettysburg, where his operational decisions contributed greatly to the Confederate defeat of Pickett's Charge.

Challenges: (1) What was his principal doctrine concerning artillery tactics that experience in the war demonstrated to be correct? Give one example where his philosophy proved superior and one where his philosophy wasn't followed that led to disaster. (2) How was his theory proven at Gettysburg? (3) Pickett's Charge was his greatest moment, but another battle showed his superior skill as artillery commander even more clearly. What was the battle and what did it prove?

Challenge #V-4

Major General George Thomas is often overlooked as a major character. Considering that he never lost a battle, served with gallantry at Shiloh, Perryville, Stones River, and of course Chickamauga, and was responsible for the victories at Missionary Ridge and Nashville, this is almost incomprehensible. His reputation as a slow and deliberate planner who turned down promotions makes him an unappealing figure at first, but he deserves substantial historical acclaim.

Challenges: (1) His promotions to lieutenant colonel and colonel in 1861 came with the resignations of which men? (2) When Don Carlos Buell was demoted as commander of the Army of the Ohio, General Rosecrans was promoted but not Thomas. Why not? (3) At Chickamauga, who reported that Thomas was standing "like a rock"? (4) Who suggested him for promotion to lieutenant general?

Challenge #V-5

Major General Daniel Sickles was either an American hero or an infamous criminal and insubordinate military commander, depending on your point of view. Even 160 years later, it's not easy to decide which description is more accurate. Thomas Keneally, the author of *Schindler's List*, wrote an outstanding biography, *American Scoundrel*.

Sickles was an unscrupulous swindler who led a life that no writer of fiction could have invented. A brief synopsis: A lawyer, Tammany Hall politician, U.S. congressman, and serial adulterer, he murdered his wife's lover (Francis Scott Key's son Philip) in broad daylight across the street from the White House, pleaded temporary insanity (invented for him by his lawyer, Edwin Stanton), and won acquittal. And that was only the warm-up. Then he recruited the Excelsior Brigade, lost his leg at Gettysburg, testified against Meade at congressional hearings, had an affair with the queen of Spain, received the Medal of Honor, and championed saving the battlefield at Gettysburg as a park. He was a diplomat, playboy, beloved general, congressman, murderer, and good old boy. He looked out solely for himself and was unperturbed if other people got killed. He had zero training as a soldier. He was self-aggrandizing, selfish, corrupt, and unprincipled, but he was also brave, loyal, patriotic, and extremely enterprising. He got away with all of it because he was colorful, resourceful, and charming.

Challenge: The monument on the field at Gettysburg to his brigade was designed to include his bust. It does not, and the empty spot is conspicuous. What happened?

Challenge #V-6

Montgomery C. Meigs served as quartermaster general of the U.S. Army during the Civil War. His administration of such a sprawling organization could have been the target of corruption and graft, but his record was outstanding for effectiveness and ethical rectitude.

Challenge: What decision did he make that altered the attitude toward how Union soldiers killed in the war were buried?

Challenge #V-7

The building of a "brown water navy," or ships to operate specifically in rivers, which was so crucial to victories at Vicksburg, Mobile Bay, and other places, was not highly thought of when it was first proposed by a civilian. He designed an armored steamship that helped the Union seize and maintain control of the Mississippi River during the Civil War.

This man was an engineer who had spent his life on the Mississippi River. Before the war, he created a business that removed dangerous debris and shipwrecks from the river. After the war, he designed and built the first bridge to cross the Mississippi River at Saint Louis. His bridge provided a crucial railroad connection between Missouri and eastern cities.

In 1861, this man wrote to the U.S. attorney general to suggest that the Union needed to build a fleet of armored steamships for use on the river. Edward Bates, who had no military portfolio, summoned him to Washington to make the case for a river navy in the west. Soon after the meeting, the army advertised for bids, and this man's design won the contract to build warships. He offered to build seven steamships with iron plating in only 65 days. The ships were called "ironclads."

The first of the gunships, the *Saint Louis*, was launched five weeks after starting the work. Although he failed to build all seven ships in the proposed time, after 100 days the last of the seven entered the Mississippi River. He wrote to President Abraham Lincoln that the "St. Louis was the first iron clad built in America.... She was the first armored vessel against which the fire of a hostile battery was directed on this continent."

Challenges: (1) Who was he? (2) Why would Attorney General Bates get involved in this controversy? (3) Bonus: Name the seven ships.

2. Confederate Army

Challenge #V-8

General Robert E. Lee is celebrated as a brilliant military tactician and leader. His impeccable bearing impressed everyone with who he came in contact, except Mary Chesnut whose diary shows remarkable perception into people. She thought he appeared too perfect.

When Winfield Scott offered Lee command of the Union army, Lee had a very difficult choice to make. Obviously, this promotion was precisely what Lee had dreamed of achieving his entire career, so to turn it down must have required sincere and deep beliefs. He waited until the results of the Virginia plebiscite was known, then resigned his Union army commission when his state joined the secession movement.

One often hears the argument that Lee himself didn't own slaves, abhorred slavery, and fought for the Confederacy only because of loyalty to his state. In fact,

General Robert E. Lee by Julian Vannerson (Library of Congress).

Lee was a typical aristocratic Virginian of the 19th century in his political mindset and his views on slavery.

Challenges: (1) How many Virginia generals stayed loyal to the Union? Bonus: Name them. (2) Had Lee stayed with the Union, what would have been the financial cost to him and his family? (3) How did he treat the slaves he owned?

Challenge #V-9

General Joseph E. Johnston is acknowledged as an excellent general and a fine man, but he is also often criticized for his strategy of retreat. His strategy of falling back and stalling for time is good military doctrine when outnumbered and when trading land for time might lead to victory. Washington's victory over the British, for example, used this method. Such a strategy might have succeeded if he had had the support of President Davis, but their relationship was strident and unproductive.

Challenges: (1) What was the origin of the dispute between Johnston and Davis? (2) What setback led to further recriminations between them?

Challenge #V-10a,b

#V-10a

General Longstreet's contributions to the Confederate war effort were singular. He was probably the most effective second-in-command on either side. Interestingly, he was related by marriage to General Grant, whom he knew at West Point and with whom he spent the first two years of his career. What was their familial relationship?

#V-10b

General Longstreet clearly did not agree with some of General Lee's decisions. His reluctance to attack at Gettysburg is one of the best-known stories of the war. It is thought that Longstreet asked to be sent to the western theater prior to Gettysburg, perhaps to be made its commander or second under Johnston. Why Longstreet was never given a large independent command is one of the great mysteries of how Jefferson Davis thought. Clearly, protecting Bragg and promoting Hood over Longstreet seem in retrospect to be two of Davis's worst decisions.

Challenge: Longstreet had independent command twice in the war. Name these campaigns and the outcomes.

Section V. Military Personalities of the Civil War

Challenge #V-11a–c

#V-11a

Ambrose Powell (A.P.) Hill was the classic example of a Confederate commander who could be brilliant at times but could also make huge errors in judgment. His disappearance at Gettysburg, perhaps due to chronic effects of a venereal disease, is legendary. Nevertheless, he frequently came along at the right time to save the battle, such as at Antietam. His worst performance was at Fredericksburg.
Challenge: What did he do wrong?

#V-11b

One of the most impactful moments of the war followed the Battle of Glendale in the Seven Days campaign. As a consequence of a seies of actions, A.P. Hill, one of Longstreet's brigade commanders, was transferred to Stonewall Jackson's corps after a major disagreement.

A.P. Hill could be even more contentious than Braxton Bragg. In four years, Hill quarreled with every officer he served under. The Longstreet feud developed after the Seven Days when the two engaged in a war of the newspapers over which of them should get most credit. Finally, Hill stopped communicating with his commander and asked to be relieved of serving under him.
Challenge: (1) What was the nature of the disagreement between Longstreet and Hill? (2) How was it resolved?

#V-11c

Stonewall Jackson was not the easiest man in the world to get along with. His religious fanaticism, his penchant for lemons, and his belief that one arm was longer than the other made for a strange personality. Stonewall Jackson arrested and turned over for courts-martial Turner Ashby, Richard Garnett, A.P. Hill, as well as five of Hill's colonels for using a fence for firewood. He had running feuds with basically all of his subordinate commanders. This record exists despite the fact that he was killed before the midpoint of the war! In fact, at one point after the defeat at Kernstown, every single one of his subordinate officers was being court-martialed
Challenges: (1) How did Jackson and Hill get along? (2) What was the infamous response Hill made to this new commander? (3) How was this subsequent feud resolved? (4) In what way were the personalities of Hill and Jackson polar opposites?

Challenge #V-12

Major General George Pickett is remembered today by his last-place standing at West Point, his division's charge at Gettysburg, and his inglorious defeat in the final battle of the war. The common characterization of him as a flamboyant dandy who failed in his special moment on the big stage isn't an accurate portrayal.

Challenges: (1) Describe the contribution he made in the Mexican War. (2) What actions did he lead a brigade in prior to his promotion to division command? (3) In his final battle, Pickett was nowhere to be found. Why not? (4) What potential war crime led Pickett to escape to Canada? (5) What was the conversation Pickett had with Mosby after briefly meeting with Lee after the war? (6) Who led the postwar restoration of his accomplishments?

Challenge #V-13

P.G.T. Beauregard had a background in engineering. When the war started, he was superintendent at West Point. He commanded the defense of Charleston and captured Fort Sumter. He won at First Manassas and planned the surprise attack on Shiloh, which he led in reality from the start and in fact after Albert Sidney Johnston's death on day one. After the siege of Corinth, he returned to Charleston. In 1864, he was responsible for the defense of Petersburg, where he brilliantly delayed the Union army for months. He and General Johnston convinced Davis that the war needed to end. After the war, he advocated for black suffrage and became wealthy promoting the Louisiana Lottery.

He was an imaginative and highly regarded strategist. Despite suggestions that his ideas were unmoored to reality, he was more often correct than not. He predicted the early attacks on New Orleans and the necessity of holding Tennessee. He suggested an invasion of Illinois or Ohio; and for all those looking for how the war might have gone differently, this is the idea to think about. Nevertheless, after Corinth, he never again was given command of a major fighting army. Why he wasn't considered to replace Bragg, why Hood was promoted rather than Beauregard, and why he spent the central portions of the war in Charleston challenge our understanding. Charleston did require an outstanding military engineer, but Beauregard offered so much more. Jefferson Davis did not like him, and basically, that was enough.

Challenges: (1) At Corinth, Beauregard brilliantly deceived General Halleck into thinking he was about to attack, which caused the cautious general to move very slowly even though he far outnumbered the Confederates. What charade succeeded in fooling Halleck for weeks? (2) Beauregard ultimately withdrew to Tupelo but not out of fear of Halleck. What was the real reason he left Corinth? (3) Where Beauregard went wrong with Davis isn't exactly clear. The usual explanation is that he on went on medical leave without permission in advance, leading to his replacement by Braxton Bragg. But three other possibilities, far more likely the underlying explanation versus the cover story, also exist. What are they?

Challenge #V-14

Daniel Harvey (D.H.) Hill was intelligent, thoughtful, and courageous but also difficult, argumentative, and contentious. He was a strict teacher with a sarcastic sense of humor. He was the brother-in-law of Stonewall Jackson. He was an exceptional combat officer and very brave. He contributed greatly to the Confederate war effort in 1861–1862, but then was relegated to backwater commands. He managed to be friends with Longstreet and Johnston and to disagree with Lee and Bragg. There is no doubt Davis underutilized him.

Hill graduated from West Point, fought in the Mexican War (brevetted twice for bravery), and then became a professor of mathematics at Washington College. He wrote the standard text on algebra of his day. He owned slaves and taught one to read and write, who became a preacher.

He led his division with distinction at the Seven Days. He worked out a fair method of prisoner exchange. His division fought hard at South Mountain and with heavy casualties at the Sunken Lane at Antietam, where his leadership probably saved the day.

Then he seemed to fall out of favor. He was not engaged at Fredericksburg, was reassigned to North Carolina instead of Chancellorsville, was not promoted on Jackson's death to corps command, and was commander of the defense of Richmond when Lee invaded Pennsylvania. This is precisely what Lee did with officers he did not want to work with.

Then he was sent west where his forces were in the middle of the Battle of Chickamauga. Afterward, his criticism of Bragg led to reorganization of that army, leaving Hill without a command. He was assigned to backwater commands until he once again became a division commander under Johnston at the very end. After the war, he served as president of the University of Arkansas.

Challenges: (1) What was the prisoner exchange method called and how did it work? (2) Why did Hill and Lee not get along?

Challenge #V-15

Brigadier General Edward Porter Alexander was General Hunt's opposition in the eastern theater of the war, in charge of artillery under Longstreet. One of the problems Alexander had to overcome was that the Confederate army failed to organize as Hunt suggested and kept to the old method of assigning artillery to be under the command of infantry corps commanders. Hunt therefore remained under the command of General Longstreet and had minimal direct input into strategic decisions. As he himself wrote in his outstanding memoirs, this led to errors. For example, the multiday battle at Gettysburg had wasted a lot of ammunition and he lacked authority to concentrate the artillery he had available for day three. His memoirs are often quoted for his clear and unbiased views of Confederate strategy and particularly the errors he thought Lee made. His criticisms were direct without regard to the Lost Cause consequences. After the war, he worked as an engineer, professor of mathematics, and a railroad executive.

Challenge: Alexander is best known for his artillery command, but he made other major contributions in another aspect of warfare that is much less celebrated. Describe his original appointment in the Confederate army and his innovations in that position.

Challenge #V-16

James Ewell Brown (J.E.B.) Stuart was dashing, bold, and intrepid. His exploits enamor every young Civil War buff. His uniform sported a gold sash and a large plumed hat accented by an ostrich feather. He led his cavalry corps on two circumnavigations of the Union army in 1862, an astonishing feat of courage and planning. Stuart's outstanding results in reconnaissance earned him a high reputation, but he was also partially blamed for the defeat at Gettysburg because he got trapped behind enemy lines and was unable to let General Lee know where the Union army was located. He was killed in the Battle of Yellow Tavern.

Born in Virginia, he graduated West Point near the top of his class and was a favorite of its superintendent, Robert E. Lee. Before the war, he was stationed in Texas, Kansas, and fought against the Cherokees. He was lieutenant under Colonel Lee in ending the John Brown raid. When Virginia seceded, he resigned from the U.S. Army.

Challenges: (1) What was the critical information Stuart provided Lee with on his ride in the Peninsula Campaign? (2) What information did Stuart capture related to Second Manassas? (3) At what battle did Stuart assume command of an infantry corps?

Challenge #V-17

Nathan Bedford Forrest was undoubtedly the war's greatest raider. His exploits have assumed such legendary proportions that it's almost impossible to separate fact from interpretation.

Challenges: (1) What was Forrest's prewar occupation? (2) What was his response to General Buckner's plan to surrender Fort Donelson? (3) What was his military response at Parker's Cross Roads to being surrounded? (4) What was Forrest's greatest victory? (5) What was Forrest's involvement in the Fort Pillow massacre? (6) How many horses were shot out from under him? How many men did he personally kill? How many times was he wounded? (7) What was his involvement in the Ku Klux Klan?

J.E.B. Stuart (Library of Congress).

Challenge #V-18

Wade Hampton was a natural cavalryman—brave, audacious, and a superb horseman. He was a South Carolina plantation owner who organized and paid for "Hampton's Legion" at the outbreak of the Civil War. Although indifferent about secession, he resigned his seat in the South Carolina state senate in early 1861 and joined the Confederacy. Although he had no formal military training, his prestige helped secure him an appointment as a colonel.

He played a key role in the First Battle of Bull Run, where he was wounded. He participated in the Peninsula Campaign, when he was wounded again at Seven Pines. He participated in action at Fredericksburg. He led the pursuit of retreating Union forces after Second Manassas. He led his cavalry brigade at Brandy Station and joined J.E.B. Stuart during his ride before Gettysburg.

After General Stuart's death in May 1864, Hampton assumed command of the Confederate cavalry. During the Overland Campaign in June 1864, Hampton won a major victory at the Battle of Trevilian Station. Hampton would later defend against Union cavalry menacing Richmond and Petersburg. In September 1864, he directed the "Beefsteak Raid," a raid behind enemy lines that captured over 2,000 head of cattle.

After the Civil War, Hampton became a vocal opponent of Reconstruction. He was elected governor of South Carolina and to the U.S. Senate.

Challenges: (1) Hampton had no formal military education or experience before the war. He was one of three to achieve the rank of lieutenant general despite this deficiency. Who were the others? (2) The Battle of Trevilian Station was fought against which Union general, whose goal was what? (3) Who were the Red Shirts and what was Hampton's relationship with them?

Challenge #V-19

General Braxton Bragg famously feuded with every one of his subordinates. The famous story Grant tells in his autobiography about Bragg feuding with himself in the old army was apocryphal (perhaps), but his multiple disagreements with his subordinates, and his military losses, led to his being demoted as western commander at the end of 1863.

There is a famous episode involving Bragg and Nathan Bedford Forrest. First, we must go back a year. Forrest was placed under Brigadier General Joseph Wheeler's command, and when Wheeler committed them to an ill-conceived attack on Fort Donelson in early 1863, Forrest flew into a rage. He told Wheeler, "This is not a personal matter, but you will tell General Bragg in your report that I will be in my coffin before I will fight under you again." Forrest then ended his tirade with the ultimate military gesture of protest: "If you want my sword, you can have it."

The notorious moment came when Forrest told Bragg just what he thought of him after Bragg had twice "tampered with" Forrest's cavalry command. In reality, the event supposedly was caused when Forrest incorrectly believed that Bragg was again placing him under Wheeler. The confrontation occurred at Bragg's headquarters on Missionary Ridge during the Confederate siege of Chattanooga.

Forrest reportedly said, "I have stood your meanness as long as I intend to. You have played the part of a damned scoundrel, and are a coward, and if you were any part of a man I would slap your jaws and force you to resent it. You may as well not issue any more orders to me, for I will not obey them, and I will hold you personally responsible for any further indignities you endeavor to inflict upon me.... If you ever again try to interfere with me or cross my path, it will be at the peril of your life."

Challenges: (1) Did this event actually happen? (2) What order did Bragg actually give and did Forrest's statement cause Bragg to reverse it?

Challenge #V-20

Patrick Cleburne was one of the best battle leaders of the Confederate army. An immigrant from Ireland, his original ambition was medicine, like his father. When he failed his entrance exam, he joined the 41st Regiment of Foot in the British army. He moved to Arkansas and in 1855 worked as a pharmacist. He and his business partner, Thomas Hindman (who also rose to generalship), were shot in a street fight with Know-Nothings. Cleburne was shot in the back; he turned around and killed his attacker. The other troublemakers hid until he collapsed in the street; then he and Hindman moved to Mississippi where he studied law.

With secession, he joined the Confederate army not because of slavery, which he claimed he had no opinion about, but because the Southern people had welcomed him. Although joining as a private, he rose to become a major general, fighting with high distinction at Shiloh, Stones River, Chickamauga, and Atlanta. Throughout, his leadership was courageous and very active. Bragg called him "one of the best and truest officers in our cause." The Confederate Congress officially thanked him for his actions at Missionary Ridge and Ringgold Gap. General Lee referred to him as "a meteor shining from a clouded sky," which, after all, is an amazing compliment from the general himself.

Yet despite these accolades, Cleburne was passed over for promotion to corps commander three times. He was killed leading a charge at Franklin. Sam Watkins described that his horse was halfway over the parapet and that Cleburne had been hit 49 times. The memoir he never wrote is probably the greatest disappointment in the Civil War genre.

Challenge: He was never promoted past the division command level. Who was Cleburne in conflict with that led to a lack of promotion, and why?

Challenge #V-21

Without General Samuel Cooper, who served throughout the war as Confederate quartermaster general, the successes of Lee, Beauregard, and

Johnston could never have happened. Moreover, although few have heard of him, it was his final official act that indebts all of us to him.

Challenge: Who was he and what did he do?

Challenge #V-22

Generals make mistakes, like all humans. In war, hundreds, even thousands, may die as a consequence of an incorrect decision taken in a critical circumstance. Some generals use the experience to succeed the next time, a good lesson for all of us. Grant and Lee, for example, both had bad days, but they also had some pretty impressive victories.

Challenges: Given a second chance, these generals showed their true strength of character. All were promoted despite a failure that resulted in massive casualties. Name both their original failure and their later success. State for each (1) the mistake these men committed at a crucial moment and (2) their redemptive action that later brought them high visibility.

- O.O. Howard
- William Sherman
- Thomas Wood
- Edward Ord
- Stonewall Jackson
- William Mahone
- John C. Breckinridge
- Joseph Hooker
- Lew Wallace

Answers

Answer #V-1

All the rumored occasions of Grant's drinking are presented in Ron Chernow's biography *Grant*. Sylvanus Cadwallader was a war correspondent for the *Chicago Times*, attached to General Grant's headquarters from 1862 to 1865. He wrote a memoir that was not printed until 1955 claiming that Grant had a barrel of whiskey for his exclusive use. Supposedly, Cadwallader was in conversation in the tent of Colonel William Duff, Grant's chief of artillery. Grant walked in, and Duff pulled out a cup, dipped it into a barrel, and handed the cup to Grant. Grant drank the contents and handed the cup back to Duff; this sequence was repeated two more times. Grant then left the tent. Cadwallader claimed that Duff had been ordered by Grant to keep the barrel of whiskey handy. This allegation has never been confirmed by anyone else.

Cadwallader recounted the most well-known story of Grant's drinking, on June 3, 1863, during an inspection tour to Satartia, Mississippi, on the Yazoo River. The siege of Vicksburg was agonizingly slow. Grant had been separated from his wife, Julia, since April. During his trip, Grant encountered the steamboat *Diligence* and decided to board. According to the reporter, "I was not long in perceiving that Grant had been drinking heavily, and that he was still keeping it up. He made several trips to the bar room of the boat in a short time, and became stupid in speech and staggering in gait. This was the first time he had shown symptoms of intoxication in my presence, and I was greatly alarmed by his condition, which was fast becoming worse."

One can wonder how the world would be different if President Lincoln had heeded these stories. Shelby Foote in the Ken Burns series gave an opinion that Grant resorted to the bottle when separated from his wife. A sexual trigger to alcohol abuse is well known, but the evidence in Grant's case isn't definitive. John Rawlins, his law partner from before the war, was supposedly his guardian and perhaps his protector in this regard. Lincoln sent four officers to check on his drinking habits: James McPherson, Lorenzo Thomas, Charles Dana, and David Hunter. Not one ever reported to Lincoln or Stanton that Grant was ever drunk.

Further Reading
- Chernow, Ron. *Grant*. Penguin Press, 2017.

- https://www.americanheritage.com/users/sylvanus-cadwallader
- https://www.amazon.com/General-John-Rawlins-Ordinary/dp/0253057302/ref=sr_1_1?crid=3HTXBQ016X6VT&dchild=1&keywords=john+rawlins+no+ordinary+man&qid=1632540927&s=books&sprefix=john+rawlins%2Cstripbooks%2C167&sr=1-1
- https://www.historynet.com/ulysses-s-grants-lifelong-struggle-with-alcohol.htm

Answers #V-2

#V-2a

(1) On Christmas Eve, 1860, Sherman predicted what would happen if a war came, according to David French Boyd, a professor at Louisiana State Seminary, where Sherman was the superintendent. Boyd reported in his postwar memoir that Sherman told him,

> You, you people of the South, ... don't know what you are doing. ....This country will be drenched in blood. God only knows how it will end. ....It is all folly, madness, a crime against civilization!
>
> ....Besides, where are your men and appliances of war to contend against them? .... The North can make a steam-engine, locomotive, or railway car; hardly a yard of cloth or pair of shoes can you make. You are rushing into war with one of the most powerful, ingeniously mechanical, and determined people on Earth—right at your doors.
>
> You are bound to fail. Only in your spirit and determination are you prepared for war. In all else you are totally unprepared, with a bad cause to start with. At first you will make headway, but as your limited resources begin to fail, and shut out from the markets of Europe ... as you will be, your cause will begin to wane. ... If your people would but stop and think, they must see in the end that you will surely fail.

(2) Sherman was quoted in Exhibit No. 14, which was published by the *New York Tribune* on October 30, 1861. Secretary of War Simon Cameron purposely released the report to the press, probably to embarrass Sherman. The report was widely interpreted that Sherman had an unstable character.

Sherman, commanding Union forces in Kentucky, told Secretary of War Simon Cameron he needed 60,000 men to defend his territory; and when asked how many to go on the offensive, Sherman "promptly replied 200,000 men.... The Secretary of War replied that ... he thought Gen. Sherman over-estimated the number and power of the rebel forces; that the Government would furnish troops … but that he [the Secretary] was tired of defensive war.… He begged Gen. Sherman to assume the offensive and to keep the rebels hereafter on the defensive."

Cameron called Sherman's request "insane" and removed the general from command. Sherman was put on 30-day leave soon thereafter.

In February 1862, Sherman was assigned to Paducah, Kentucky, under Ulysses S. Grant, who recognized Sherman's potential. Later in the war, when a civilian disparaged Grant, Sherman responded, "General Grant is a great general. He stood by me when I was crazy, and I stood by him when he was drunk; and now, sir, we stand by each other always."

FURTHER READING
- https://www.americanheritage.com/new-sherman-letters
- https://thehistorianshut.com/2018/07/27/in-1861-several-u-s-newspapers-implied-that-general-william-tecumseh-sherman-was-a-lunatic/
- https://historyofyesterday.com/william-tecumseh-shermans-spot-on-prophecy-about-the-civil-war-abc406276fa1

#V-2b

1. "I am tired and sick of war. Its glory is all moonshine. It is only those who have neither fired a shot nor heard the shrieks and groans of the wounded who cry aloud for blood, for vengeance, for desolation. War is hell."

2. "If the people raise a howl against my barbarity and cruelty, I will answer that war is war and not popularity seeking. If they want peace, they and their relatives must stop the war."

3. "I make up my opinions from facts and reasoning, and not to suit anybody but myself. If people don't like my opinions, it makes little difference as I don't solicit their opinions or votes."

Answers #V-3

1. The organization of artillery within an army primarily composed of infantry posed significant logistic difficulties. What was the best way to coordinate the two arms? Such problems were critical both in campaigning (transporting artillery required horses and moved more slowly) and in battle (where they should be positioned relative to the infantry, both in defense and during an attack). Hunt

was the chief proponent of the organizational concept that infantry brigades should retain artillery batteries for close-in support but that batteries assigned to divisions and corps be assigned to an artillery reserve at the army level for more strategic control. A critical aspect of his theory was for batteries to fire slowly (once a minute), taking careful aim, and not to fire rapidly and haphazardly. Antietam proved him correct, and when Hooker reorganized things for Chancellorsville, disaster followed.

2. Confederate authority dictated that artillery remain under control of their corps command. The Confederate configuration was based on corps location. The artillery stayed with their commander. As a result, there was insufficient concentration of Confederate fire on the objective.

Whereas Hunt, the most well-known artillerist of his day, had argued that that was not the best management system and that a single commander of artillery should be in charge. At Gettysburg, Hunt's artillery positioning and strategy won the battle.

3. Hunt's use of the artillery reserve at Malvern Hill involved massing 250 guns to defeat repeated infantry assaults. He himself commanded 60 as a single battery. His positioning of artillery to create enfilading cross fire devastated Pickett's Charge. His ideas made Napoleonic methods of war obsolete, even if at the time, no one quite realized it.

Answers #V-4

1. Robert E. Lee and Albert Sidney Johnston
2. He was offered the position but rejected it, as he did not think he was qualified.
3. Future president James Garfield
4. President Johnson, who wanted to replace Grant with him as general-in-chief. Once again, Thomas asked his nomination be withdrawn.

Answer #V-5

He stole the money given as charitable donations and kept it for himself. He argued that the entire battlefield was a monument to him. This isn't surprising given the size of his ego. "American scoundrel" is truly the right descriptor for this man.

Answer #V-6

He made Arlington National Cemetery happen on Lee's front lawn, at the Custis-Lee Mansion, then called Arlington House. Meigs confiscated the home on the grounds that Mrs. Lee did not pay property taxes levied against the Arlington estate in person. The property was officially offered "for sale" on January 11, 1864, and was purchased for "government use, for war, military, charitable and educational purposes."

His intention was to make the house forever uninhabitable to prevent the Lee family from returning. A stone and masonry burial vault in the rose garden, 20 feet wide and 10 feet deep, contains the remains of 1,800 Bull Run casualties. Meigs himself was buried there with his wife, father, and son. Thousands of others were buried in the grounds surrounding the home.

Neither General Lee nor his wife ever attempted to recover control. After General Lee's death in 1870, George Washington Custis Lee brought legal action as eldest son of General and Mrs. Lee, claiming that the land had been illegally confiscated and that, according to his grandfather's will, he was the legal owner. In 1882, the U.S. Supreme Court in a 5–4 decision returned the property to Custis Lee. In 1883, Congress purchased the property for $150,000.

Answers #V-7

1. James Buchanan Eads
2. Bates was from Missouri, so Eads was his constituent.

The initial seven ironclads were the *Cairo, Carondelet, Cincinnati, Louisville, Mound City, Pittsburg* [sic], and *St. Louis*. The river ironclads were vital to the offensives in Tennessee, Kentucky, and upper Mississippi. Eads corresponded with navy officers who sailed his ships and used their experience in battle to improve the vessels. Modifications were made during post-combat repairs and improvements were designed for later generations of gunboats.

By the end of the war, he had built over 30 river ironclads. The last were so strong and well built that the navy sent them into service in the Gulf of Mexico, where they supported the successful Federal attack on the Confederate port city of Mobile. All senior officers in the western theater, including Grant and Sherman, agreed that Eads and his vessels had been vital to victory in the west.

Answers #V-8

(1) Although 78 Virginia generals joined the Confederacy, 10 others stayed in the Union:

a. Winfield Scott
b. George Thomas
c. William Terrill
d. Jesse Reno
e. Philip St. George Cooke (J.E.B. Stuart's father-in-law)
f. Alexander Dyer
g. John Newton
h. George Ramsey
i. William T. Ward
j. Rear Admiral Samuel Phillips Lee (cousin of General Lee)

Many generals on both sides chose sides that placed them in opposition to their state. John C. Breckinridge was a Confederate general and political figure despite the fact that Kentucky didn't secede. Bushrod Johnson (Ohio), Samuel Cooper (New York), and John C. Pemberton (Pennsylvania) were born in the North but fought for the South. David Farragut was born in Tennessee. John Buford was born in Kentucky. Montgomery Meigs was born in Augusta, Georgia. John C. Fremont was born in Savannah, Georgia. Solomon Meredith was born in North Carolina. David William Birney was born in Alabama and John Gibbon was raised in North Carolina in a slave-owning family but both fought for the Union.

(2) General Lee had a hard choice, no doubt. Lee chose on the basis of what was best for his family, his family history, his land holdings, and his thoughts on race. His choice was the only one a man of his time and place could make unless he turned his back on everything he had. Few thoughtful people would argue his decision was easy.

A man of loyalty and character, the choice he made was about his sense of identity. Elizabeth Pryor's outstanding interpretation is that Lee was a Southerner who believed in slavery, whose family and friends believed likewise, and whose heritage all influenced him to choose against his duty. Lee took at least two oaths to the United States. He was a man to whom duty and loyalty were critical elements of character. Pryor suggests that he chose the only way a man of his unique circumstances could and resolved the conflicts in his mind by reinterpretation of his duty.

Think about what Lee would have lost if he had stayed with the Union. Three estates with thousands of acres, almost 200 slaves, all the wealth that his father had lost and then some, his family's "property," his standing in Virginia's society, his reputation and that of the Lee name (which had been tarnished by his father) would all have been lost almost immediately if he had not resigned.

(3) Lee was a pretty typical slaveholding aristocrat of the Old Dominion. Lee said almost nothing in public about slavery, but in a widely quoted

letter to his wife in 1856, he described slavery as an evil but one that had more deleterious effects on whites than blacks. He felt that the "painful discipline" to which they were subjected elevated them from barbarism to civilization and introduced them to Christianity. He suggested that the end of slavery would come in "God's good time," but this might take quite a while since to God, a thousand years was just a moment. Meanwhile, the greatest danger to the "liberty" of white Southerners was the "evil course" pursued by the abolitionists, who stirred up sectional hatred. Lee voted for John C. Breckinridge, the extreme pro-slavery candidate in 1860 although the more moderate Southerner John Bell carried Virginia.

Lee owned a few slaves that he inherited from his mother (his son, Robert E. Lee Jr., said three or four families). Following the death of his father-in-law, George Washington Parke Custis, in 1857, Lee became master of 189 enslaved people. Custis's will stipulated that the enslaved people inherited be freed within five years. Lee, as executor and supervisor of Custis's estates, drove this labor force hard to lift those estates from debt. Concerned that it might take longer than the five years stipulated, Lee petitioned state courts to extend his control. The Custis bondspeople, aware of their former owner's intent, resisted Lee's efforts to enforce stricter work discipline. Resentment resulted in escape attempts. In 1859, Wesley Norris, his sister Mary, and their cousin George Parks escaped to Maryland where they were captured and returned to Arlington. In an 1866 account, Norris described being whipped under Lee's watch.

Virginia courts in 1858 and 1862 denied Lee's petition to indefinitely postpone the emancipation of his wife's enslaved people. Finally, on December 29, 1862, Lee officially freed the enslaved workers and their families on the estate. Lee freed his slaves because it was required under the terms of his father-in-law's will. Even then, he kept them enslaved longer than the terms of the will.

Further Reading

- Foner, Eric. "The Making and the Breaking of the Legend of Robert E. Lee." *New York Times*, August 28, 2017. https://www.nytimes.com/2017/08/28/books/review/eric-foner-robert-e-lee.html
- Freeman, Douglas Southall. *Lee*. Abridged. Scribner, 1997.
- Pryor, Elizabeth Brown. *Reading the Man: A Portrait of Robert E. Lee through His Private Letters*. Penguin Books, 2008.
- https://angrystaffofficer.com/2019/04/01/debunking-the-myth-of-southern-hegemony-southerners-who-stayed-loyal-to-the-us-in-the-civil-war/?fbclid=IwAR0Ak2TYD2s-B_MfaAupSOERZrPOtyKa6QroZTPuHTfp_amo9NBra6ZKgFU

Answers #V-9

1. Johnston was promoted by Davis to full general following First Manassas at which Johnston reinforced Beauregard. However, three other men he had outranked in the "old army" now outranked him. Johnston felt that since he was the senior officer to leave the U.S. Army and join the Confederacy, he should not be ranked behind Samuel Cooper, Albert Sidney Johnston, and Robert E. Lee. Only Beauregard was placed behind Johnston on the list of five new generals. Davis's reasoning was that Johnston's U.S. commission as a brigadier general was as a staff officer and that his highest line commission was as a lieutenant colonel; both Sidney Johnston and Lee had been full colonels. Johnston sent an undiplomatic letter of protest to Davis, who was offended. Their relationship never recovered.

2. The relationship between Johnston and Davis became acrimonious as public allegations surfaced regarding who was to blame for Vicksburg. Johnston was especially angered that blame was placed on him, considering the lack of resources he was given, both in terms of manpower and supplies, Pemberton's refusal to abandon Vicksburg as he had suggested, and President Davis's habit of communicating directly to Johnston's subordinates. (Davis considered firing Johnston, but he remained a popular officer and had many political allies, most notably Senator Louis Wigfall.) Bragg's army was removed from Johnston's command, setting the stage for the Chattanooga Campaign and ultimately Bragg's resignation as commander.

Answers #V-10

#V-10a

Fourth cousins by marriage: Longstreet was Julia's fourth cousin. Longstreet and Grant also had spent three years together at West Point and served together in the Mexican-American War. Longstreet was in the wedding party at the Grants' wedding.

#V-10b

In the Suffolk Campaign, he obtained sufficient supplies to feed the Army of Northern Virginia for two months, missing the Battle of Chancellorsville. The Knoxville Campaign is discussed separately.

Answers #V-11

#V-11a

He failed to identify a problem in the deployment of his troops. There was a 600-yard gap in the line created by swampy terrain and dense vegetation. This gap was exploited by the Union advance, leading to two-thirds of the Confederate casualties in Jackson's corps.

#V-11b

At the Battle of Glendale, Stonewall Jackson got lost and didn't take part. Longstreet essentially managed half of the Army of Northern Virginia. Instead of arranging his men in lines of combat, he chose to string them out as a single file. After Seven Days, Lee recognized Longstreet's leadership and he was made commander of 28 brigades (up from 6) and leader of the right wing, later First Corps.

An editorial appeared in the *Richmond Examiner* claiming incorrectly that A.P. Hill alone fought at Glendale. Longstreet wrote a letter in response published in the *Richmond Whig* denying that version of events.

Hill took offense and requested to be transferred. Longstreet gladly accepted the request, adding a sarcastic note that it was necessary "to exchange the troops or to exchange the commander."

Lee made no move at first.

After Hill's refusal to forward even routine reports to headquarters, Longstreet placed him under arrest and confined him to quarters. Hill took the next step, issuing a challenge to his commanding officer to duel.

Obviously, Lee did not want his best battle commanders harmed in a personal duel. So he transferred Hill and his command to Stonewall Jackson in the valley.

#V-11c

1. It took exactly one week after Hill's transfer before Hill and Jackson began an even more disputatious relationship than Hill with Longstreet. Hill was upset at Jackson's command style. Jackson kept Hill uninformed about his plans and changed the order of march and neglected to inform Hill. Jackson and Hill exchanged words over his division straggling. Jackson asked Lee to reduce the size of Hill's division. At the Battle of Cedar Mountain, Hill once again saved Jackson's army by arriving just in time to stop the Union advance. One

of the broken units he had assisted was Jackson's old Stonewall Brigade, a point he was only too pleased to note.

    2. In the Maryland Campaign, Jackson was displeased with Hill's response to his orders, so he began personally issuing orders to Hill's brigade commanders. Hill said, " General Jackson, you have assumed command of my division, here is my sword; I have no use for it."

    3. Hill was ordered to march in the rear of his division for the rest of the campaign. Jackson charged him for allowing his command to straggle. After Antietam, which Hill—arriving last on the field just in the nick of time after an astounding 17-mile forced march—saved, each officially made charges against the other. Jackson was killed at Chancellorsville before any resolution was reached. Hill was then advanced to corps command so he wouldn't need to report to either Longstreet or Ewell.

    4. Jackson was unable to get along with subordinates, in contrast to Hill, who was unable to get along with superiors.

Further Reading

- https://warfarehistorynetwork.com/2015/11/15/civil-war-generals-stonewall-jackson-and-a-p-hill/
- https://www.historynet.com/souths-feuding-generals-november-99-americas-civil-war-feature.htm

Answers #V-12

    1. Pickett carried the flag over the parapet during the Battle of Chapultepec in September 1847. Wounded at the base of the wall, Pickett's friend and colleague Lieutenant James Longstreet handed him the flag. Pickett carried the flag over the wall and made his way to the roof of the palace, unfurling it over the fortress and announcing its surrender.

    2. Pickett was an excellent brigade commander at Williamsburg and Seven Pines. At Gaines's Mill, he was wounded in the shoulder leading his men in an attack. He missed Antietam due to his wound, was lightly used at Fredericksburg, and missed Chancellorsville as part of Longstreet's Suffolk Campaign.

    3. He was hosting a fish fry, attended by other Confederate officers, resulting in a crushing defeat against Union cavalry under Sheridan supported by an infantry corps under Warren at Five Forks. It was said that there was an acoustic shadow that prevented anyone from hearing sounds of the battle.

4. After Gettysburg, he commanded the Department of North Carolina. At the Battle of New Bern, which was a defeat, he had 22 Union captured soldiers executed. After the war, an investigation seemed to suggest he was in the wrong until General Grant ended the investigation so that Pickett could return to the United States.

5. A brief meeting between Lee and Pickett ended quickly. Afterward, he told Mosby, "That man destroyed my division," to which Mosby replied, "Yes, but he made you immortal."

6. His widow, LaSalle, became a writer and lecturer intent on describing her husband as the perfect Southern gentleman.

Answers #V-13

1. Beauregard ran empty trains up and down the city with the locomotives whistling and his soldiers cheering. The idea was to make it appear that reinforcements were arriving constantly.

2. Malaria was rampant in Corinth and the water was contaminated. Perhaps half of his men had recurrent fever.

3. Leaving the important rail junction of Corinth without a battle could not have enamored him with Davis. He did so knowing he was outnumbered and that many of his troops were ill. Another possibility is that Bragg and Beauregard had a competitive relationship. Bragg was appointed head of the Louisiana Guards at the start of the war, which was the position Beauregard coveted. When he became head of the Confederate army instead, Bragg was envious. And of course, Bragg was Davis's friend. Finally, his Creole background and French appearance led to some cultural misunderstandings particularly in regard to infidelity, a reputed Creole characteristic. Hence, he was charged with having a train of concubines, a wagon of champagne, and so on.

In 1893, Longstreet told the *Washington Post*, "The same may be said of Beauregard, a brave, mettlesome soldier in action, and a strategist of the first order. He was, like Johnston, equal to any command. He labored under the same disadvantage with Johnston—he had aroused the personal displeasure and jealousy of the President, and never had his full confidence. He was very resourceful, made excellent plans, and was intensely patriotic. His military suggestions received little heed at Richmond. He undoubtedly saved the capital from Butler."

FURTHER READING
- https://www.thoughtco.com/general-p-g-t-beauregard-2360577

Answers #V-14

1. The Dix-Hill Cartel was agreed to on July 22, 1862, with Major General John Dix. A scale of equivalents was developed wherein an officer might be exchanged for a certain number of enlisted men or might entail a parole in which no military capacity was allowed until officially exchanged. Soldiers of equivalent ranks would be exchanged on a one-to-one value. The table lists the equivalents:

Officer	Equivalent in Privates
Corporal and Sergeant	2
Lieutenant	4
Captain	6
Major	8
Lieutenant Colonel	10
Colonel	15
Brigadier General	20
Major General	40
Commanding General	60

The cartel worked initially but failed when President Davis refused to honor the arrangement in regard to black Union soldiers.

2. Hill was critical of Lee a number of times, and General Lee did not like it. Of the Battle of Malvern Hill, Hill said, "It wasn't war; it was murder." The loss of Special Orders 191 was often blamed on Hill both during and after the war, and it may be that Lee thought Hill was responsible.

Further Reading

- https://www.americancivilwarforum.com/why-did-d-h-hill-not-get-along-with-r-e-lee-53994.html
- https://www.historynet.com/the-abrupt-demise-of-a-maverick-daniel-harvey-hill.htm

Answer #V-15

After graduating from West Point, he worked as an assistant to Major Albert Myer, who developed the Signal Corps and developed the code for signal flags. He was the first to use signal flags during combat, at First Manassas. His appointment in the Confederate army was as chief engineer and signal officer. This involved him in intelligence gathering, so he was involved with the spy ring in Washington. He was also involved in the use of observation balloons in the Peninsula Campaign, giving General Lee accurate information at Gaines's Mill.

Answers #V-16

1. When Lee became commander of the Army of Northern Virginia, he sent Stuart on a reconnaissance mission to determine whether the right flank of the Union army was vulnerable. Stuart and 1,200 troopers made a complete circumnavigation of the Union army position, riding 150 miles in four days. He determined that the flank was indeed vulnerable. He also captured many Union soldiers, 260 horses and mules, and numerous supplies. His men met no serious opposition from the Union cavalry, coincidentally commanded by his father-in-law, Colonel Philip St. George Cooke.

2. Stuart led a highly courageous raid on General John Pope's headquarters. He retrieved intelligence and a staff document from which Lee could learn the strength and position of Federal forces, allowing him to plan for the coming battle. Moreover, he also captured Pope's dress uniform from the Union general's tent.

3. The second day of Chancellorsville, after Jackson's and A.P. Hill's wounding.

Further Reading

- https://encyclopediavirginia.org/entries/stuart-j-e-b-1833-1864/
- https://www.history.com/topics/american-civil-war/j-e-b-stuart

Answers #V-17

1. He was a slave trader as well as land and cotton dealer.
2. He and his men rode out of the fort through the snow and escaped.
3. He ordered, "Charge 'em both ways, boys," and he did, and he escaped.
4. At Brice's Cross Roads, he defeated an infantry force twice his

size. Forrest used his more mobile cavalry to threaten both ends of the Union infantry line simultaneously and his artillery to hold the center.

5. He was the leader of the unit that engaged in massacring black Union troops, although there is no definitive evidence that he ordered it or participated in it. The action was one of the most notorious war crimes of the conflict.

6. He had 29 horses shot from under him, killed 30 enemy soldiers in hand-to-hand combat, and was wounded four times.

7. No one knows for sure. It's hard to conceive that the "Wizard of the Saddle" and the "Grand Wizard" of the Ku Klux Klan having the same name was coincidental. His testimony to Congress was a blueprint for evasion. He had the benefit of intervention by Grant and Sherman, who wanted an immediate reconciliation between the Northern and Southern states.

Further Reading

- Hurst, Jack. *Nathan Bedford Forrest: A Biography.* Knopf, 1993.
- https://www.americancivilwarforum.com/general-nathan-bedford-forrest-2027716.html
- https://www.battlefields.org/learn/civil-war/battles/brices-cross-roads
- https://www.cnn.com/2020/10/01/opinions/nathan-bedford-forrest-connor-towne-oneill-carr/index.html
- https://heritagepost.org/article/brices-crossroads/

Answers #V-18

1. Nathan Bedford Forrest and Richard Taylor. (The Confederate States of America Congress never formally approved John B. Gordon's promotion to lieutenant general.)

2. At Trevilian Station, Hampton and Fitzhugh Lee repulsed repeated attacks by Union general Philip Sheridan and prevented the destruction of the Virginia Central Railroad. It was one of the largest cavalry battles of the war, with the highest casualties of any cavalry battle. The battle was a tactical victory for the Confederates, as Sheridan failed to achieve his goal of destroying the Virginia Central Railroad. The distraction it created, however, contributed to Grant's successful crossing of the James River.

3. Hampton was leader of the Redeemers, a political party during Reconstruction whose goal was to restore white rule. His campaign

for governor was notable for violence by the Red Shirts, a paramilitary group that served the Democratic Party by disrupting elections and suppressing black and Republican voting. They were a much more violent and organized group than the Ku Klux Klan, and their goal was intimidating nonwhite, non–Democratic voters.

FURTHER READING

- https://www.history.com/topics/american-civil-war/wade-hampton

Answers #V-19

1. This famous story originated in John Wyeth's 1899 biography *The Life of General Nathan Forrest*. The official records seem to show a respectful relationship between Bragg and Forrest. The original source was James Cowan, a surgeon in the Confederate army and a cousin of Forrest, who was the only actual eyewitness. However, Cowan's version suggests that Jefferson Davis was also there, which is not possible. In Wyeth's second edition, he removed this story. It is also hard to imagine Bragg not immediately firing Forrest for such insubordination.
2. Whatever actually happened, Bragg transferred three of Forrest's brigades into Wheeler's corps but not Forrest himself.

FURTHER READING

- https://emergingcivilwar.com/2013/09/24/post-chickamauga-
- https://www.historynet.com/did-forrest-really-threaten-braggs-life.htm
- bragg-vs-forrest/
- https://www.thegreatcoursesdaily.com/american-civil-war-braggs-problems-and-the-siege-of-chattanooga/

Answer #V-20

The fact that he was an immigrant and not a Virginian and who did not study at West Point would have been well outside the usual Davis formula for promotion.

Certainly, his famous suggestion to the top leadership of the Army of Tennessee that the South should consider the emancipation of slaves to enlist them in the army, recognizing that his country was losing the war, may have been one reason. Allowing slaves to fight in the Confederate army due to pragmatic (diminishing Confederate soldiers) and moral reasons (to show the North and perhaps posterity that the war wasn't only about slavery but also about a broader way of life he had grown fond of in the South since leaving Ireland) was not widely countenanced by his colleagues. Obviously, Cleburne's suggestion was not politically correct in his environment.

Moreover, his statement that slavery was the Confederacy's "most vulnerable point, a continued embarrassment, and in some respects an insidious weakness" was poorly received by Confederate politicians and other military leaders. Davis directed the proposal be suppressed; this could not have been a career-enhancing moment. John Bell Hood undoubtedly held this against him in blaming him in part for Schofield's slipping past him on the way to Franklin.

FURTHER READING

- https://www.battlefields.org/learn/biographies/patrick-r-cleburne
- https://www.theirishstory.com/2021/03/16/major-general-patrick-ronanye-cleburne-corks-confederate-general/#.Yars5BaIYlQ

Answer #V-21

Cooper's loyalties were with the South: his wife's family was from Virginia, and he had a close friendship with Jefferson Davis. He resigned his U.S. commission and traveled to Montgomery to join the Confederate army. He was immediately appointed as brigadier general and adjutant general and inspector general of the Confederate army, a post he held until the end of the war. On May 16, 1861, he was promoted to full general in the Confederate army, one of five men promoted at that time and one of just eight total. His was the earliest date of rank, and thus, despite his relative obscurity today, he outranked Generals Albert S. Johnston, Robert E. Lee, Joseph E. Johnston, and P.G.T. Beauregard. He reported directly to President Davis.

His last official act in office was to preserve the official records of the Confederate army and turn them over intact to the U.S. government, where they form a part of the *Official Records, the War of the Rebellion: A Compilation of the Official Records of the Union and Confederate Armies*, published starting in 1880. We would not have these records to study were it not for General Cooper.

Section V. Military Personalities of the Civil War   113

FURTHER READING

- https://www.mycivilwar.com/leaders/cooper_samuel.html?fbc lid=IwAR1qnTbSBeK0NYpib2z5BHjkxOjEAkJVdsxO_fHpm_ alFLiKU3GuLB4_Zo0

Answers #V-22

Howard: (1) Failed to entrench and be prepared for Jackson's flank attack at Chancellorsville. Another failure was his poor positioning of the defensive line of Brigadier General Francis C. Barlow on day one of Gettysburg, which was exploited by the Confederate corps of Lieutenant General Richard S. Ewell and once again the 11th Corps collapsed, leaving many men behind to be taken prisoner. (2) Transferred to the west, he became an excellent corps commander during the Atlanta Campaign and March to the Sea. General Sherman would commend Howard as a corps commander of "the utmost skill, nicety and precision." He went on after the war to direct the Freedmen's Bureau.

Sherman: (1) Failed to entrench or heed warnings of Confederate troops at the beginning of the Battle of Shiloh. (2) Led the western army in the Atlanta Campaign and March to the Sea.

Wood: (1) Moved his men in a defensive position at Chickamauga, (perhaps) knowing the order to do so was faulty. (2) Wood redeemed himself during the successful assault on Missionary Ridge, when Wood's division was the first division to reach the rebel positions atop the heights and the first division to drive defenders from their fortifications. He also excelled at the Battle of Lovejoy's Station on August 20, 1864, where despite a badly shattered leg, he stayed on the field encouraging his men.

Ord: (1) Ord was sent with a detachment of two divisions along with Major General William S. Rosecrans's forces to intercept Sterling Price at the town of Iuka. Due to a possible acoustic shadow, Ord's forces were never engaged and Rosecrans fought alone. (2) Major General John Gibbon's corps of Ord's army played a significant role in the breakthrough at Petersburg. On April 9, he led a forced march to Appomattox Court House to relieve Major General Philip H. Sheridan's cavalry and force Lee's surrender.

Jackson: (1) Performed poorly at the Seven Days battles. He arrived late at Mechanicsville and inexplicably ordered his men to bivouac for the night within clear earshot of the battle. He was late at Gaines's Mill and Savage's Station. At White Oak Swamp, he failed to employ fording places to cross White Oak Swamp Creek, attempting for hours to rebuild a bridge, which limited his involvement to an ineffectual artillery duel and a missed opportunity to intervene decisively at the Battle of Glendale, which was raging nearby. Thousands of men died. It has been suggested by McPherson that his troops were lethargic from the travel from the valley and that Jackson, who required more than the usual amount of sleep, was both sleep deprived and suffering from stress fatigue. (2) The importance and number of Jackson's subsequent victories and hard fighting are the stuff of legend: he was outstanding at Second Manassas, Antietam, Fredericksburg, and Chancellorsville.

Mahone: (1) Unaccountably failed to engage his troops on day two at Gettysburg despite orders but (2) became a hero at the Battle of the Crater and Lee's go-to man during the Petersburg siege.

Breckinridge: Bragg charged that Breckinridge's drunkenness had contributed to defeats at Stones River and Missionary Ridge, but (2) he redeemed himself at New Market and Second Kernstown and saved the Confederate military records when Richmond fell. Breckinridge should probably have been president or secretary of war much sooner; executive decisions were his strength.

Hooker: (1) Got conked in the head and made awful command decisions at Chancellorsville but (2) redeemed himself with his preparations prior to Gettysburg and his attack at Lookout Mountain. He resigned rather than accept Howard as his commander, the man he held responsible for the loss at Chancellorsville.

Wallace: (1) Got lost finding his way to the Shiloh battlefield on day one but (2) redeemed himself at the Battle of Monocacy and as the author of *Ben-Hur*.

SECTION VI

1861 Battles and Campaigns

Challenges

Challenge #VI-1

"War does not determine who is right—only who is left."
—Bertrand Russell

The Revolutionary War concerned the separation or independence of the 13 colonies from England, generated by a desire for a change in the form of government, while the American Civil War resolved whether the United States would remain one country and what its moral core would be. A revolutionary war is often thought of as a war of independence, while a civil war is fought between factions in one country.

Do these distinctions in terminology hold up to scrutiny? President Davis would say that the Confederacy was seeking independence. They had no intention of changing the U.S. government. Didn't King George think that the colonies were part of his country?

Challenge: What is the difference between a civil war and a revolution? Bonus: Within that distinction, what is a rebellion? And what is an insurrection?

Your answer must consider whether the Civil War was a revolutionary war and whether the Revolutionary War was a civil war.

Challenge #VI-2

The firing on Fort Sumter was the immediate action that started the Civil War. Once the Confederates under P.G.T. Beauregard fired on U.S. federal property, a line had been crossed and a rebellion had begun.

Charleston, South Carolina, was the most important port on the southeast coast. The harbor was defended by three Federal forts: Sumter; Castle Pinckney, one mile off the city's Battery; and heavily armed Fort Moultrie on Sullivan's Island. The Union defense under Major Robert Anderson was originally at Fort Moultrie. On December 26, 1860, Anderson and his command of 90 men slipped away from Fort Moultrie to the more defensible Fort Sumter. Some consider this movement a provocation, but of course, both were U.S. federal forts.

Meanwhile, Union supplies began to dwindle. On January 5, 1861, the *Star of the West* departed from New York with 200 reinforcements and provisions. As the ship approached Charleston Harbor on January 9, cadets from the Citadel fired, forcing the ship to abandon its mission. On March 1, Jefferson Davis ordered Brigadier General P.G.T. Beauregard to take command of the Confederates in Charleston. On April 4, Lincoln informed Southern delegates that he intended to attempt to resupply Fort Sumter, as its garrison was now critically in need. In the views of South Carolinians, any attempt to reinforce Sumter would mean war. "Now the issue of battle is to be forced upon us," declared the *Charleston Mercury*.

Challenges: (1) Was an attempt made to have Anderson to surrender peaceably? (2) Who fired the first shot into the fort from Charleston? (3) Who fired the first return salvo from the fort? (4) With the surrender of the fort, how many casualties had been sustained? (5) Who received the surrender? (6) What was the relationship between Beauregard and Anderson? Bonus: Why was Fort Sumter more defensible than Fort Moultrie?

Challenge #VI-3

The First Battle of Bull Run or Manassas was the first major battle of the war. The battlefield is located about 30 miles southwest of Washington, D.C. The forces on both sides were badly led and poorly trained. Irvin McDowall led the Union army and P.G.T. Beauregard led the Confederate army.

General McDowell was a graduate of West Point and taught tactics there for four years to many of the generals who went on to great fame for their skills. His primary army experience was as a supply officer under General Winfield Scott. Although he had never actually commanded an army on a battlefield, he was given this responsibility despite his protests that he was a supply officer, not a combat commander. Convinced that his troops were not ready, he was nevertheless pressured to attack by President Lincoln. His attack plan was clever enough but his army too inexperienced to carry it out.

There was essentially no strategic value to the battle, but its major lessons were that the war was not going to end anytime soon and that it was going to be much more violent than anyone had realized. About the only memorable aspect was the stand of a brigade of Virginia troops who stood "like a stonewall" under the leadership of an unknown brigadier general and notoriously unpopular science teacher at Virginia Military Institute named Thomas J. Jackson.

Challenges: (1) McDowell's plans for First Manassas included a diversionary attack and a flanking action by a corps, yet none of these maneuvers were actually performed. The reasons were partly because no one in his army had a clue how to carry them out and partly because he was rushed. Who rushed him? Why? (2) In what ways were the tactics used illustrative of the poor training and leadership? (3) What other problems did the battle illustrate? (4) What two new innovations, used perhaps for the first time in war, led to the Confederate victory? (5) Who made the famous statement about Jackson and what happened to him?

Lieutenant General Pierre Gustave Toutant de Beauregard by Mathew Brady.

Challenge #VI-4

General Winfield Scott knew that a civil war would be a prolonged affair when everyone else thought it would be over in weeks. He was a top-notch military strategist who was a hero of the Mexican War. He saw long in advance that the weakness of a Southern nation was its absence of manufacturing, supplies, and weapons production. Therefore, he developed what came to be known as the Anaconda Plan, after the snake that squeezes its victims and suffocates them to death. The idea was that by blockading the Southern ocean ports and the Mississippi River, the Confederate military would slowly die as its supplies dwindled, isolated from its foreign trading partners.

Other Union commanders were not sanguine about the idea, preferring a rapid attack strategy to a slow suffocation. Although Anaconda was not implemented fully, President Lincoln proclaimed a blockade in April 1861. This required the monitoring of 3,500 miles of Atlantic and Gulf coastline, including 12 major ports, notably New Orleans and Mobile.

Challenges: How well did the blockade work? How did its effectiveness change over the course of the war?

Challenge #VI-5

Railroads were crucial strategic and tactical resources during the Civil War, serving as supply and transportation means for both sides. Soldiers, food and fodder, and armaments were transported by rail to keep the war effort progressing. Critical crossroads and segments of track became military targets because they were vital to transportation of manpower and material. Supplies could be transported more quickly and efficiently by railcar than on horse-drawn wagons.

Southern railway design concentrated on short lines linking cotton regions to oceanic or river ports. The absence of an interconnected network became a major handicap during the Civil War. An agrarian society, its rails were primarily intended as commercial lines linking agricultural centers to ports for the sale and transportation of goods.

In contradistinction, the North and Midwest constructed networks that linked cities to each other by 1860. Over 80 percent of farms were within 10 miles of a railway, facilitating the shipment of grain, hogs, and cattle to national and international markets. Two-thirds of the rail miles and four-fifths of the manufacturing power of the nation were located in Northern states.

At the start of the war, over 200 railroads were in existence. Those in the North could run from one place to another without any problem. But in the South, trains of one railroad line could not run on the others.

Challenge: What was the reason for this difference, and how did it impact the war efforts and military strategy?

Challenge #VI-6

The Civil War was, of course, a conflict between the blue and the gray. But really, the color of the Confederate uniform was butternut, a light brown color. The Union at the start of the war had myriad colors and styles, including zouaves, cadet gray, and a mix of light and dark blue.

Challenge: Why did the Union ultimately choose dark blue and the South light gray? Bonus: Why are modern police mostly clad in blue?

Answers

Answer #VI-1

A rebellion is the more general term encompassing all civil uprisings, while an insurrection is a rebellion on a smaller scale. A revolution is precipitated by an existing power gradient (political, economic) and a desire to change the form or philosophy of government, while seeking independence. A civil war is fought by civilians/citizens of the same country to gain control of that country (e.g., English), whereas a revolution is a forcible overthrow of a government or social order in favor of a new system (e.g., French, Russian).

The problems with this distinction are who decides if there are one country or two and what defines a new system? Every military is run by professionals: clearly, Lee, Johnston, Davis, and so forth were not mere citizens but highly trained and experienced soldiers. Another is that the Civil War would fall somewhere between.

One major distinction between a revolutionary war and a civil war is in whose perspective things are interpreted. In 1776, "we" declared independence, so it was a revolution; the British considered it an insurrection. In 1861, the Confederacy declared itself independent, so they called it a revolution, but the Union fought to remain one country, thus a civil war and a rebellion.

There is also a political/propaganda aspect to the terminology: a revolution for independence sounds like a worthy cause, to gain freedom and liberty and rights that are overdue, while a civil war sounds divisive and a war merely over control. Lincoln wanted it to be a civil war, to deny nation status to the Confederacy, while Davis wanted it to be the Second American Revolution; both had political purposes. How conflicts are labeled is a political construct, aimed at conferring legitimacy on one entity or the other. History is indeed written by the victors, and it begins with the name of the conflict.

Answers #VI-2

1. On April 9, Davis ordered Beauregard to take the fort. On April 10, a courteous demand for surrender was delivered in person, and equally courteously, Anderson refused. The two men who delivered

the request were Captain Stephen D. Lee and General James Chesnut, Jr. (husband of Mary, the diarist), both of whom would play important roles in the war.

2. A 36-hour mortar and cannon attack then occurred. The first shot of the battle and the war was a signal shot by Lieutenant Henry S. Farley from Fort Johnson under the command of Captain George S. James, according to Stephen Lee. James was killed at the Battle of South Mountain in 1862. Edmund Ruffin did shoot one of the first signal shots but not the first as is legendary.

3. The first return cannon round was fired by Captain Abner Doubleday, the second-in-command.

4. There were no casualties on either side during the battle, but buildings in the fort were set on fire and resources were running low, so Anderson surrendered. However, a 100-gun salute after the battle resulted in two Union deaths when a round exploded prematurely. One death was immediate, the other a mortal wounding.

5. Louis Wigfall, a former U.S. senator from Texas, then a Confederate officer. He would become a member of the Confederate Senate and be a powerful force there.

6. Anderson's valor and commitment to duty was recognized in the Union. Beauregard was honored in the South for its first victory. He was ordered to direct the troops at Bull Run. Anderson had been Beauregard's artillery instructor at West Point, and Beauregard was serving as superintendent there until secession.

Bonus: Two reasons: (1) Moultrie was vulnerable to an overland attack and (2) its guns were pointed out to sea, which was the intended purpose of these forts, not toward the town, which is where the threat was located.

Further Reading

- https://www.battlefields.org/learn/civil-war/battles/fort-sumter
- http://www.eyewitnesstohistory.com/sumter.htm
- https://www.history.com/topics/american-civil-war/fort-sumter

Answers VI-3

1. President Lincoln was adamant that an attack be made: "You are green, it is true; but they are green also. You are all green alike." Also, there were rumors (which were accurate) that Johnston's troops were ready to move by train to reinforce Beauregard, which would

increase the size of the force facing him from 22,000 to 34,000. Another reason was that many Union troops had volunteered for 90-day service, which was about to expire.

 2. (a) The various regiments were advanced piecemeal. (b) All of the attacks were frontal; there was no attempt at flank attacks. (c) Artillery units were left exposed without infantry defense. (d) Neither commander put into the fight much more than 50 percent of their troops.

 3. (a) Lack of similar uniforms led to confusion about friend versus foe, (b) lack of a standard national flag confused rebel troops, leading Beauregard to design one, (c) many different weapon types made defective or obsolete ones difficult to support, and (d) Lincoln pushed the Union into battle before they were ready.

 4. (a) Railroads used to transport troops to the front for the first time. When reinforcements under General Joseph Johnston arrived from Shenandoah Valley by rail, the battle quickly turned into a rout as Union troops panicked. (b) Colonel E.P. Alexander's newly established "system of field signals" that notified "Shanks" Evans that "his left is turned" turned the tide.

 5. General Barnard Bee, who was killed very soon after his comment.

Answer #VI-4

 The Union blockade was a powerful weapon that eventually destroyed the Southern economy, at the cost of very few lives, just as General Scott planned it. The measure of the blockade's success was not the few ships that slipped through but the thousands that never tried. Ordinary freighters had no reasonable hope of evading the blockade and stopped calling at Southern ports. The interdiction of coastal traffic meant that long-distance interior travel depended on the rickety railroad system and never overcame the devastating impact of the blockade.

 When the blockade began in 1861, it was only partially effective. It has been estimated that only one in ten ships trying to evade the blockade were intercepted. However, the Union navy gradually increased in size throughout the war and was able to drastically reduce shipments into Confederate ports. By 1864, one in every three ships attempting to run the blockade were being intercepted; in the final two years of the war, the only ships with a reasonable chance of evading the blockade were blockade runners specifically designed for speed. Lee's army, at the end of the supply line, nearly always was short of supplies as the war progressed into its final two years.

Answer #VI-5

The South had two disadvantages regarding railroads. First, it had only about one-third the mileage as the North, and second, the gauges of the rails varied widely. Much of the Confederate rail network was in the 5 ft (1,524 mm) broad gauge format, but much of North Carolina and Virginia had 4 ft 8½ in (1,435 mm) standard gauge lines. Sometimes, for example in Montgomery, Alabama, a city was served by two railroads with different gauges and different depots. Thus, cargo had to be unloaded from one railroad and moved by animal-powered transportation to the other company's station, where it would be reloaded. Southern railroads west of the Mississippi were isolated, disconnected, and differed widely in gauge.

In the South, travel was mainly confined to east-to-west in the east and north-to-south in the west. There were minimal interconnections between the various regions: the only east-to-west routes went through Knoxville, Chattanooga, and Atlanta. These familiar names where important battles were fought were strategic locations precisely because of the railroad. Conversely, the Southern system did have its lines placed well behind the battlegrounds in the early stages of the war. These interior lines were a huge advantage to the Confederate strategy of transporting critical manpower and supplies to where they were in immediate demand.

By contrast, almost all of the Northern rails were in the 4 ft 8½ in (1,435 mm) standard. Consequently, the North could transport troops and material to more places with minimal transfers due to gauge. In the North, the lines went east-to-west with little interconnection south of New Jersey.

Southern military authorities were quicker to recognize the potential of railroads and to use the rails it had to transport troops from one theater to another, to support troops in a threatened area. The North was not as quick to learn this trick.

When Ulysses S. Grant was promoted to command all of the Union armies, he understood the advantage the South had in its interior lines of supply and the part railroads played. As long as the Northern strategy involved uncoordinated attacks on different regions, the rebels would be able to transport troops from one area to another in order to halt any Union advance. By applying pressure to all points of the South at the same time, advances could be made without the Confederates reinforcing threatened zones from other areas.

Further Reading

- Confederate Railroads in the American Civil War. https://pipiwiki.com/wiki/Confederate_railroads_in_the_American_Civil_War

- History of Rail Transport in the United States. https://www.americanhistoryusa.com/topic/history-of-rail-transport-in-the-united-states/
- Klein, L.W. "The Critical Role of Railroads in Influencing Military Strategy in the Civil War." *Emerging Civil War Blog*. https://emergingcivilwar.com/2022/02/15/the-critical-role-of-railroads-in-influencing-military-strategy-in-the-civil-war/#more-208332
- Railroads in the Civil War. http://www.gatewaynmra.org/2004/railroads-in-the-civil-war/; http://www.civilwar.com/history/weapons-44543/railroads-79476.html

Answers #VI-6

At the start of the war, Confederate soldiers wore clothes from home and homespun. When cloth became scarce, the principal source of Confederate uniforms was captured Union uniforms. The dark blue uniforms were boiled in a solution with walnut hulls, acorns, and lye. The resulting color was light tan, which the Southerners called "butternut." Weathered and faded gray uniforms also took on a light brownish appearance.

Gray was chosen for Confederate uniforms because gray dye could be made relatively cheaply. Also, the standard uniform color of state militias was a shade of cadet gray, which is not suitable for combat wear, as it gives away the position of the individual easily from its bright blue-gray tones. Generals didn't need to worry about this, so they wore beautiful gray uniforms that they purchased on their own.

Since the American Revolution, the American infantry had worn dark blue coats (to separate them from the Redcoats). In the Mexican War, this was supplemented by pale blue pants. With mass production necessary for the Civil War, everything became dark blue. The blue dye was called Barlow's indigo blue. Before the mass production of cheap chemical dyes was perfected in Prussia in the late 19th century, natural indigo was more expensive than gray dyes.

Ironically, most indigo production was in the South; this caused the Union to briefly resort to logwood dyes that immediately changed to brown reacting to sunlight. For this reason, some preserved uniforms have brown thread, as they continued to use logwood (as well other cheaper materials) as dye. These dyes were too difficult to make in the South in large quantities given limitations in resources.

Bonus: The first U.S. professional policemen wore blue to give usage to the surplus Civil War uniforms from the Union side.

Section VII

1862 Battles and Campaigns

Challenges

1. East

Challenge #VII-1a,b

#VII-1a

The Shenandoah Campaign of 1862 was undoubtedly the pinnacle of Stonewall Jackson's career. His unpredictability, speed, and aggressiveness all rightly make this campaign one that is taught as a standard of military strategy. His 17,000 men marched 646 miles in 48 days, defeating three Union armies in succession, winning at least five significant battles. As a diversion of Union forces away from the Peninsula Campaign, it was plainly brilliant.

However, Peter Cozzens suggests that it wasn't so much that Jackson was brilliant as that his opponents were extraordinarily incompetent. Moreover, he concludes that Jackson was actually an awful leader.

Challenges: (1) Name the Union generals he defeated. (2) What could the Union army have done better that would have made Jackson's task much harder, and why didn't they do it? (3) By the end of the victorious campaign, Jackson had charged basically all of his subordinates with incompetence, and many were facing courts-martial as a result. Why didn't they follow his orders?

#VII-1b

Although Jackson's Shenandoah Campaign is acknowledged to be a work of military genius, he did lose one battle. Jackson received incorrect intelligence that a small detachment of Union soldiers was vulnerable, but it was in fact a full infantry division more than twice the size of Jackson's force. His initial cavalry attack was forced to retreat. He reinforced it with a small infantry brigade. With his other two brigades, Jackson sought to envelop the Union right, but a single Union brigade drove Jackson from the field.

Challenge: Name the battle and the Union commander who defeated Jackson (the only one ever).

Lieutenant General Thomas Jonathan "Stonewall" Jackson. This is the "Chancellorsville" portrait, taken at a Spotsylvania County farm on April 26, 1863, seven days before he was wounded.

Challenge #VII-2a–f

#VII-2a

In March 1862, General McClellan decided on a turning movement by water. The plan was to land troops on the peninsula and use the Union navy to secure his supply lines and from that base advance against Richmond. Seventy thousand Federal troops boarded naval transports headed for Fort Monroe, located at the tip of the Virginia Peninsula. General Irvin McDowell with 35,000 troops also moved to Fredericksburg, 50 miles north of Richmond, and General Nathaniel P. Banks commanded another 25,000 men in the Shenandoah Valley.

In the spring and summer of 1862, General McClellan advanced a Union force westward on the Virginia Peninsula from Fort Monroe at the mouth of Hampton Roads. His goal was to invade and occupy the Confederate capital of Richmond. The Confederates enjoyed interior lines between General Johnston's army, near Manassas, and the peninsula. Johnston benefited from this geographic advantage to shift his forces down to reinforce Confederate troops.

By early April, McClellan had as many as 110,000 troops in position. In fact, there were only between 13,000 to 20,000 Confederates opposing him near Yorktown. Still, he convinced himself that 200,000 Confederates were opposing him, so he did nothing. But the Confederate commander, a West Point graduate, was hopelessly outnumbered and knew it.

Challenge: Who was the commanding officer? What did he do to hold off the Union army?

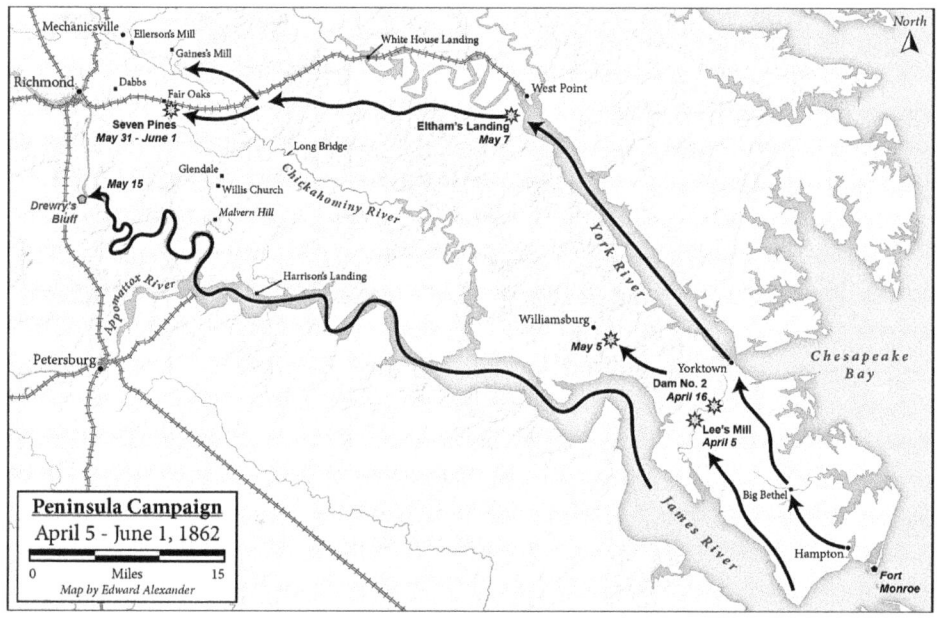

Map: Peninsula Campaign. Note advances by land abetted by support on two rivers.

#VII-2b

During the Confederate retreat from Yorktown, Brigadier General Joseph Hooker's division confronted the Confederate rear near Williamsburg. The Battle of Williamsburg was the first large battle of the Peninsula Campaign. Forty-one thousand Union and 32,000 Confederate troops were engaged.

Hooker attacked an earthen fortification alongside the Williamsburg Road called Fort Magruder but was repulsed. Confederate counterattacks directed by Major General James Longstreet threatened to overwhelm the Union left flank, but the arrival of Brigadier General Philip Kearny's division stabilized the Federal position. The battle was inconclusive, resulting in the Confederates continuing their withdrawal.

A Union brigade advanced on the Confederate left flank, occupying two abandoned redoubts. The Union commander in charge was ordered to withdraw numerous times, but he would not, first holding the ground against an attack and then leading a bayonet charge in a counterattack.

Challenges: (1) Who was the brigadier general who led this gallant brigade, and what did McClellan say about him? (2) What was this general's first postwar assignment?

#VII-2c

After McClellan's troops had taken Yorktown and Williamsburg, which is located on high ground between the York and James Rivers, the Confederates retreated northwest. They crossed another river, which is the only natural barrier between the Peninsula and Richmond. Part of the Union army followed, while other portions remained east of the river.

Soon after the Union forces were positioned on both sides of the apparently calm river, heavy rains developed. The river and swamps became so flooded that they were completely impassable. The Union army was divided; although the two segments were close together, there was no direct connection. General Johnston attacked the two (of five) corps that were south of the river to try to destroy them before the rest of the army could come to their aid. The attack was made in two locations, at the railroad station of Fair Oaks and a mile away at the crossroads of Seven Pines. His plan was elaborate, which led to Longstreet's corps getting lost. General D.H. Hill led the attack and all possible reinforcements sent in. However, Johnston's plan did not succeed, and McClellan defended successfully.

After the battle, mosquitos surrounded the area from the rains and floods. Soldiers on both sides became severely ill with an infection of ambiguous origin.

Challenges: (1) Name the river and (2) name the illness was given at the time.

#VII-2d

At this critical moment, near the end of the battle, Johnston was hit in the right shoulder by a bullet and in the chest by a shell fragment. He fell from his horse and was knocked unconscious. He suffered a broken shoulder and two cracked ribs. His aides carried him to the rear, where he regained consciousness. He immediately asked for his sword (and pistols), which had fallen to the ground when he fell from his horse.

Challenges: (1) Why was the sword so important to him? (2) Which general took command?

#VII-2e

On June 25, a surprise attack by McClellan began a series of six major battles over the next week—the Seven Days Battles, which were the culmination of the Peninsula Campaign. Despite a series of draws and minor skirmishes, McClellan progressively retreated toward the safety of Harrison's Landing on the James River. Although Lee deserves the accolades he has received as a master tactician for taking an aggressive stance with a smaller force to ward off a much larger one, the military reality is that all of these fights were essentially draws.

Except one. In that battle, the Confederates launched numerous failed charges. A final concerted effort caused the Union line to fall back, which resulted in the only clear Confederate victory during the Seven Days. The victory was obtained despite one general leading his men in the wrong direction while another led his men seemingly in yet another desperate attack that surprisingly succeeded.

General Fitz John Porter and Fifth Corps had been successful at Mechanicsville defending against Lee's attack. Nevertheless, McClellan ordered him to retreat east where he established a strong position overlooking Boatswain's Swamp, a river boundary that wasn't on Lee's map. Thus, when Lee continued his movement, he came up against a strong perimeter. Lee renewed his attacks against the right flank of the Union army, isolated on the northern side of the Chickahominy River. Lee committed all six divisions (57,000 men) that were up in frontal attacks that were not well coordinated and did not dislodge Porter.

However, to continue holding out, Porter needed reinforcements. The majority of McClellan's army was across the Chickahominy River. Jackson's division was in the rear, marching to the battlefield, after getting lost on the way.

At this point, McClellan could have done one of several things:

    a. Send substantial reinforcements across the river to Porter and engage Lee in a defensive battle.

    b. Send substantial reinforcements across the river and attack Lee's left flank, held by D.H. Hill.

    c. Take the bulk of the army west and attack Richmond.

    d. Send minimal reinforcements to assist in a holding defense.

    e. None of the above.

Challenges: (1) Name the single battle Lee actually won at the Seven Days. (2) If you were McClellan, which option would you have chosen? And which option did he select? (3) Name the general with the high reputation who got lost. (4) Name the general whose desperate charge won the battle. (5) What did the general who led the charge do on inspecting the position later? And what did the general who got lost say? And what did McClellan say?

#VII-2f

Lee's final opportunity to defeat the Union army was at the Battle of Glendale on June 30, but his orders were poorly executed and Stonewall Jackson's troops were delayed, allowing the Union army to find a strong defensive position on Malvern Hill.

At the Battle of Malvern Hill on July 1, Lee launched a series of unsuccessful frontal assaults against strong infantry and artillery defenses, resulting in heavy casualties. At the climax of the Seven Days Battles, the Union army was located on a 130-foot elevation on Poindexter's Farm. McClellan wasn't present, some of the Confederate army arrived too late due to faulty maps, and Stonewall Jackson couldn't collect his artillery until too late. At least three unsupported Confederate charges were made across open ground each repulsed by Union artillery. Yet after the battle, the Union army retreated, and Lee was praised as having saved Richmond.

The Battle of Malvern Hill has several eerie parallels with Pickett's Charge one year later. Lee ordered frontal charges against a strongly defended position with artillery. This was the work of Major General Henry Jackson Hunt, the Union artillery commander. He massed 250 guns to defeat repeated infantry assaults. It has been noted that the classic "Napoleonic" strategy of large infantry attacks could not be effective against such weaponry. The main difference was the outcome: at Malvern Hill, the Union army retreated after defeating the Confederates, snatching defeat from the jaws of victory.

One Confederate general cautioned against direct charges and was laughed at by another. One charge was led by a heroic brigadier general who would go on to lead another famous charge the next year.

Challenges: (1) The commanding general of the Union army was not present at this battle. He also hadn't been present at the Battle of Glendale. So who was running the Union army during these intense battles? (2) Where was the commanding general while his men were fighting and dying? (3) Name the general who opposed the charges, the one who laughed at him, and the one who led the first charge. (4) What were the consequences of the Seven Days Battles?

Challenge #VII-3

The Second Battle of Manassas was the climax of the Northern Virginia Campaign. Robert E. Lee's Army of Northern Virginia, despite being numerically inferior, pursued Union major general John Pope's Army of Virginia.

Pope had become convinced incorrectly that General Jackson was trapped. Thus, he concentrated his army to complete the assault. On August 29, Pope launched an offensive against Jackson's corps comprised of multiple attacks. Jackson was in a good defensive position along an unfinished railroad grade. The attacks were unsuccessful, with heavy casualties on both sides. Jackson was not in any difficulty whatsoever. At noon, Longstreet's corps arrived on the field, taking position on Jackson's right flank.

On August 30, Pope renewed the attack, unaware that Longstreet was on the field. He moved no force to oppose Longstreet. Confederate artillery shattered an assault by Major General Fitz John Porter's Fifth Corps. Then in the largest infantry attack of the war, Longstreet's wing composed of 25,000 men attacked the unprepared Union flank. The Union left flank was destroyed and the Union army driven back to Bull Run. Only a highly effective Union rearguard action prevented disaster.

Challenges: (1) What did Generals Pope and McDowell do wrong at Second Manassas? (2) What did Porter do wrong? (3) Why was Longstreet's counterattack so effective? Contrast it to Pickett's Charge at Gettysburg. (4) What was the strategic result of this battle? (5) Estimate the ratio of dead and total casualties on the Union and Confederate sides. (6) Explain why this is surprising but shouldn't be.

Challenge #VII-4

Following the battle at Manassas, Stonewall Jackson attempted to cut off the retreat of the Union army toward Washington. The Union army was attempting a retreat to Washington when General Halleck ordered an attack. Lee sent one of his corps to envelop the Union army while keeping Longstreet in place to deceive the Union commander into thinking the whole army was still in his front. The Confederates sent its cavalry as a vanguard for the infantry. Exhausted, the infantry stopped on a hill and its commander slept in the morning. That afternoon, a Union division attacked the hill during a thunderstorm resulting in bayonet and hand-to-hand fighting. Two Union generals were killed, and the Union army retreated to Washington.

Challenges: (1) Name the battle. (2) Name both Union generals killed that day.

Challenge #VII-5a,b

#VII-5a

General Robert E. Lee issued Special Order 191, which has become known as "The Lost Order," on September 9, 1862, during the Maryland Campaign to his corps commanders directing their movements for the campaign. Soldiers of the Union army found a copy of this order on September 13. The military intelligence gained allowed General McClellan to advance his army with confidence and thus was a decisive element in the Battles of South Mountain and Antietam.

In Special Order 191, General Lee outlined the routes to be taken and the timing for the attack of Harpers Ferry. It provided specific details of the movements his army would take during the invasion of Maryland. The crucial point was that Lee divided his army, which he planned to regroup later.

Consequently, when General McClellan came into its possession, he had an accurate and timely picture of exactly where the components of the Confederate army were located and what routes they were going to be using in the next several days. He knew that the Confederate army was divided, and he knew exactly where they were.

Copies of General Lee's order were sent by courier to each of the generals involved. A total of eight copies of the order were transcribed and sent to Generals Jackson, Longstreet, Walker, Stuart, McLaws, Taylor, and D.H. Hill, as well as President Jefferson Davis.

The order was found by complete happenstance in a farm field in an envelope with three cigars wrapped in a piece of paper lying in the grass at a campground that General Hill had recently vacated. The Union soldier who found the order recognized immediately the importance of the document.

Challenges: (1) Who actually wrote and signed the Lost Order? (2) Since the Lost Order were lost, who didn't receive his copy? And how did he know where to go without it? (3) Who lost it? (4) Who found it?

#VII-5b

At the Battle of Antietam, more Americans died in a single day (September 17, 1862) than on any other day in the nation's history (although the

The Sunken Road at Antietam (photograph by Lloyd W. Klein).

bloodiest battle in American history was Gettysburg; its more than 46,000 casualties occurred over three days).

At dawn, Hooker's corps assaulted Lee's left flank across Miller's Cornfield. The battle continued around the Dunker Church. A series of Union assaults against the Sunken Road ultimately crushed the Confederate center with huge casualties, as the road was a great defense when the attackers rushed it but a detriment when it was used to flank those inside. However, the resulting advantage was squandered. In the afternoon, Burnside's corps captured a stone bridge over Antietam Creek and advanced against the Confederate right. At this critical moment, Jackson's subordinate, Major General A.P. Hill, arrived at the last minute from Harpers Ferry, which Jackson had taken several days prior.

McClellan has been criticized ever since for advancing portions of his line at different times rather than at once and holding back an entire corps entirely. McClellan far outnumbered Lee but consistently sent in his reserves too late and held back too many men for fear that Lee outnumbered him. In fact, had McClellan ordered Major General Fitz John Porter to attack the Sunken Road, the battle would have turned out much differently.

Challenges: (1) Who told McClellan to hold back his corps and why? (2) Where were A.P. Hill and his light division earlier in the day? (3) What was the strategic result of this battle? (4) Estimate the ratio of dead and total casualties on the Union and Confederate sides.

Challenge #VII-6

"Mr. Brady has done something to bring home to us the terrible reality and earnestness of war. If he has not brought bodies and laid them in our dooryards and along the streets, he has done something very like it." So wrote a correspondent for the *New York Times* after visiting Mathew Brady's Manhattan gallery in October 1862 to view the famed photographer's latest exhibit, "The Dead of Antietam."

Two photographs from "The Dead of Antietam" (Library of Congress). See Answers for full credits. The first shows the casualties of war near a fence along Hagerstown Road, near the current location of the visitor center. The second shows the Dunker Church from what is now the visitors' parking lot.

It is said that a picture is worth a thousand words. Mathew Brady exhibited a series of 97 photographs taken immediately after the Battle of Antietam. These images were the first to show dead bodies on the battlefield. Two of the many photographers Brady hired to document the war produced these images at Antietam. The impact of this exhibit changed how noncombatants viewed war and, indeed, war news reporting ever since. The accompanying photographs are two of the best-known Antietam photographs, showing Confederate victims at the Dunker Church and along a road that still exists. The others remain graphic and disturbing even by modern standards.

The *New York Times* review continued:

"You will see hushed, reverent groups standing around these weird copies of carnage, bending down to look in the pale faces of the dead, chained by the strange spell that dwells in the dead men's eyes."

Challenge: Brady arranged for the photographers to travel to the battlefield. Who were the photographers who made these unbelievable photographs that changed war reporting forever?

Challenge #VII-7

The Battle of Fredericksburg featured numerous futile frontal attacks by the Union army on December 13, 1862, against entrenched Confederate defenders. The Confederates lined up behind a stone wall on the heights

Marye's Heights (photograph by Lloyd W. Klein). The Confederates were lined up behind this stone wall. A small portion of the slope that the Union soldiers had to traverse is shown.

behind the city. It is usually considered the most one-sided large battle of the war. General Ambrose Burnside ordered multiple futile frontal attacks on Marye's Heights. His advance had been delayed, eliminating surprise, but he attacked anyway.

Challenges: (1) Why was the Union army delayed in its attack? (2) What was the strategic result of this battle? (3) Estimate the ratio of dead and total casualties on the Union and Confederate sides. (4) Explain why this is surprising but shouldn't be.

2. West

Challenge #VII-8

The surrender of Fort Donelson was the start of the meteoric rise of an obscure brigadier general named Ulysses Grant and the decline of an otherwise excellent officer, Simon Bolivar Buckner.

In early 1862, the Confederacy's most promising soldier, Albert Sidney Johnston, commanded forces from Arkansas to the strategic Cumberland Gap. General Polk remained in Columbus with about 12,000 men. Forts Henry and Donelson defended the Tennessee and Cumberland Rivers, and in Bowling Green, General Buckner was positioned with about 4,000 men. The rising river had made Fort Henry an easy target and Donelson was also easy prey.

On February 6, Fort Henry on the Tennessee River was captured, which made Donelson, just 12 miles distant, untenable. Johnston recognized that this defensive line could not hold. He abandoned his position in Bowling Green and moved Beauregard's 12,000 men to Donelson. Because of the direct route to Nashville that would be opened, Johnston decided to defend the undefendable fort.

Grant advanced to invest Fort Donelson on the Cumberland River by February 13. Grant had surrounded the fort with about 25,000 men while Confederate commander Brigadier General John B. Floyd led a garrison of three divisions of about 16,000 troops. Union navy gunboats attacked the fort but were beaten back by Confederate artillery. On February 15, with the fort surrounded, Brigadier General John B. Floyd launched a surprise attack against Grant's right flank led by Brigadier General Gideon Johnson Pillow. The plan was to open an escape route to Nashville. Grant rallied his men and counterattacked. Although Pillow's attack opened the route, Floyd did not escape and ordered his men back to the fort. On February 16, Floyd, Pillow, and other senior commanders escaped the fort, turning over command to Brigadier General Simon Bolivar Buckner, a friend of Grant from West Point. Later that day, Buckner surrendered the garrison to his old friend unconditionally.

Challenges: (1) What was the brilliant strategy Grant employed to so easily capture two forts and an entire army without actually attacking either? (2) What were the consequences of the battle?

Challenge #VII-9

Shiloh (April 6–7, 1862) was the place where Grant and Sherman came into their own, but it was almost the end of their careers. P.G.T. Beauregard planned a surprise advance and attack at Pittsburg Landing on the west bank of the Tennessee River. Exactly how involved Albert Sidney Johnston was in the planning is controversial; Larry J. Daniel suggests he was totally out of his depth. The Northern newspapers exaggerated the nature of the surprise at the time; there was no entrenchment, but Sherman had been forewarned and elements of the army found the Southern lines quite soon. Despite being routed early, Sherman showed tenacity and skill despite adversity on the first day, proving to himself and to others that he had the emotional and cognitive skills necessary to lead an army.

Challenges: (1) What was the major error made by the Confederate leadership in planning this battle? (2) Where was Lew Wallace on day one? Why was this error made and why didn't Grant forgive him? (3) Why was the west bank of the river a terrible strategic mistake? Who chose this ground? (4) The death of Albert Sidney Johnston, of course, was a major event in the war; the Confederate western theater never really found its general. A bullet to the back of Johnston's knee, where the popliteal artery is located, killed him. This wound should not have resulted in death; a simple tourniquet would have been lifesaving. Why did his wound go unnoticed until too late? (5) Which general was killed in the toughest part of the battle on day one? At which location? Who was supposed to be there commanding but wasn't? Bonus: The night of the first day, Sherman said to Grant, "We've had the Devil's own day." What was Grant's response? (6) Who appeared the night of April 6 to provide reinforcements? (Trick question: There are two answers.) (7) Which side suffered the most casualties?

Challenge #VII-10

As Grant launched his spring offensive, two armies moved toward Richmond and one toward the valley. Another army consisting of three brigades marched across the Appalachian Mountains into southwest Virginia to destroy the Virginia and Tennessee Railroads. The Confederate general was highly experienced but had only a small force and had just assumed command. He decided to take a stand at a mountain. The Union commander decided to attempt an envelopment of the right flank with one brigade while the others under a colonel who became a future U.S. president attacked frontally. Serving as a major under him was yet another future U.S. president. The railroad was destroyed, and the Confederates lost 23 percent of their total force.

Challenge: Name the battle, the two future presidents who fought, and the name of their division.

Challenge #VII-11

In July 1862, General Braxton Bragg realized that holding Kentucky was crucial to western defense. Despite the setback at Shiloh, he determined to invade that state and threaten Indiana and western Ohio while Halleck was besieging Corinth. He split his army into two and sent his cavalry under John Hunt Morgan north into Ohio.

General Buell went in pursuit of Bragg knowing that the other half of the army under Kirby Smith was distant. He took his much larger army and approached the crossroads town of Perryville, Kentucky, where Bragg was camped. Despite his advantage, he delayed an attack. Instead, Bragg ordered a division to attack the Union left flank. Buell was two miles behind and did not even know he was under attack. More troops were sent by Bragg but not by Buell, resulting in a retreat until finally reinforced. Bragg, recognizing that he was outnumbered and short of supplies, withdrew.

Buell had failed to engage his entire army, and the next day he did not heed his general's advice to counterattack because he did not know the size of the forces he faced. In fact, he outnumbered them 60,000 to 16,000.

Challenges: (1) What battle describes this ludicrous series of events? (2) What was the strategic result of this battle? (3) Estimate the ratio of dead and total casualties on the Union and Confederate sides. (4) Explain why this is surprising but shouldn't be.

Challenge #VII-12

As the commanding general, you can make all the wonderful plans you want, but on the battlefield, it often works out differently than how it was planned.

Grant intended to converge three armies to attack one Confederate army before it merged with another. He had one army in close contact with the Confederate army and a second nearby. He had both of them halt until the third army arrived; the plan was to wait until the first two armies heard the sound of fighting the next morning, then attack.

However, that third Union army, which had gotten lost, was 20 miles away. The next day, to get back on track, instead of taking two roads, its general decided to take one and ran into the retreating Confederate army attempting to merge. Neither Grant nor the other army came to his aid.

Thus, what actually happened was that two armies ran into each other by accident and fought all day without reinforcements despite other armies being close by.

Challenges: Name the battle, the Union general who led the attack, and the reason why no reinforcements came to his aid.

Challenge #VII-13

Major General William Rosecrans is one of the most interesting personalities of the war. He was highly intelligent, very effective in command, and brave under fire, but he was also brusque, arrogant, and nasty to superiors.

Stones River was his greatest moment, but at the outset, it didn't look that way. He had replaced General Buell because he would not move to attack General Bragg, yet Rosecrans remained in Nashville for months. General Henry Halleck threatened to remove him too if he did not move within a week. Finally in December 1862, he was ready to attack the enemy camped outside Murfreesboro, Tennessee.

On the morning of New Year's Eve 1862, Rosecrans was getting ready to make a surprise attack when he was surprised first by Bragg. The Union army was driven back on the defensive.

At that critical moment, with disaster looming, the commanding general rallied his men personally, gave direct orders to groups of men, large and small, disregarding his own safety as he rode near the front of his line and, supposedly, in no man's land. He was covered in blood when his chief of staff was beheaded by a cannon ball. He personally took control of artillery placements and rushed units to the point of danger.

His magnificent personal leadership saved the day, preventing an impending defeat. The next day, Bragg attacked him again and was repulsed with heavy losses. This battle had the highest percentage of casualties of any battle on *both* sides: 29.7 percent Union, 33.5 percent Confederate. Often, veterans of this battle in later years said it was the worst fight in which they were ever engaged.

Section VII. 1862 Battles and Campaigns

Challenges: (1) Why was Rosecrans surprised, and what was the nature of the two generals' strategies? (2) Which Union general saved the destruction of the army by anticipating the attack? (3) By mistake, a gap in the Confederate line of attack developed; which general filled it? (4) Which blunder did Bragg make that probably saved the day for Rosecrans?

Answers

Answers #VII-1

#VII-1a

1. Jackson defeated armies led by Nathaniel Banks (McDowell, Front Royal, Winchester), John Fremont (Cross Keys, Port Republic), and Irvin McDowell.

2. Jackson was outnumbered about 50,000 to 17,000 in total, but the various Union commanders never joined forces, allowing Jackson to fight each separately. In part, their orders were based on holding positions in the valley, and in part, the generals' egos demanded that they defeat the enemy individually.

3. None of Jackson's subordinates understood what their role in each battle was, and thus whether they should retreat, attack, or stay put had to be determined solely from their local situation. The operational goal was often never clarified to them. His subordinates also were often not consulted about key decisions. Consequently, piecemeal deployment of troops was a serious problem, which might have resulted in even better results.

#VII-1b

The First Battle of Kernstown, Colonel Erastus B. Tyler. Although the battle was a tactical defeat for Jackson, it was a strategic victory because he was able to regroup and continue his offensive. The single loss at Kernstown resulted in Garnett retreating before he had orders, resulting in his humiliation and court-martial. Jackson also had a significant fight with Turner Ashby as he retreated down the valley.

FURTHER READING
- Cozzens, Peter. *Shenandoah 1862: Stonewall Jackson's Valley Campaign.* University of North Carolina Press, 2008.

Answers #VII-2

#VII-2a

Major General John Bankhead Magruder. He decided to bluff McClellan by constantly marching his forces back and forth, making loud noises, and using sporadic artillery barrages to create the illusion of a much larger military presence. The effect worked and persuaded McClellan to call for a siege of Yorktown. That decision allowed time for Johnston to come to Magruder's aid.

Although the hero of this battle, Magruder was later blamed for the defeat at Malvern Hill. After the Peninsula Campaign, he became the general administrating a number of departments. Magruder was successful in lifting the naval blockade at Galveston and recapturing the city temporarily in 1863. After the war, Magruder fled to Mexico. He worked under Emperor Maximillian I before returning to the United States in 1867.

#VII-2b

1. Brigadier General William Hancock. McClellan reported that his performance was "superb"; and he was forever after nicknamed "Hancock the Superb." And he was indeed.

2. At the close of the war, Hancock supervised the execution of the Lincoln assassination conspirators.

#VII-2c

The Chickahominy River and Chickahominy fever. Its cause has never been entirely worked out. The illness had symptoms of both typhoid fever and malaria, and so it is today officially termed "typhomalarial fever" but at that time was called bilious fever. Most likely it was an epidemic of several illnesses including malaria, typhoid, dengue fever, and perhaps shigellosis.

FURTHER READING
- https://www.historynet.com/details-bridging-the-chickahominy-river.htm

#VII-2d

1. Johnston said, "The sword was the one worn by my father in the Revolutionary War, and I would not lose it for ten thousand dollars;

will not someone please go back and get it and the pistols for me?" It was retrieved with a fight by Drury Armistead of the Third Virginia Cavalry.

    2. Major General Gustavus W. Smith assumed temporary command. Smith, who had chronic ill health, was indecisive about the next steps. The attack was renewed but without vigor. After the end of fighting the next day, Davis replaced Smith with Robert E. Lee. McClellan said he preferred Lee to Johnston. Lee had made a poor showing early in the war and he thought Lee "wanting in moral firmness when pressed by heavy responsibility & is likely to be timid and irresolute in action." McClellan was clearly not a good judge of men, as he demonstrated repeatedly.

#VII-2e

    1. Battle of Gaines's Mill. Lee followed up on the action at Mechanicsville the day before which he initiated to prevent a siege of the capital by McClellan, which he did not think he could defeat.

    2. Had McClellan chosen a, b, or c, it would likely have ended the war. Instead, he did what he did best: d and e, retreat. He sent Slocum's division only, and only with hesitation, so that Lee was able to better coordinate his attacks and bring Jackson, finally, into the battle. He attacked with 16 brigades (32,000 men) against about the same number on defense.

    3. Stonewall Jackson famously arrived late. D.H. Hill, instead of being in the rear, ended up in front and joined the attack on the Union left.

    4. Brigadier General John Bell Hood. It was Hood's brigade of Longstreet's command that finally broke through an exhausted Union line.

    5. Over 400 men and most of the officers in Hood's Texas brigade were killed or wounded. He cried at the sight of the dead and dying men on the field. After inspecting the Union entrenchments, Jackson remarked, "The men who carried this position were truly soldiers indeed." McClellan wrote to his wife, "I am tired of the sickening sight of the battlefield, with its mangled corpses & poor suffering wounded! Victory has no charms for me when purchased at such cost." But he didn't win that battle.

The parallels with the actions at Gettysburg almost exactly a year later are one of the most fascinating aspects of this battle. Many of the brigade and division leaders in this battle would become famous, making not dissimilar charges and decisions at Gettysburg.

Section VII. 1862 Battles and Campaigns

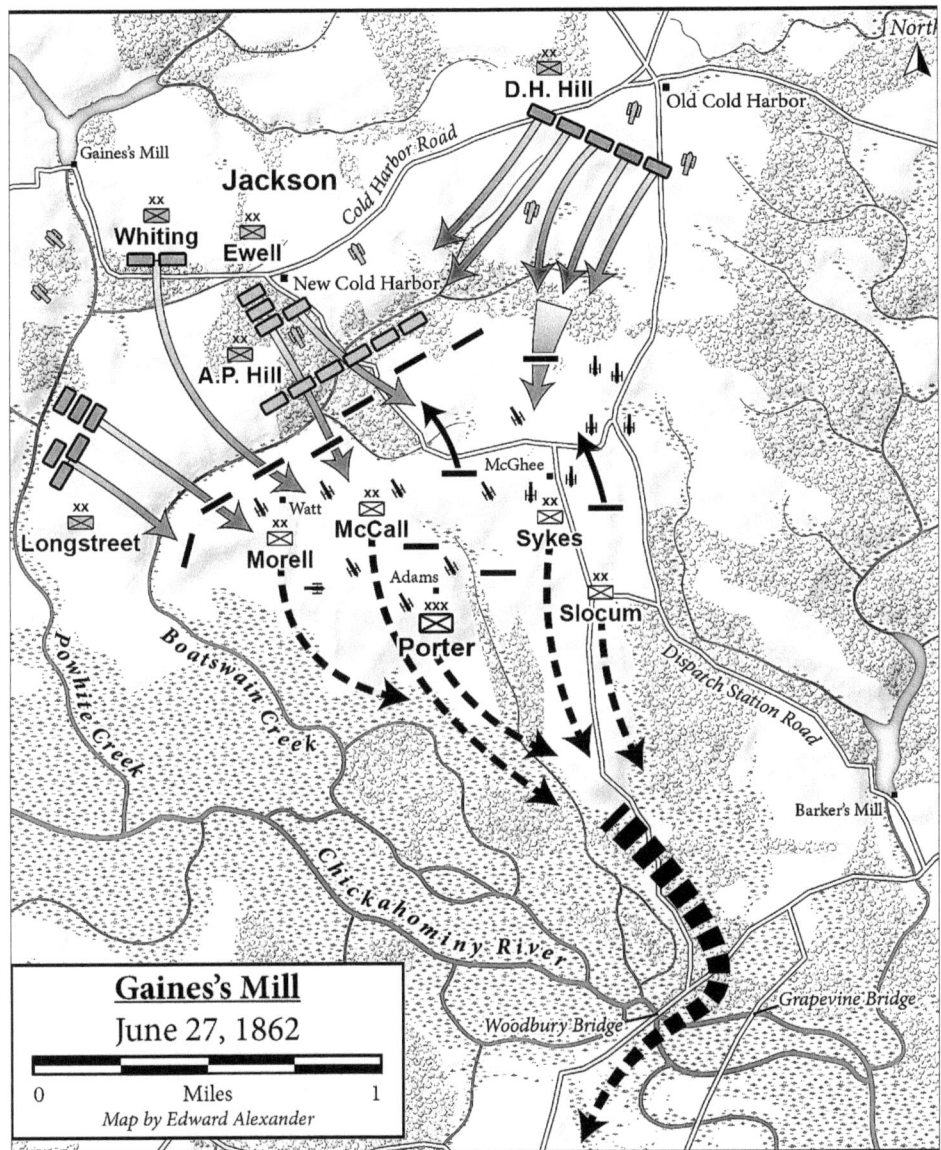

Map of the Battle of Gaines's Mill. Note that A.P. Hill attacked frontally in the late afternoon, before Jackson was in position, doing so without orders from General Lee. D.H. Hill's later attack exposed his left flank, protected only by cavalry; a counterattack by Porter in this location might have turned the tide. Hood's advance on the opposite flank was decisive when, at around 7:00 p.m., Lee was finally able to coordinate his attack, breaking the Union defense.

Jackson's poor performance remains the biggest criticism of his military record. General Ewell was Jackson's first division commander and had to be instructed to move into the battle immediately by Lee's aide, Walter Taylor. His brigade commander, Isaac Trimble, lost 20 percent of his men in the attack. Pickett's brigade attempted a frontal attack and was defeated by artillery fire with severe losses; Pickett was wounded in the action. Hood's Texas brigade under James Longstreet ultimately led to a crack in the defense, leading to the retreat.

The tactical defeat led McClellan to retreat. He believed he was in a trap, caught between two rivers. When General Grant was in almost the same position in 1864 after the Battle of Cold Harbor (the battlefield is almost adjacent), he found in it an opportunity.

FURTHER READING
- Spruill, Matthew. *Decisions of the Seven Days*. University of Tennessee Press, 2021.

#VII-2f

1. In both battles, effective command of the army fell to his friend and Fifth Corps commander Brigadier General Fitz John Porter. In fact, McClellan never officially gave control of the army to anyone.

2. At Glendale, McClellan was five miles away, positioned behind Malvern Hill. He had no telegraph communications and was too distant to command his army. He was on a gunboat, the USS *Galena*, during the battle of Malvern Hill. At one point, he was 10 miles away from the fighting, downstream on the James River. Editorial cartoons were published during the 1864 presidential campaign deriding McClellan for having taken safety on board a ship while his army was in a severe fight.

3. D.H. Hill, James Longstreet, Lewis Armistead. D.H. Hill argued against the attack, James Longstreet laughed at him, and Lewis Armistead spearheaded the attack. When viewed from the standpoint of Pickett's Charge one year later, these coincidences are thought provoking.

4. Lee's victory saved Richmond and the Confederacy in 1862. On June 24, 1862, McClellan and the Army of the Potomac were within six miles of Richmond; it was said that Union soldiers heard church bells ringing in the city. Despite being so close, the Union army retreated. It would be two years before it was again in such a favorable position. McClellan was briefly replaced by Pope.

Answers #VII-3

1. Buford's cavalry was under McDowell. He reported during the day of August 29 that Longstreet's men were advancing by Thoroughfare Gap. This report was not forwarded to Pope until that evening. The next day, Pope ordered him to take a position that would have placed him appropriately, had anyone known where Longstreet was; but McDowell declined, saying he had no idea what was there.

2. Porter had personally criticized Pope and did not want to serve under him. Pope had ordered a charge that Porter knew was an error, leaving his flank and that of the army open to Longstreet. Pope again ordered the attack the next morning, resulting in disaster. After the battle, Pope was looking for a scapegoat and settled on Porter, who was court-martialed. He was restored by McClellan at Antietam, but when he lost command, Porter was vulnerable.

3. Longstreet's charge of 25,000 men (five divisions) counterattacked in the largest mass assault of the war. It was perhaps twice as large as Pickett's Charge. Although the attack crossed 1–1.5 miles, there was minimal artillery fire. Pope was engaging the Confederate right almost entirely and had ignored his left flank despite repeated warnings by many subordinates.

4. Lee had wanted to attack the day before, but Longstreet delayed. Many have seen in this the seeds of their disagreement at Gettysburg. Pope was relieved of command, McClellan reinstated, and Lee invaded Maryland, where Antietam occurred just three weeks later.

5. Strength: Union 77,000: 51,000 (Army of Virginia); 26,000 (Army of the Potomac); 62,000 engaged; Confederates (Army of Northern Virginia) 50,000. Casualties and losses: Union: 14,462 total casualties; 1,747 killed; 8,452 wounded; 4,263 captured/missing; Confederates: 7,298 total casualties; 1,096 killed; 6,202 wounded. Union casualties were about 22.5 percent; the Confederates about 16 percent.

A Confederate victory no doubt, but the difference, especially in killed, is underwhelming. How many times can an army lose 16 percent in a victory?

Further Reading

- https://www.battlefields.org/learn/maps/second-manassas-unfinished-railroad-august-29-1862-8am-10am

- https://www.essentialcivilwarcurriculum.com/the-second-battle-of-bull-run.html
- http://npshistory.com/publications/civil_war_series/18/sec2.htm

Answers #VII-4

1. Battle of Ox Hill or Chantilly; the battlefield today is a small park near Dulles airport.
2. Philip Kearny and Isaac Stevens

Answers #VII-5

#VII-5a

1. Robert H. Chilton was assistant adjutant general with the rank of lieutenant colonel serving on the staff of General E. Lee, rising later to chief of staff, and was promoted to brigadier general. He wrote eight copies of the order and signed them in Lee's name. A copy was sent to each general and to General Cooper.

2. The copy of Special Order 191 recovered by Union troops is addressed to General D.H. Hill. But the strange thing is, Hill received a copy of the order. We know this because it still exists; actually, both copies do. And both are authentic.

R.H. Chilton undoubtedly wrote the order found in the field. The copy Hill actually received is in Stonewall Jackson's handwriting. D.H. Hill was adamant he received only one copy of the order.

At the time that Special Order 191 was made, D.H. Hill was under the command of Jackson. Jackson in turn copied the document for Hill because once the army crossed into Maryland, Hill was to exercise independent command as the rear guard. For this reason, Jackson copied and sent Hill the order because he didn't know Chilton had done so. But since Special Order 191 conveyed Hill's having an independent command once entering Maryland, Chilton sent Hill a copy as well. The mystery of the loss of the order centers on the existence of duplicate orders to the same general. Hill received Jackson's copy, which he kept forever, but the order from Chilton he said he never received and didn't miss, since Jackson was his commander. That copy is the "Lost Order."

3. No one really knows.

Chilton insisted his copy of the order made it to Hill; however, because he did not learn of the order having gone missing until much

Section VII. 1862 Battles and Campaigns

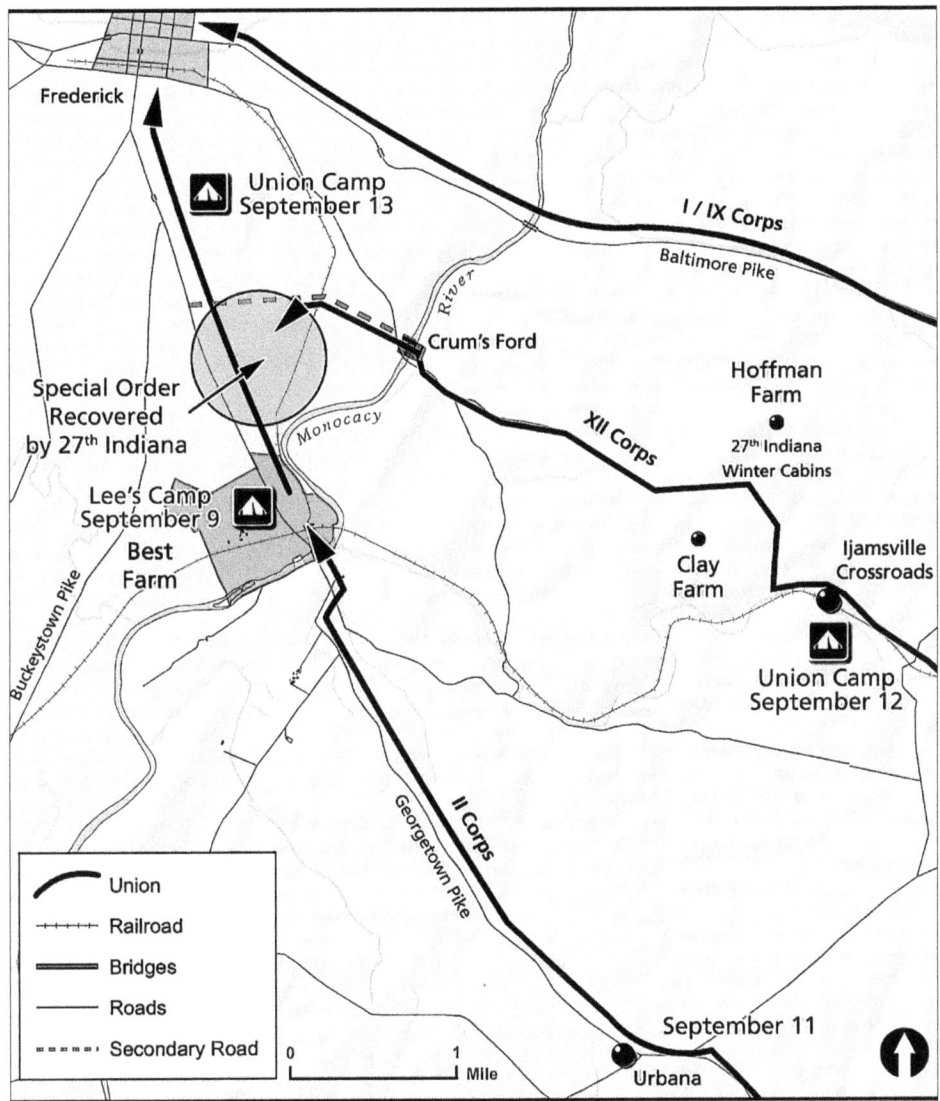

Map showing Lee's camp on the Best Farm and the close proximity to where Special Order 191 was recovered. This location is today a large field fronting the Monocacy Battlefield Visitors Center (National Park Service, Monocacy National Battlefield, Maryland).

later, he was certain that the signed envelope would have been returned or an investigation would have followed. Years later, Chilton could not remember which officer he had dispatched as a courier to Hill. So why was the order not delivered to Hill? This order dictates the overall strategy of the Army of Northern Virginia and therefore is a critical movement order. It should have been delivered directly to D.H. Hill himself. And how did such an important document end up in a field wrapped around three cigars?

Lee wrote the order in a field on the Best Farm right behind the house and barn. The field it was found in is located less than a half mile up the road, now in front of the National Park Service headquarters. The Best Farm is located outside of Frederick, Maryland, and was a key Confederate artillery position in the 1864 Battle of Monocacy. A historical marker on the Monocacy National Battlefield commemorates the finding of Special Order 191 during the Maryland Campaign.

See for one theory:

- Klein, L.W. "Who Lost the 'Lost Order'?" *Emerging Civil War Blog.* https://emergingcivilwar.com/2022/02/24/who-lost-the-lost-order/#comment-96195

4. Around noon on September 13, a Union soldier on a skirmish line found an envelope. On opening it, Corporal Barton W. Mitchell of the 27th Indiana Volunteers, part of the Union 12th Corps, found three cigars inside wrapped inside a note. Mitchell did not read every word, but he noticed that it concluded with the phrase "By command of General Robert E. Lee" and was signed "R.H. Chilton, Assistant Adjutant General."

Mitchell recognized the significance of the document and showed it immediately to Sergeant John M. Bloss. The note was elevated up the 27th Indiana's chain of command: to Captain Peter Kop, Colonel Silas Colgrove, then to Brigadier General Alpheus Starkey Williams, commander of the 12th Corps.

Further Reading

- Sears, Stephen W. *Landscape Turned Red: The Battle of Antietam.* Houghton Mifflin, 1983.
- Thorp, GM & Rossino, AB. *The Tale Untwisted: General George B. McClellan*, the Maryland Campaign, and the Discovery of Lee's Lost Orders. Savas Beatie, 2023.
- https://www.battlefields.org/learn/primary-sources/general-robert-e-lees-lost-order-no-191
- https://civilwarintheeast.com/things/the-lost-order/
- https://encyclopediavirginia.org/6294hpr-3355bd52ffcf2c6/

#VII-5b

1. The notorious story is that the reserve troops belonging to McClellan's most trusted corps commander, General Fitz John Porter,

was ready to attack at the Sunken Road. McClellan was ready to commit these reserves under Porter. Porter supposedly slowly shook his head with disapproval and said to McClellan, "Remember, General! I command the last reserve of the last army of the Republic." For this reason, McClellan did not commit these troops, which would have assuredly carried the day.

Modern scholarship suggests that this never happened and that Porter was blamed after the fact. Two months later, he was court-martialed for his actions at Second Bull Run and dismissed from the army. This story may have been manufactured for that purpose. Then 16 years later, a special commission exonerated him, and in 1886, his commission was restored to an infantry colonel. He enjoyed a very successful postwar career.

    2. A.P. Hill was on the way from Harpers Ferry, where he had been detailed to parole the capture of the Union garrison there.

    3. This was a major Union strategic victory. Lee's Northern invasion ended. Lincoln thought it a sufficient victory to announce the Emancipation Proclamation. Internationally, it was the end of any hope that Britain would recognize the Confederacy. There is some controversy whether it was a tactical victory or a draw, but the casualties suggest a tactical Union victory. Lincoln believed a more substantial operational victory should have been obtained. McClellan did not pursue despite myriad orders to do so and was relieved for the second time as commander.

    4. Army of the Potomac: 87,164 total troops
    Casualties and losses: 12,410 total (2,108 killed, 9,549 wounded, 753 captured/missing)
    Army of Northern Virginia: 38,000 "engaged" troops
    Casualties and losses: 12,051 total (3,281 killed, 7,752 wounded, 1,018 captured/missing)

Answer #VII-6

Mathew Brady decided to move on from studio portraits and cartes de visite to document the war, and with permission from President Lincoln, he organized and self-financed a team of photographers who took thousands of photographs documenting camp life and battlefield scenes. One of these photographers on Brady's team, Alexander Gardner, took all the photographs featured, and James Gibson assisted.

In 1862, Brady's exhibit *The Dead of Antietam* showed the public the first-ever photographs of a battlefield before the dead had been removed.

The exhibition took place at Brady's studio on Broadway in New York City. In modern society, we have seen live battlefield scenes on television and movie images of graphic content and have become desensitized. It is hard for us today to fully comprehend the shocking impression this exhibit made.

Gardner arrived on the battlefield on September 19, 1862, two days after the battle had ended. He photographed the dead and the living who handled their remains, demonstrating without protecting the viewer from the sight of those who had grisly wounds and those who fell over rocks in their final moments, as well as the bodies bloating under the hot sun.

These images received extensive media attention. The *New York Times* review conveys the impact of these photos perhaps as well as the photos themselves:

> The living that throng Broadway care little perhaps for the Dead at Antietam, but we fancy they would jostle less carelessly down the great thoroughfare, saunter less at their ease, were a few dripping bodies, fresh from the field, laid along the pavement. There would be a gathering up of skirts and a careful picking of way; conversation would be less lively, and the general air of pedestrians more subdued. As it is, the dead of the battlefield come up to us very rarely, even in dreams. We see the list in the morning paper at breakfast, but dismiss its recollection with the coffee.

The photos are searchable online and in the Library of Congress. The link is for the *New York Times* review: *https://www.nytimes.com/1862/10/20/archives/bradys-photographs-pictures-of-the-dead-at-antietam.html*

Answers #VII-7

1. Burnside proposed moving the Union army to Falmouth, directly across the Rappahannock River from Fredericksburg, then making a direct attack on the Confederate capital of Richmond, Virginia, avoiding Lee's forces who were then in Culpepper. Burnside arrived in Falmouth by November 19, but the pontoons that he planned to use to cross the Rappahannock were delayed. The army was delayed because some functionary in Washington had failed to send the pontoons when Burnside asked for them. They were supposed to be there when he got there but didn't arrive for 10 days. Then heavy snowfall prevented all military operations for a week after they did arrive.

2. Although the boats necessary to build a single pontoon bridge arrived on November 25, that was too late to cross the river without opposition because the element of surprise had been lost. Still, Burnside

had an opportunity because at that time, only half of Lee's army had arrived and were not yet dug in. Had Burnside acted quickly, he might have been able to attack Longstreet and defeat him before Jackson arrived.

3. Once again, he squandered his opportunity. During this delay, Lee anticipated Burnside's crossing the Rappahannock. He ordered Lieutenant General James Longstreet and Lieutenant General T. "Stonewall" Jackson to defend a line along the river just outside the town of Fredericksburg.

4. Actually, none. Despite this being the most one-sided and complete Confederate victory in the war, it had minimal effect strategically. Confederate morale rose; they were outnumbered but still prevailed with an unmistakable victory. On the other side, Union morale was already low after Burnside had replaced McClellan, who was popular with the troops. Burnside's errors in planning and leadership led to rising insubordination and his ineffective second offensive against Lee in January 1863, derisively called the "Mud March."

5. Army of the Potomac: 122,009 troops (114,000 engaged)

Casualties and losses: 12,653 total (1,284 killed, 9,600 wounded, 1,769 captured/missing)

Army of Northern Virginia: 78,513 (72,500 engaged)

Casualties and losses: 5,377 total (608 killed, 4,116 wounded, 653 captured/missing)

The ratio is about 1.5:1; when stated as percentages, 11.1 percent versus 7.4 percent. This is a clear Confederate victory but not as one-sided as history suggests.

6. Most accounts fail to note that the first day, the attack went very well for the Union army, causing many Southern casualties. Lee's formidable defense had an unforeseen flaw. In A.P. Hill's line, a triangular-shaped patch of woods extending beyond the railroad was swampy and covered with thick underbrush and the Confederates had left a 600-yard gap there between the brigades of Brigadier Generals James H. Lane and James J. Archer. Brigadier General Maxcy Gregg's brigade was deployed about a quarter mile behind the gap. Meade's First Brigade entered the gap, climbed the railroad embankment, and turned right into the underbrush, striking Lane's brigade in the flank. Despite this promising beginning, Burnside failed to take advantage.

Answers #VII-8

1. Grant synchronized his movements with Admiral Andrew Foote so that naval and infantry attacks were coordinated. The

central strategy of using rivers as a transportation system by which to transport and capture the large area of the South could only have succeeded in this way. Thus, the Tennessee and Cumberland Rivers, rather than being geographic obstacles, became a high-speed highway for invasion and supplies. Moreover, the attacks were coordinated by both land and sea. In modern military parlance, this is called combined arms warfare.

2. Of 16,000 Confederates engaged, more than 12,000 were captured or missing, and 1,400 others were wounded or killed. Of the 24,500 Union troops who fought at Fort Donelson, there were 2,700 total casualties.

When the rebels asked for terms of surrender, Grant replied that no terms "except unconditional and immediate surrender" would be acceptable. This earned him the nickname "Unconditional Surrender." President Lincoln promoted Grant to major general after the battle. The Battle of Fort Donelson was the first major Union victory and made Grant famous. The loss of Forts Henry and Donelson was a disaster for the Confederates, who were depending on these river forts to keep control of Kentucky and eastern Tennessee. The Cumberland River and Tennessee River became integral parts of Union supply lines. Nashville fell to Union troops shortly afterward. Johnston, who was thought to be the best general on either side, was embarrassed and under pressure to demonstrate his super-iority.

FURTHER READING
- Cooling, Benjamin Franklin. *The Campaign for Fort Donelson.* U.S. National Park Service and Eastern National, 1999.
- https://www.battlefields.org/learn/civil-war/battles/fort-donelson?fbclid=IwAR2qTCXfrR3C80iKToAPHKUGen5-dXWS_svwl8mGlUsSracP5Zt3eFpFX6w

Answers #VII-9

1. Beauregard underestimated the length of time to march from their camps to the area of Pittsburg Landing. This resulted in many of their troops not having enough rations and they then stopped their initially successful assault in order to feast at the Union campsites. Another error was that the rains had slowed travel from their base in Corinth. Had they arrived a day sooner, Buell might not have gotten there in time for day two. In fact, the whole idea was to attack Grant before Buell joined him.

2. Wallace took a road that was correct if the lines were where they had been at the start of the day, but by the time he arrived, those lines were pushed back, so Wallace was behind enemy lines. He had to countermarch.

3. Grant's back was to the river; he could have been entirely destroyed. His defense at Pittsburg Landing in the afternoon of day one saved his army. General Charles Ferguson Smith was at the time commander of the army, as Halleck tried to dump Grant behind the scenes. Sherman went upstream with his division to raid the Memphis and Charleston Railroad but on the way noted Pittsburg Landing and sent a recommendation to Smith that he occupy it. Smith sent Hurlbut, who occupied the landing. Upon Sherman's return from his unsuccessful raid, he landed there, decided the ground was good, and took charge of the forces around the landing and occupied Shiloh Church.

4. Johnston was shot while leading a charge. Why the commanding general was doing this has been speculated about ever since. More importantly, he had received a wound to that leg in the Mexican War, decreasing his sensation substantially. He very likely did not appreciate that he had been significantly wounded because of a lack of pain. The bleeding became severe and filled his boot with blood. He exsanguinated on the field from what ought to have been a nonfatal wound.

5. General Smith was in charge but developed a leg infection just prior to the battle. In fact, he died of it a couple of weeks later. General William H.L. Wallace took command; yes, there were two General Wallaces in the same army in this battle. This Wallace ended up defending the Hornet's Nest for six hours, eventually being killed there.

Bonus: "Lick 'em tomorrow though" was Grant's famous response.

6. Don Carlos Buell's Army of the Ohio arrived. And so did Lew Wallace's division. The Union counterattacked the morning of day two. The Confederate lines had become confused the day before and now were outnumbered.

7. The Union had 63,000 men engaged, with 13,000 casualties (1,754 killed, 8,400 wounded, 2,900 captured) versus the Confederates with 40,000 men with 10,700 casualties (1,728 killed, 8,000 wounded, 1,000 captured). The Union on a percentage basis had a slightly lower rate of casualties.

Further Reading

- Daniel, Larry J. *Shiloh: The Battle That Changed the Civil War.* Simon & Schuster, 1997.

Answers #VII-10

Battle of Cloyd's Mountain; Colonel Rutherford B. Hayes and Major William McKinley; the Kanawha Division.

Answers #VII-11

1. Perryville
2. Bragg had won a tactical victory against larger numbers. He had pushed his opponent back for over a mile. But his precarious strategic situation was clear, and he retreated. Kentucky remained in Union control for the rest of the war. This is considered one of the turning points of the war.
3. Union forces numbered 22,000 against 16,000 Confederates, which is rather a small battle considering its importance. The Union suffered more than 4,200 casualties, with about 900 killed, while the Confederates suffered over 3,400 casualties, with about 500 killed. By percentage, the difference is not large. But the 20 percent casualty rate overall shows that this was one of the most desperate fights of the war.
4. Dividing a smaller force to invade the state with an army in the rear was risky. The strategy of invading the North was appealing, but there was no supply line to support it.

Answers #VII-12

Battle of Iuka; William Rosecrans. Before modern battlefield communication, military commanders would frequently give orders contingent on hearing sounds of battle.

On September 19, 1862, General Grant planned an attack against Confederate major general Sterling Price near Iuka, Mississippi. The plan was for General William Rosecrans to attack Price first. After hearing sounds indicating that the battle was under way, Major General Edward Ord would move in Price's rear to prevent a retreat. But the sounds of battle were never heard. Rosecrans's army fought the Confederates all afternoon. Ord and his army waited for the battle sounds, but they never heard any, so they never attacked. Price was able to retreat and saved his army.

It is believed that an acoustic shadow suppressed the sound and prevented them from realizing that the battle had begun. Anomalous sound propagation can occur when either sound waves are suppressed due to blocking by trees or mountains, or when wind, temperature, and pressure conditions cause the sound waves to "bounce" over certain areas. The colloquial expression for this is "bad acoustics"; the principle of physics is that sound can travel in refraction channels above the ground over long distances until returning to the earth's surface and thus not heard in intervening locations. At the Battle of Iuka, a northerly wind prevented General Grant, located to the south, from hearing the sounds of battle and sending more troops. Ord and his troops likely were situated in an acoustic shadow.

This episode was the start of the feud between Grant and Rosecrans. Northern newspapers gave very favorable accounts to Rosecrans, while Grant was criticized. Rumors started that Ord's column did not attack in conjunction with Rosecrans because Grant was drunk and/or incompetent. The fact that the battle was inaudible was not mentioned.

Acoustic shadowing was reported in several other Civil War battles including Fort Donelson, Gaines's Mill, Seven Pines, Perryville, Chancellorsville, and Five Forks. At Gettysburg on day two, Ewell was supposed to attack Culp's Hill when Longstreet's artillery started firing, but he never heard them, allowing Meade to shift his army to his left flank.

FURTHER READING

- https://www.battlefields.org/learn/civil-war/battles/iuka
- https://blog.echobarrier.com/blog/acoustic-shadow-explained
- http://mshistorynow.mdah.state.ms.us/articles/386/iuka-a-strange-civil-war-battle-in-northeast-mississippi
- https://www.thermaxxjackets.com/sound-wave-refraction-acoustic-shadows/

Answers #VII-13

1. Rosecrans's plan was to attack Bragg's right flank after breakfast. But Bragg attacked Rosecrans right flank at dawn. It's interesting that each had exactly the same strategy.

This was the *third* early morning attack catching the Union army by surprise in 1862. (Fort Donelson and Shiloh were the other two.) General Hardee attacked with 10,000 men in one wave.

2. The ubiquitous Brigadier General Philip Sheridan was prepared for an attack by 4:00 a.m. in the center of the right half of the line. Sheridan had his men up early (which reportedly upset them). His

defense slowed Bragg's attack until a new defensive line could be set up along the railroad. One-third of his men were casualties in an area called the Slaughter Pen.

3. Patrick Cleburne was coming up behind the first line and filled it in.

On day one, Bragg and Breckenridge didn't communicate well, and Breckenridge never threw his troops into the attack, which might have overwhelmed Rosecrans's line.

4. On day two, Breckinridge was slow to attack. Bragg received a false report of Union reinforcements, so he held Breckinridge back.

Bragg also made the mistake of sending Breckenridge to try to flank Rosecrans on day three. It was a disaster. Breckenridge lost 1,800 men and blamed Bragg forever after over the loss of his "orphan" brigade.

Section VIII

1863 Battles and Campaigns (Except Gettysburg)

Challenges

1. East

Challenge #VIII-1a–c

#VIII-1a

The Battle of Chancellorsville is often considered Lee's most remarkable victory. He took huge risks, but he calculated the options available to his opponent, Joseph, and knew he could bluff successfully. The battle resulted in the end of the Union invasion of Virginia and ultimately Hooker's time as commander in chief, but the price to the Confederate side was Jackson's death by friendly fire and an enormous casualty rate.

Hooker planned a double envelopment and, in fact, fooled Lee. Hooker, however, made a series of tactical errors including leaving only Sedgwick behind at Fredericksburg, which was transparent in being only a diversion. Having dropped into Lee's rear, an aggressive attack might have caught Lee in a bad position forcing him to retreat with the Union army chasing him. But Hooker stopped and waited for Lee to attack him, ceding the initiative to Lee.

Challenges: (1) What was the great gamble Lee took in the campaign that goes against all military logic and common sense? (2) Where did Hooker go wrong? (3) What about his concussion?

#VIII-1b

The stunning victory occurred in large part because Stonewall Jackson found a road not on maps of the day that led around the right of the Union lines. On May 1, realizing that they were outnumbered, Jackson sent a brilliant aide to find a route.

Challenges: (1) Who discovered the road Jackson used? It branched off at a junction where what industrial plant was located? (2) Why did Hooker not suspect Jackson's march? (3) How did Jackson convince General Lee to make perhaps the riskiest gamble of all of the gambles Lee ever made? Why was it such a risk? (4) Why didn't the Union cavalry show Hooker where Jackson's corps was moving? (5) Which Union general didn't entrench despite warnings?

#VIII-1c

Even after the Union army was stunned by Jackson's attack, Hooker's defensive position was still stronger. Lee's army remained divided, and Hooker's lines outnumbered Lee in every location. It was a situation that could have led to victory.

By the morning of May 3, Howard's 11th Corps had been defeated, but the Army of the Potomac remained a potent force and Reynolds's First Corps had arrived overnight, which replaced Howard's losses. About 76,000 Union men faced 43,000 Confederate at the Chancellorsville front. The two halves of Lee's army at Chancellorsville were separated by Sickles's Third Corps, which occupied a strong position on high ground at Hazel Grove.

And the Army of Northern Virginia was split. Sickles's troops at Hazel Grove were right in between. Hooker could have attacked either part and destroyed it. Stuart was completely aware of this predicament. He was not in a position for a defensive battle. Instead, he prepared an attack at dawn on Hazel Grove rather than await one.

And Hooker, who continually made the wrong decisions in this battle, then made his most disastrous decision.

Challenges: (1) Who replaced Jackson in corps command on the second day? (2) What did Hooker order in the morning and why? (3) What was the Confederate response? (4) What is a Pyrrhic victory and does that describe this battle?

Challenge #VIII-2

Lee's army had stolen a march, passing around a mountain, threatening the Union right flank. A Confederate corps stumbled upon two

Section VIII. 1863 Battles and Campaigns (Except Gettysburg)

Union corps retreating. The Union army was posted behind a railroad track, ambushing two brigades of Confederates who had no idea how many troops were in their front. The Union defense held under the outmanned Confederate attack. A Union counterattack led to the death of a Confederate brigadier general. After the battle, the Union retreat continued, and Lee's offensive stopped. The Confederate commander lost standing in General Lee's eyes, who told him to bury his dead and say no more about it.

Challenges: (1) Name the battle that these events describe. (2) Name the Confederate general who attacked without knowing what size force he was attacking and the general who died. (3) Which side lost more men?

2. WEST

Challenge #VIII-3a–d

#VIII-3a

Vicksburg was probably the definitive turning point of the war. Short of some disaster, it is impossible to see how the Confederacy can win independence by military action once the Mississippi River is in Union hands.

Grant tried and failed myriad strategies before finding the one that worked. The Vicksburg Campaign was an unmistakable sign of the man's steely determination and shrewd mind. Grant failed over and over, but he never gave up. No other commander on the Union side had the emotional toughness to have succeeded.

Of all the various plans that failed, one in particular deserves attention. Union navy forces attempted to capture the city of Vicksburg in 1862 but were unable to accomplish it without army support. Grant's Canal was an attempt to create a canal through De Soto Point in Louisiana, across the Mississippi River from Vicksburg, Mississippi. Brigadier General Thomas Williams was sent to De Soto Point with 3,200 men to dig a canal capable of bypassing the Confederate defenses. Diseases, especially malaria and dysentery, and falling river levels prevented Williams from successfully constructing the canal, and the project was abandoned until January 1863, when Grant took an interest in it.

Recognizing that there were extensive engineering obstacles to the project, Grant began by moving the upstream entrance where there was a stronger current. Reports suggested that the water standing in the canal was stagnant and without a current. A much deeper channel was needed before the Union navy ironclads could pass through it. Grant also ordered that the canal be widened. By the end of the month, Grant knew the canal project would not succeed. Visiting Union officers later found that the water was only 2 feet and noted the lack of a current, although depths of up to 8 feet and widths up to 12 feet were reported in places.

Challenge: Obviously, Grant thought up a better plan. But what was the final result of this ingenious plan to dig a canal?

#VIII-3b

Grant marched the Army of Tennessee down the west side of the Mississippi River. The troops had to rendezvous with the Union navy, which provided transport for the river crossing into Confederate territory. On the evening of April 16, an acting rear admiral sneaked his Union fleet past the Confederate batteries at Vicksburg to meet up with Grant. As the boats rounded De Soto Point, they were spotted by Confederate lookouts who spread the alarm. Although each vessel was hit by Confederate fire, the fleet successfully fought its way past the Confederate batteries to rendezvous with Grant.

This man was chosen by Secretary Welles for this mission, but there were serious doubts. Here is what he wrote in his diary:

> …is but a Commander. He has, however, stirring and positive qualities, is fertile in resources, has great energy, excessive and sometimes not over-scrupulous ambition, is impressed with and boastful of his own powers, given to exaggeration in relation to himself … is not generous to older and superior living officers, whom he is too ready to traduce, but is kind and patronizing to favorites who are juniors, and generally to official inferiors. Is given to cliquism but is brave and daring like all his family.… It is a question, with his mixture of good and bad traits, how he will succeed.

Challenge: Who was this man and what became of him after the war?

#VIII-3c

All of the bayou operations were failures, but Grant was determined and would not quit. He chose a course that was bold but precarious. The army marched south on the west side of the Mississippi River and crossed the river south of Vicksburg. At that stage, Grant had several options, including attacking Vicksburg from the south and the east or to join forces with General Banks, capture Port Hudson, and then march on Vicksburg as a combined force. To succeed, though, Porter had to sneak his navy past the guns defending Vicksburg. There had to be a sufficient number of gunboats and transport ships south of the city for the plan to work. Once the navy had made this downstream passage, there was no return: the river current would slow them too much.

After crossing the river and advancing toward Port Gibson, the Union army skirmished with Confederate outposts for three hours. At dawn, the Confederates made a strong resistance against the Union advance and a battle ensued. The Confederates continued to fall back and establish new defensive positions at different times during the day. Eventually, they conceded and left the field in the early evening. Grant was now in control of Port Gibson and Grand Gulf.

Grant now had to make a choice. His orders were to join up with General Banks and take Port Hudson, then together attack Vicksburg. He did not follow these orders. Instead, he sent a message to Halleck that Banks was in the middle of his own operations, so he would advance on his own. He was well aware that it would take eight days for the message to be received and responded to.

Challenges: (1) What was the real reason Grant made this decision? (2) What was Lincoln's response after Vicksburg fell?

#VIII-3d

The Battle of Champion Hill (May 16, 1863) was the decisive battle of the Vicksburg Campaign. It was the moment when Pemberton had the single chance to hold off Grant.

Pemberton was out of line for the battle, with his right flank forward, as he hadn't decided his course. John A. McClernand's corps attacked Pemberton on the Union left and James B. McPherson on the right, with Stephen Lee providing an excellent defense. At 1:00 p.m., the Union took the crest of the hill. McPherson's corps advanced, capturing a critical crossroads and closing the Jackson Road escape route. A counterattack pushed the Federals back beyond the Champion Hill crest before their surge was halted, but they were too few to hold the position. Grant now also counterattacked, committing all of his forces. Pemberton's men could not stop this assault, and he ordered his men to use the one escape route still open, the Raymond Road crossing of Baker's Creek.

A single Confederate brigade led by a courageous general held the rear guard at all costs. The general was killed by artillery fire. His teenage son was on the field and hugged his father as he died.

Challenge: Who was this brave Confederate general? Bonus: What was the irony in his death that came to pass several weeks later?

Challenge #VIII-4a,b

#VIII-4a

July 1863 is remembered for the great Union victories at Gettysburg and Vicksburg. But often overlooked because it occurred at the same time is the Tullahoma Campaign, which also had a huge impact on the course of the war.

After Stones River, General Braxton Bragg withdrew to Tullahoma, located near Guy's Gap, toward Shelbyville. The Confederate Army of Tennessee held a strong defensive position in the mountains. But through a series of feints, Major General William Rosecrans captured the key passes. The Confederate command experienced marked dissension and discord, a lack of confidence in General Bragg, and a lack of supplies.

Bragg expected to be attacked from the direction of his left flank, threatening Chattanooga. Consequently, that town and flank was heavily fortified awaiting attack.

Meanwhile, Rosecrans spent six months in Murfreesboro training and refused to attack until he was ready despite increasingly peremptory entreaties from the entire Washington command including Lincoln. Finally on June 23, he began his advance. Despite severe rain and mud, Rosecrans had planned a surprise.

Challenge: Lincoln called it "the most splendid piece of strategy I know of." Describe the strategy Rosecrans employed.

#VIII-4b

Tullahoma is a classic example of catastrophe when an army's command and control structure fails due to personal antagonism and breakdown in communication.

Rosecrans had a major advantage: his troops had possession of the seven-shot Spencer repeating rifle. Bragg also was not supplied from Richmond well at this time because of preoccupation with other fronts. Rosecrans did not receive the public acclaim this campaign deserved. Under different circumstances, the significance of this campaign would have been better appreciated. The following day, Vicksburg surrendered to Grant. Secretary of War Stanton telegraphed Rosecrans, "Lee's Army overthrown; Grant victorious. You and your noble army now have a chance to give the finishing blow to the rebellion. Will you neglect the chance?"

Challenges: (1) Why was this victory so lightly regarded? (2) What was General Rosecrans's response to this telegram?

Section VIII. 1863 Battles and Campaigns (Except Gettysburg) 163

Challenge #VIII-5

Before the war, he had an uninteresting military and civilian career despite graduating high in his class at West Point. He later taught there but had never served in battle. He was the victorious commander in several prominent western theater battles. His brusque, outspoken manner and willingness to quarrel openly with superiors limited his advancement. He made a single poorly worded order that led to a disastrous defeat, and his career was effectively ended despite his other military successes. He was considered for running with Lincoln as vice president in 1864. Interestingly, he had the distinction of watching both his direct superior and his chief of staff elected president.

Challenges: (1) Who was he? (2) Who was his superior and subordinate who became president? (3) Why wasn't he selected to run with Lincoln (he would have become president in 1865 if he had!)?

Challenge #VIII-6

Chickamauga was the only authentic Confederate victory in the western theater. When Rosecrans failed to follow up on his almost-bloodless tactical victory at Tullahoma, Bragg abandoned Chattanooga. Rosecrans divided up into three columns and moving toward his rear. Bragg went south, into the mountains of Georgia.

Thinking Bragg was in full retreat, Rosecrans pursued vigorously but almost had an entire corps ambushed when he divided his army over three routes. He gathered his men at Chickamauga Creek. Neither Bragg nor Rosecrans could ascertain precisely the location of the enemy, leading to many lost opportunities for flanking and attack.

The battle began in the morning of September 19. Bragg attacked through numerous fields and woods, but the Union defense held.

But on day two, disaster struck. Bragg resumed his assault. In the late morning, Rosecrans was under the impression that he had a gap in his line. In moving units to shore up the supposed gap, Rosecrans accidentally created an actual gap, directly in the path of an eight-brigade assault on a narrow front by Confederate lieutenant general James Longstreet. His corps was detached from the Army of Northern Virginia and arrived on the battlefield via a detour by railroad. Longstreet's attack, which just coincidentally was aimed toward this gap, resulted in a massive rout. The attack caused one-third of the Union army, including Rosecrans himself, to retreat from the field.

Union units spontaneously rallied to create a defensive line on Horseshoe Ridge ("Snodgrass Hill"), forming a new right wing for the line, and held until twilight. Union forces retreated to Chattanooga. The Confederates occupied the surrounding heights and started a siege of the city.

Challenges: (1) Why did a gap develop in the Union lines? (2) Which general took advantage of this error with a highly effective attack? (3) Where was Rosecrans as disaster hit? Why didn't he lead as he did at Stones River? (4) Which Union general saved the destruction of the army? And which staff man was instrumental in arranging that defense? (5) What was the strategic result of this battle? (6) Estimate the ratio of dead and total casualties on the Union and Confederate sides. (7) Explain why this is surprising but shouldn't be.

Challenge #VIII-7a,b

#VIII-7a

Lots of people argue whether Antietam, Gettysburg, or Vicksburg was the "turning point" of the war. Some of this discussion revolves around what is meant by a turning point. In theory, you can have lots of turning points. A turning point in a war should be a decisive moment at which the direction of the war changes. If we accept that definition, then a great argument can be made that that moment occurred at the Battles of Lookout Mountain and Missionary Ridge.

After the defeat at Chickamauga, General Braxton Bragg began a siege of the Union army holding Chattanooga. Rosecrans was replaced by Thomas and reinforced by Sherman's army of 20,000. The Confederates pinned the Union army inside Chattanooga for two months and attempted a siege. They were not able to completely surround the city. They occupied Lookout Mountain and Missionary Ridge to the south and east of the city instead. General Ulysses S. Grant arrived to take command in this disastrous situation in late October. He immediately planned an offensive. Within one month, Grant had completely turned the situation around and was ready to lift the siege. First, he established a supply line and then he took control of the river.

On November 23, Grant began to attack the center of the Confederate line using Thomas's and Sherman's troops. Lookout Mountain was located on the Union's far right; General Joseph Hooker was in command of the wing covering this location. Ordered to create a diversion, Hooker advanced toward the fog-covered peak. Surprisingly, what was intended to be a demonstration carried what was thought to be an impregnable mountain. The next day, Union forces launched an overwhelming offensive on Missionary Ridge. This resulted in the complete collapse of the Confederate lines around Chattanooga.

Section VIII. 1863 Battles and Campaigns (Except Gettysburg) 165

Challenges: (1) What was the name of the supply line Grant opened to relieve the siege? (2) Why didn't Bragg defend Lookout Mountain intensively, as it was obviously the key to his defensive line?

#VIII-7b

The Battle of Missionary Ridge is one of the Union's greatest victories in the war, and it illustrates just how superior Grant and his corps commanders (Sherman, Thomas, Hooker) were to Bragg. Indeed, this was not only the greatest leadership of any army in the war but perhaps the most powerful army of the 19th century. And the victory on this day would have made Wellington and Napoleon proud.

The Battle of Chattanooga was launched on November 23 when Grant sent General Thomas to probe the center of the Confederate line. This rather straightforward strategic plan set up ultimate victory when the Union captured Orchard Knob, causing the rebels to retreat higher up Missionary Ridge. On November 24, General Hooker had captured Lookout Mountain, on the extreme right of the Union lines. The Battle of Lookout Mountain was the antecedent to the Battle of Missionary Ridge.

The attack took place in three parts. On the Union left, General Sherman attacked troops commanded by General Patrick Cleburne at Tunnel Hill. This ridge was an extension of Missionary Ridge. Cleburne ultimately held the hill despite severe fighting. Hooker also advanced from Lookout Mountain, but the difficult terrain caused him to have little impact on the battle.

The Union achieved success in the center of the line. Both sides issued orders that were confusing and a bit separated from the conditions on the ground. Some Union troops thought they were only supposed to take the rifle pits at the base of the ridge and then stop. But others understood that they were to advance to the top if they could. Similarly, some Confederates thought their orders were to hold the pits at all costs, while others thought they were to delay any advance, then fall back to the top of Missionary Ridge.

Challenges: (1) What tactical errors did Bragg make in defending the mountain? (2) What were the strategic and tactical outcomes? (3) What was the casualty rate and why is this surprising?

Answers

Answers #VIII-1

#VIII-1a

1. Lee divided his smaller army twice in the face of a larger army. This created the possibility of being defeated in detail. In addition, some of Longstreet's divisions were still detached, and Early's division was also divided in the latter stages.

2. General Hooker defeated himself. Hooker never considered what Lee might do and thought Lee could not discern his plan; he underestimated his enemy and never thought about the responses Lee might make. Lee, on the other hand, calculated very carefully the situation of the new Union commander, understood what choices he would not make, leaving him with a window into what he would do. Hooker made plans and had only limited flexibility when that plan met obstacles, and he had little ability to analyze how the enemy would respond to situations.

Hooker began the battle overconfident (Lee would be forced to either give battle or "ingloriously fly"). He expected Lee to retreat, but he surrendered the initiative and didn't anticipate Lee's tactics. Hooker refused to recognize intelligence reports that didn't support his preconceived notions.

3. On May 3 at 9:15 a.m., a Confederate cannonball hit a wooden pillar he was leaning against at his headquarters. He later wrote that half of the pillar "violently [struck me] … in an erect position from my head to my feet." He suffered a concussion, which caused him to be unconscious for over an hour. Hooker's concussion didn't lead to any change in his poor decisions, which he made both before and after. The myth has permeated usual discussions of the battle and prevents deeper analysis of Hooker's command decisions.

#VIII-1b

1. Investigations of a route to be used to reach the right flank identified the proprietor of Catharine Furnace, Charles C. Wellford, who showed Jedidiah Hotchkiss, Jackson's cartographer, a recently constructed

Section VIII. 1863 Battles and Campaigns (Except Gettysburg)

road through the forest that would shield marchers from the observation of Union pickets. Investigations of the route were made by Hotchkiss and the Reverend Beverly Tucker Lacy, Jackson's "chaplain general."

2. When reports were coming in about a large troop movement, Hooker believed the Confederate troops were retreating. He sent Sickles to chase after them, thus guaranteeing that he would be out of place and unable to support Howard.

3. At dawn on May 2, Lee and Jackson studied Hotchkiss's hastily drawn map and decided to undertake one of the biggest gambles in American military history. Jackson's corps, about 30,000 troops, would follow a series of country roads and woods paths to reach the Union right. Lee, with the remaining 14,000 infantry, would occupy a position more than three miles long and divert Hooker's main army of three to four times that many during Jackson's dangerous trek. Lee therefore divided his small army once again: his army was now in four disconnected parts, all of them facing larger forces. Had Hooker attacked, Lee had insufficient men to defend.

4. Stoneman's cavalry was carrying out a long-distance raid against the Confederate supply lines, so they weren't available to screen or divert. Hooker had sent the cavalry off to cut Lee's line of supply by tearing up the railroad in Lee's rear. Unfortunately, the mission failed.

5. General Oliver Otis Howard. Believing he was in the rear and held in reserve, he didn't anticipate an attack on his position.

#VIII-1c

1. J.E.B. Stuart

2. The Union position at Hazel Grove was separated from the main army position with tentative connection and support. Hooker pulled Sickles back because he was thinking defensively, not offensively. Hooker ordered Sickles off the high ground and to fall back to a much lower position called Fairview. Hooker felt he was losing and couldn't see the advantage of his position, so he retreated to what he erroneously thought was a safe defensible position. As previously noted, Hooker was unimaginative; if you are losing, you fall back.

Sickles would remember this moment two months later at the Peach Orchard. He wouldn't make the mistake again of following orders he knew to be wrong, and he would not again let the high ground in his front be captured by the enemy for their artillery.

3. Stuart had been ready to fight for that ground and now it had been given to him. He took control of the high ground and blasted Sickles at Fairview, where he was a sitting duck for Stuart's artillery.

4. A Pyrrhic victory is a military victory in which the winning army has incurred such a devastating toll that it is tantamount to defeat. The phrase originates from Pyrrhus of Epirus, whose triumph against the Romans in the Battle of Asculum in 279 BC destroyed much of his forces.

    a. At Chancellorsville, the Union army had 106,000 engaged, suffering 12,000 casualties, and the Confederate army of 60,000 had almost 13,000 casualties. This doesn't include the Union losses in the Fredericksburg and Salem Church portions of the battle, which also adds another 4,500 to the Confederate side. One can calculate that Lee lost 22 percent of his army in victory—obviously, this casualty rate could not be sustained for only a minimal strategic advantage.

FURTHER READING
- Sears, Stephen W. *Chancellorsville*. Mariner Books, 1996.
- https://www.historynet.com/battle-of-chancellorsville

Answers #VIII-2

(1) The Battle of Bristoe Station occurred on October 14, 1863, between Union forces under Major General Gouverneur K. Warren and Confederate forces under A.P. Hill. The Union Second Corps under Warren surprised and repelled a Confederate attack by Hill on the Union rear guard. (2) Lieutenant General A.P. Hill; Carnot Posey. (3) There were 1,380 casualties (8.1 percent) of 17,000 Confederate troops engaged versus 540 casualties (6.4 percent) of 8,500 Union troops.

Answers #VIII-3

#VIII-3a

In April 1876, the Mississippi River actually changed course, forming a channel through De Soto Point. Vicksburg became isolated from the riverfront after the oxbow lake formed by the course change became cut off from the river. Vicksburg would not be located on the river again until the completion of the Yazoo Diversion Canal in 1903. Although most of Grant's Canal has since been destroyed by agriculture, a small section still remains. Yes, General Grant succeeded in changing the course of the

Mississippi River, an astonishing accomplishment, just too late to be of military value.

FURTHER READING

- https://www.nps.gov/vick/learn/nature/river-course-changes.htm?fbclid=IwAR3mflQUgR8JaUEIcrm2v_lLlfdGup44_XwzxIcJ1mTAyyCT2h_umfcT2Sc
- https://www.vicksburgpost.com/2003/01/27/water-returned-to-citys-doorstep-100-years-ago/?fbclid=IwAR1X5nFZ8F-l_0sbr3Ki1HBygBiPb-GCgxl4aBCznjSOgKAvVdURVJUvJDA

#VIII-3b

Rear Admiral David Dixon Porter.

He became superintendent of the Naval Academy when it was restored to Annapolis. Porter was de facto secretary of the navy early in the Grant administration. When his adoptive brother David G. Farragut was promoted to admiral, Porter became vice admiral; likewise, when Farragut died, Porter became the second man to hold the rank of admiral. His grandson won the Medal of Honor in 1901 for actions in the Philippines.

#VIII-3c

1. Banks ranked Grant as a major general; if the two had joined, Grant would have been subordinate. Grant knew Banks was incompetent and he had no desire to have Banks mess things up. So Grant just avoided joining Banks and pursued his own plans without hindrance. Grant was in position to accept Pemberton's surrender, and Banks was in Port Hudson. He might have felt that he had a great plan and that including a below-average political general would only have slowed him down.

2. Lincoln's letter of congratulations:

My dear General

I do not remember that you and I ever met personally. I write this now as a grateful acknowledgment for the almost inestimable service you have done the country. I wish to say a word further. When you first reached the vicinity of Vicksburg, I thought you should do, what you finally did—march the troops across the neck, run the batteries with the transports, and thus go below; and I never had any faith, except a general hope that you knew better than I, that the Yazoo Pass expedition, and the like, could succeed. When you got below, and took Port Gibson, Grand Gulf, and vicinity, I thought you should go down the river and join Gen. Banks; and when you turned

Northward East of the Big Black, I feared it was a mistake. I now wish to make the personal acknowledgment that you were right, and I was wrong.

Yours very truly,
A. Lincoln

#VIII-3d

Brigadier General Lloyd Tilghman. He was exchanged for General Reynolds when both were prisoners. It is ironic that both were killed within three weeks of each other.

Further Reading

- Miller, Donald L. *Vicksburg: Grant's Campaign That Broke the Confederacy.* Simon & Schuster, 2019.
- https://www.battlefields.org/learn/civil-war/battles/vicksburg
- https://www.historynet.com/battle-of-vicksburg

Answers #VIII-4

#VIII-4a

The strategy was to feint on Bragg's left flank, which was exactly what he expected, but then move against Bragg's right, which was not strongly defended. Rosecrans's plan was to cover Shelbyville with one corps while the rest of the army made a giant right wheel heading toward Hoover's Gap on the Confederate right flank. Speed was of the essence. Bragg was unaware of the fighting on his right flank for three days because Forrest had not informed him how weak the Union right was and Wheeler had not told him of the wide right wheel toward Bragg's rear. Polk and Hardee were also not a great help; Hardee simply withdrew from the right, leaving Bragg exposed and forced to withdraw. Bragg was forced to retreat again. Rosecrans had won middle Tennessee with very few casualties.

#VIII-4b

1. First, the day it ended was the day Lee launched Pickett's Charge and lost the Battle of Gettysburg. Also, the lack of casualties made it appear to be of less importance than an actual battle. The strategic importance of the Union army forcing the Confederates out of Middle Tennessee with minimal losses was not appreciated at the

Section VIII. 1863 Battles and Campaigns (Except Gettysburg)

time. Union casualties were reported as 569 (83 killed, 473 wounded, and 13 captured or missing). Bragg made no formal casualty report; his losses were listed as "trifling." The Union army had captured 1,634 Confederates.

2. He was infuriated and responded, "Just received your cheering telegram announcing the fall of Vicksburg and confirming the defeat of Lee. You do not appear to observe the fact that this noble army has driven the rebels from middle Tennessee.... I beg in behalf of this army that the War Department may not overlook so great an event because it is not written in letters of blood."

Answers #V-5

1. Major General William Rosecrans
2. His chief of staff was James Garfield, and Grant was his immediate superior.
3. Garfield recommended him to Lincoln for consideration. His telegram response was intercepted by Stanton, who buried the message. Rosecrans had difficult relationships with his superiors, including Grant and Stanton.

After the war, he had many successes as an inventor, coal-oil company executive, diplomat, and congressman.

Further Reading

- https://www.battlefields.org/learn/biographies/william-s-rosecrans

Answers #VIII-6

1. The gap developed because in the dense woods one of Rosecrans's staff officers couldn't detect the Federal division that was actually in place and reported that to Rosecrans. Rosecrans was incorrectly informed by a staff officer there was a gap and then ordered it be filled. Rosecrans directed a movement order to Brigadier General *Thomas J. Wood* "to close up and support [General Joseph J.] Reynolds's [division]." However, Wood's movement actually opened up a real, very large gap in the line. General George Thomas was in charge of the left part of the line. He had been attacked in the morning. He was calling for reinforcements. Wood received orders to pull out of the line and move to help Thomas. In retrospect, the order was poorly worded and

miscalculated the situation on the ground. There was supposed to be a unit moving into the spot, but it never happened. The traditional story is that Woods knew there wasn't a gap but moved anyway because he'd been reprimanded twice for disobeying orders earlier in the campaign that he thought were wrong.

Exactly what happened next is controversial. Henry Cist reported years later that Wood moved despite knowing that the order was an error. Cozzens's *This Terrible Sound* repeats the story in which Wood waved the order in the air, knowing it was an error. Cist was a Rosecrans partisan and was defending him. Both Dave Powell and Glenn Robertson in their works on Chickamauga refute Cist's story. Also, part of it comes from a very troubled source, *Those Fateful Generals* by E.V. Westrate, which gives the story but offers zero evidence.

A modern interpretation is that Wood was hesitant to move, but McCook reminds him to follow orders—Rosecrans had criticized Wood before during that campaign for not immediately following an order. So Wood moved.

Major William Richards of McCook's staff:

"Wood peered quizzingly at the order, turned to McCook and read it aloud, adding in the familiar vernacular indulged between those two Generals: Mack, I'll move out by the right flank and rear to hide my move from the enemy. No, Tom, said McCook, just march out by the left flank and I'll order Jeff (meaning Jeff Davis) to close your gap. As Brannan's whole division intervened between Wood and Reynolds, whom he had been ordered to support, no one present thought of any other meaning than that taken by Wood." https://apps.dtic.mil/dtic/tr/fulltext/u2/a437039.pdf

It should be noted that Wood was never reprimanded or demoted, which seems inconsistent with an alleged action of such severe consequence that was intentional.

2. By coincidence, Lieutenant General James Longstreet had planned to lead a massive assault in that very area through a heavily forested area. The Confederates took advantage of the gap to full effect, shattering Rosecrans's right flank. At this moment, Longstreet had set up his line as a massed attack aimed right at the section of open line. The resulting attack split the Union line in two. Rosecrans and troops were forced to retreat.

3. Rosecrans tried to rally his retreating units but allowed the retreat to Chattanooga so he could better organize his men and the city defenses. Rosecrans began to build defensive positions for the expected Confederate attack. Thomas left his position at the end of the day and rejoined Rosecrans. These were excellent plans, and Rosecrans deserves

credit for picking up the pieces. Unfortunately, Rosecrans lost self-control, and his military career ended soon after.

4. The Union army escaped complete disaster thanks to the defense organized by Major General George H. Thomas, who commanded the remaining forces on Horseshoe Ridge, heroism that earned him the nickname "Rock of Chickamauga." The army withdrew that night to fortified positions in Chattanooga.

Rosecrans sent his chief of staff, James A. Garfield, to Major General George H. Thomas with orders to take command of the forces remaining at Chickamauga and withdraw as soon as he could. But Garfield thought Thomas's part of the army had held and, with Rosecrans's approval, headed across Missionary Ridge to survey the scene. Garfield's hunch was correct. His ride became legendary, becoming his ticket to the White House. Rosecrans's error reignited criticism about his leadership. Within a year, Garfield had been elected to the House of Representatives while Rosecrans had resigned.

5. The Confederate army secured a decisive victory at Chickamauga but lost 20 percent of its force in battle. After two days of fighting, the rebels forced the Union into a siege at Chattanooga.

6. Union ~60,000 total
   Casualties and losses: 16,170 total (1,657 killed, 9,756 wounded, 4,757 captured or missing)
   Confederates ~65,000 total
   Casualties and losses: 18,454 total (2,312 killed, 14,674 wounded, 1,468 captured or missing)

7. You would think that this massive Confederate victory would have overwhelming casualty numbers favoring the Confederate army, but in fact, the casualties might suggest a Union victory. And indeed, plenty of generals at the time thought so. The reasons are the first day, Bragg's attacks failed, and Thomas's defense on the second day caused substantial Confederate casualties. Still, you can see why there was dissatisfaction with General Rosecrans.

Answers #VIII-7

#VIII-7a

1. The "Cracker Line"
2. Hooker did not plan to attack the entire mountain because he believed the steep terrain and shelter in the rocks would be difficult to overcome. A layer of fog masked the Union advance. Consequently, Hooker's troops advanced easily.

On November 23, 1863, a reconnaissance in force by Thomas overran the Confederate position on Orchard Knob and gave Bragg deep concerns about the strength of the center of his line along Missionary Ridge. Bragg moved General William H.T. Walker's division from the base of Lookout Mountain to further protect this portion of the Confederate position. That movement left General Carter Stevenson just two brigades to hold the plateau near the Cravens House, which was insufficient for the onslaught that developed.

The Confederates overestimated the advantages offered by the mountain. Bragg left just 1,200 rebels to oppose 12,000 Union men. Artillery was not effective in this terrain because the hill was so steep that the attackers could not be seen until they appeared near the summit. Bragg did not send reinforcements because the Union attacks against the Confederate center were more threatening than the movement around Lookout Mountain. The Confederates abandoned their positions on Lookout Mountain in the afternoon. By 2:00 p.m., the "Battle among the Clouds" had ended as a surprising Union victory.

FURTHER READING

- https://www.battlefields.org/learn/biographies/george-thomas
- https://www.history.com/this-day-in-history/battle-of-lookout-mountain

#VIII-7b

1. Bragg's deployments were flawed. His line was on the crest and should have been below it on the "military" crest so that the line of fire could be directed downhill. There were also conflicting orders as to whether the men in the rifle pits at the base of the mountain were supposed to hold their ground or fight a holding action. When the Union army reached the rifle pits, they came under fire, which caused them to charge uphill even without orders to get out of the line of fire, and Bragg had no lines along the way. Bragg also had no tactical reserve; his line had no one behind them in case of a breach. So once the line was cracked by Wood's brigade, reinforcements had to come from the flanks, opening up more gaps.

2. Grant had saved Chattanooga, defeated an army in fabulous defensive positions, and opened up the entire South to invasion. Sherman advanced to Atlanta the next spring after Grant was promoted to general in chief of all federal forces. If Gettysburg and Vicksburg were the beginning of the end, then Missionary Ridge was the dagger.

Section VIII. 1863 Battles and Campaigns (Except Gettysburg)

There was no realistic chance of the Confederacy coming back militarily after this point.

The attack on the Confederate center resulted in a major Union victory. After the Confederate center collapsed, they retreated, and Bragg pulled his troops away from Chattanooga on November 26. He resigned soon thereafter, having lost the confidence of his subordinates and of his army.

3. The Union had about 5,800 casualties, while the Confederates' casualties were around 6,600. Rarely does the attacking force have fewer casualties than the defending force, and remember, this was attacking a major mountain defense. Strategically, this "little battle" often overlooked even by aficionados changed the war.

FURTHER READING

- https://www.history.com/topics/american-civil-war/battle-of-chattanooga

Section IX

Gettysburg

Challenges

1. Pennsylvania Campaign

Challenge #IX-1

Exactly what General Lee had in mind for his invasion of the North in June 1863 remains a mystery; it is most perplexing that we don't fully understand what the central general of the war was thinking about perhaps the central moment of the war. Coming off his victories at Fredericksburg and Chancellorsville, Lee (with Davis) made a decision to take the war to the North rather than reinforce Vicksburg.

The division of his forces as he advanced over the Potomac, as he did in his first Northern invasion and at Chancellorsville, might suggest that he was looking for an open space to battle and not attack a fort or make a direct siege of a city. The very western route he took exiting in western Pennsylvania seems rather indirect if Baltimore, D.C., or Philadelphia were truly his ambition. We hear often that Harrisburg was his target; if so, he was planning on its capture with just one corps.

Challenges: (1) Which raises an interesting point: What *was* Lee trying to accomplish, as best we know? (2) Lee was a deft strategist and a thoughtful psychologist. Why would Lee gamble on an invasion without a plan? What were his goals? Your answer must conform to reality, as stated above. (3) If these were his goals, what was the purpose of having his army spread out over such a wide area? (4) General Lee was certainly a fantastic tactical battlefield general, but his two invasions suggest that his army wasn't constructed for that purpose. Explain. (5) How did the Union commander respond?

Section IX. Gettysburg

Challenge #IX-2a,b

#IX-2a

One of the most controversial aspects of the Gettysburg Campaign was Jeb Stuart's absence until late in the battle. It is frequently speculated that had Stuart screened the front of Lee's army, Lee wouldn't have been surprised by the proximity of the Union army. Stuart was attempting to ride around the Union army, starting in its rear, which to his surprise, turned out to become its east flank as the Union army moved north to meet the threat.

In fact, Stuart had sent a dispatch to General Lee on June 27 that Hooker had crossed the Potomac River. It never reached General Lee, but a copy did reach Richmond; no one there bothered to confirm this with the commanding general.

Moreover, at least 5,000 cavalry had been left behind with Lee, and the commander of that force knew that Hooker had crossed the Potomac June 25–27 but failed to inform Generals Longstreet and Lee. Further, despite direct orders by Stuart to join Lee in force when Hooker advanced, this general instead guarded mountain gaps and the baggage train and never arrived at the battle.

Challenge: Who was the Confederate cavalry general who was lackadaisical in his duty?

#IX-2b

Part of the reason for Stuart's tardiness was that he was caught up in the rear and flank of the Union army. From the time he crossed the Potomac to arriving at Gettysburg required nearly eight days of nonstop marching for over 200 miles and fighting nearly every day. In fact, Stuart engaged in four skirmishes and three actual battles trying to make his way to find Ewell. Few accounts of Stuart's ride explains that he wasn't lost or just lollygagging; he was in fact in some real trouble, and it took great shrewdness merely to get to Gettysburg at all with his command intact.

Challenge: How close was Stuart to Ewell and Early on June 30? Why does that matter? Bonus: Where were the locations of these actions?

Challenge #IX-3

By June 27, 1863, General Lee had accomplished his objective of wrecking the B&O Railroad and was moving up the Cumberland Valley.

J.E.B. Stuart had torn up telegraph lines and rail north of D.C. General Richard S. Ewell's forces, moving ahead of the main body of Lee's army in south-central Pennsylvania, had already disrupted railroad operations on the Gettysburg Railroad east of Gettysburg and on the Northern Central Railway near York. A major battle was about to start, Meade and Lee were searching for each other, and the Union rail system required to transport men, ammunition, supplies, and horses was nonfunctional.

Stanton sent a civilian engineer, his chief of railroads, with complete authority to manage the railroads including civilian lines. This man knew the area well; by coincidence, he owned a house in Gettysburg, Pennsylvania. On June 30, he reported to General Halleck that the Confederates were going to gather near there. On July 1, he took a line with just one set of tracks, directed that five or six 10-car trains would run immediately from Baltimore to Westminster, one behind another, and instructed Meade's quartermasters to have troops ready to unload them all, then send them all back. On their return, there was already another convoy loaded and ready to go. Three round trips per day were organized. Because the telegraph lines were also down, he arranged a pony express type of communication line to follow the tracks.

See Challenge #IX-4. Identify this man, seated on the porch of his home in Gettysburg. Photo by Mathew Brady (Library of Congress).

By July 3, this train had moved 1,500 tons of cargo to the battlefield and returned 2,000 wounded soldiers to hospitals in Baltimore. When Lincoln gave his address that November, he took a train to Baltimore, then traveled on this same line to Gettysburg.

Challenges: (1) Who was this civilian engineer who made the Gettysburg victory possible? (2) Since no one knew where the battle would be fought, where were the supplies delivered?

2. July 1

Challenge #IX-4

If you have visited Gettysburg, you have seen the First Shot Marker at the Wisler house on the corner of Chambersburg Pike and Knoxlyn Road. And you probably know that Lieutenant Marcellus Jones fired that shot with a borrowed Sharps carbine at around 7:30 a.m. This has been accepted history for 160 years.

Except it's not correct. A Union corporal is known to have been shot and killed in a skirmish earlier that morning.

Challenge: Where were the real first shots of the battle fired? Bonus: Who is the man in the porch photo, why are his crutches and rifle prominently seen, and why is he relevant to this challenge?

Challenge #IX-5

Major General Henry Heth commanded a brigade under A.P. Hill. He is traditionally assigned blame for unintentionally commencing the Battle of Gettysburg. He sent half of his division toward the town as a reconnaissance in force, although he later claimed that he was looking for supplies, including shoes. He apparently did not know that Early's

Major General Henry Heth (Library of Congress).

division had been through the village a few days previously, and any supplies were long gone.

On June 30, Brigadier General Johnston Pettigrew, a brigade commander in Heth's division, encountered what he thought was Union cavalry, but Heth and Corps Commander A.P. Hill believed it to be a volunteer militia.

On the morning of July 1, Pettigrew marched down the Chambersburg Pike to perform a reconnaissance in force. At about 7:30 a.m., three miles outside of town near the McPherson barn, the first shots of the battle were fired.

Challenges: (1) If Pettigrew thought there was cavalry in town on June 30, why wasn't he believed? What was incorrect in his line of march on July 1? (2) How outnumbered was Buford? (3) Heth was knocked unconscious on day one by a bullet that struck him in the head. What saved his life?

Challenge #IX-6

The General John Buford Multiple-Choice Challenge

General Buford was the hero of day one at Gettysburg. His decision to defend the west part of the town allowed the Union army to ultimately occupy and defend the heights at the south part of town. Holding that ground was vital to the Union victory. His light cavalry held off more than twice their number in veteran Confederate infantry for five hours. In the morning alone, his two brigades of cavalry held off two divisions of Hill's corps for three hours. The conduct of his troops was valiant and their courage conspicuous.

Challenge: Following are five statements about General Buford at Gettysburg by well-known historians, but only one is actually correct. Your challenges are (1) tell which choice is true, (2) then for every choice, explain why each answer is correct or incorrect.

Besides his judgment and his men's gallantry, which of the following was the fundamental reason for the impressive performance by Buford and his men?

   a. Buford's troopers carried newly issued Spencer 7 shot repeating rifles into the battle for the first time.

   b. Buford's tactical strategy defined a covering force action in which space is traded for time.

   c. Buford's cavalry initiated a classic cavalry attack in the afternoon on General Lane's brigade of Pender's division, causing them to form a Napoleonic square defense, saving the retreating southern flank retreating from Seminary Ridge into the town.

d. Both Buford and Heth were entirely surprised to find a large force of their enemy on their fronts the morning of July 1, which is why it is called a "meeting engagement."

e. Buford set up his line early July 1 when Heth's division was seen marching down Chambersburg Pike, but after that, a series of generals positioned the men, including Reynolds, Doubleday, and Howard.

Challenge #IX-7a,b

Brigadier General John Buford by Mathew Brady (Library of Congress).

#IX-7a

The battle in the railroad cut, or unfinished railroad, was the site of multiple bloody attacks and counterattacks. Located near the McPherson farmhouse, it was an excavation in which railroad tracks had not yet been placed but which provided a deep entrenchment. Multiple units from the Union army were deployed near the railway cut to contest the attacks of the Confederate army. The Confederates were held off during the morning and early afternoon but were able to drive off the Union army due to superior numbers.

In the critical action at around 10:00 a.m., the Confederates so outnumbered the Union defenders that they overlapped their right flank and attacked. Three regiments moved to the railroad cut and faced south, with half of the brigade jumping into the cut to use it as a trench and the other half halting on the northern edge.

Challenges: (1) At this point, a Union counterattack was organized by the division commander James Wadsworth and his commanding officer. Who was that? (2) A repetitive theme in the Civil War was that a depression in the ground over three feet deep was good for cover when the enemy was far away but a very negative position when they are above you. Explain.

#IX-7b

Brigadier General Alfred Iverson's brigade walked into an infamous ambush at around 2:30 p.m. Iverson's men formed into a line of battle while the Union army located at Oak Ridge took position behind a stone wall. The Confederates advanced without skirmishers screening their advance; thus, there was no warning of the Federals that lay in their front. Within 20 minutes, the Confederates surrendered. Of Iverson's 1,384 men, over 900 had been killed, wounded, or captured.

Challenge: What did Iverson think was happening and why?

Challenge #IX-8

After Barlow was defeated at the base of Culp's Hill and 11th Corps beaten once again in the town, Ewell was given discretionary orders to take the hill. He did not immediately try, and when later he sent Johnson's division, they ran into the Union line digging in.

Ewell's failure to take Culp's Hill/Cemetery Hill the evening of July 1 is often considered one of the great missed opportunities of the battle. But a logical, informed understanding suggests that it was probably not possible under those circumstances to take that hill.

Challenges: (1) Give six rational reasons why Ewell did not try to take Culp's Hill the afternoon of July 1. (2) Which troops were on Culp's Hill that Early's division ran into? (3) If General Lee wanted the hill taken, why didn't he just say so? (4) Which troops and commander arrived the next morning that ensured that Culp's Hill would not be taken? Bonus: Of what places had the Union commander been in charge of before the war and after?

3. July 2

Challenge #IX-9

In the early morning hours of July 2, 1863, this officer performed an important reconnaissance mission. His undertaking was one of the most controversial moments of the war.

When the battle ended on July 1, General Robert E. Lee did not know the location of the remainder of the Army of the Potomac. He also was uncertain how far south along Cemetery Ridge the Union line extended.

Brigadier General William N. Pendleton had conducted a reconnaissance on the evening of July 1 to locate artillery positions on the northern part of Seminary Ridge but did not observe infantry positions.

Lee, needing more information to plan his attack, sent for a staff officer at about 4:00 a.m. on July 2. After the war, this officer recalled that the order he received from Lee was to "reconnoiter along the enemy's left and return as soon as possible." Although nothing was said about finding a concealed route, that wasn't necessary "as that was part of my duty as a reconnoitering Officer, and would be attended to without special instructions, indeed he said nothing about the movement of troops at all, and left me with only that knowledge of what he wanted which I had obtained after long service with him, and that was that he wanted me to consider every contingency, which might arise."

We can only guess retrospectively where he went, but the precise route is critical to understanding what happened during the battle on July 2. Most likely, he left Lee's headquarters near the Lutheran Theological Seminary and traveled south along the west slope of Seminary Ridge and into the Willoughby Run valley. This path would have taken him past the Samuel Pitzer farm and the Pitzer schoolhouse. He likely then turned east, ascending the west slope of Warfield Ridge, at about the location where McLaws formed his troops later that afternoon. Then he noted he was "following along that ridge in the direction of the round top across the Emmitsburg road and got up on the slope of round top, where I had a commanding view." This would place him on Little Round Top at about 5:30 a.m.

He reported to General Lee that there was a route that could not be detected from the Union lines. Crucially, he noted that the large hill in the distance "with a commanding view," which was Little Round Top, was unoccupied. Lee then designed the July 2 attack based on this reconnaissance.

Of course, we know now that hill was occupied, and there was no concealed route. It was dark, and it is highly doubtful he was on Little Round Top at that hour.

Challenges: (1) Who was this staff officer? (2) Where was he when he thought he was at Little Round Top? (3) Why is it nearly impossible that the officer was where he said he was?

Challenge #IX-10

Major General Daniel Sickles, Third Corps commander, made perhaps the most controversial decision of the war. His advance to the Peach

Orchard, bordering the Emmitsburg Turnpike, must count as one of the most crucial movements of the entire war. By uncovering both of his flanks and leaving Little Round Top uncovered, he clearly put Meade in a dangerous position.

General Sickles was not at all happy with the position on the line General Meade assigned him between Little Round Top and Cemetery Ridge. He felt the higher, more elevated ground to his front would be more defensible and offer his artillery a better field of fire. So without authorization, General Sickles moved his entire corps forward. This act unhinged the Union line, leaving his corps vulnerable to attack from multiple directions. Since both of his flanks were in the air, reinforcements had to be sent to protect him and the Union line. What Sickles could not have known was that his movement placed an entire corps right on the spot where General Lee had planned to start his attack.

The great debate of Sickles's move is whether it was a smart move or a dumb move. Certainly, it led to the destruction of Third Corps and threatened the entire left flank of the Union defense; but serendipitously, it may have saved the battle. There is no doubt that not following orders isn't a sign of working well with others, but Sickles wasn't the kind of man to let that bother him.

Challenge: Did Sickles's movement actually save the Battle of Gettysburg?

Challenge #IX-11

This hero immigrated from Ireland at the age of one. He was the first Irish immigrant to attend West Point and graduated first in his class in 1861 on an accelerated basis because officers were needed: the same class in which George Armstrong Custer graduated last. He fought at First Bull Run where his horse was shot from under him just one month after graduating from West Point. He was promoted to colonel and fought at Fredericksburg and

Major General Daniel Sickles by Mathew Brady (Library of Congress).

Chancellorsville. As he entered the battlefield at Gettysburg, his regiment was diverted from where it was supposed to go for an urgent assignment. He led his men to the crest of a hill and charged the Confederates, driving them down the slope. He was killed during the counterattack.

Challenges: (1) Who was he? (2) Who is the statue of, and where is it located?

See Answers for details (photograph by Lloyd W. Klein).

Challenge #IX-12a–b

#IX-12a

The staff officer depicted in the previous challenge recognized that Little Round Top was undefended as well as its tactical importance. He urgently sought Union troops to occupy it before the Confederates could.

Colonel Strong Vincent's brigade was in the ideal position to defend Little Round Top. Without consulting his superior officers, he took it on himself to position his brigade where it was most needed. Private Oliver Willcox Norton, together with Vincent, made a reconnaissance of the Confederate forces as the brigade was moving into position: "While our line was forming on the hill at Gettysburg I came out with him in full view of the rebel lines. They opened two batteries on us instantly, firing at the colors."

Colonel Strong Vincent (Library of Congress).

He mounted a large boulder while brandishing a riding crop and shouted, "Don't give an inch!" A bullet struck him and he fell mortally wounded. The determination of his brigades and its component regiments, the 20th Maine, the 44th New York, the 83rd Pennsylvania, and the 16th Michigan Infantry, saved the position. Vincent was carried from the hill to a nearby farm, where he died five days later.

Challenges: (1) What recognition did Vincent receive for his bravery? (2) How did he deploy his brigade to cover both the west- and south-facing portions of Little Round Top?

#IX-12b

Joshua Lawrence Chamberlain was an American college professor from Maine who volunteered to join the Union Army. He became a highly decorated officer, achieving the rank of brigadier general and brevet major general. He is best known for his action at Little Round Top on July 2, for which he was awarded the Medal of Honor.

Chamberlain became the lieutenant colonel in the 20th Maine Volunteer

Infantry Regiment in 1862. He fought at the Battle of Fredericksburg, where his men were pinned down on Marye's Heights overnight. He became commander of the regiment in June 1863 when losses at the Battle of Chancellorsville elevated the original commander, Colonel Adelbert Ames, to brigade command.

Arriving late in the afternoon on July 2, Chamberlain's regiment was ordered by Colonel Vincent to occupy the extreme left of the Union lines at Little Round Top and to hold it at all costs. Chamberlain's men withstood repeated assaults from the 15th Alabama Infantry Regiment and eventually held off the Confederates. Chamberlain was severely wounded commanding a brigade during the Second Battle of Petersburg in June 1864 and

Colonel Joshua Chamberlain by Mathew Brady.

was given what was intended to be a deathbed promotion to brigadier general, but he survived and in April 1865, he fought at the Battle of Five Forks. He was given the honor of commanding the Union troops at the surrender ceremony at Appomattox Court House, where he and his men saluted the surrendering army.

After the war, he served as governor of Maine, then he returned to Bowdoin College as its president until 1883. He died at age 85 due to complications from the wound that he received at Petersburg.

Challenges: (1) In 1861, Chamberlain was professor of languages and wanted to enlist in the army. What did his college's administration say to that, and how did he respond? (2) What tactic did Chamberlain utilize to save the line at Gettysburg? (3) What were his war injuries and why did he die of them 50 years later?

Challenge #IX-13

He was a lawyer and newspaper editor in a small town and he had no military education or experience. His politics were Democratic but anti-secession. As a Union Democrat, he supported Stephen Douglas for president. He volunteered at the start of the war, and his regiment elected him captain. He fought with gallantry at First Manassas and in the Seven Days, where he was wounded. He fought again in the thick of the battle at Antietam and was promoted to lieutenant colonel. He was again promoted to colonel and command of his regiment after Fredericksburg. His horse was shot out from under him at the Battle of Haymarket by J.E.B. Stuart's cavalry. Then he was arrested for allowing his men to ford a river on logs chasing the Confederate army into Maryland. His regiment arrived in Gettysburg on the morning of July 2 after traveling 14 miles every day for 11 days, finally resting on Cemetery Ridge. Due to heroic action there, he was severely wounded, requiring a cane for the rest of his life.

Challenge: Name the man and his regiment.

Challenge #IX-14

General Alpheus Williams played a prominent role because of a miscommunication between General Meade and Williams's superior officer. As a consequence, Williams commanded the 12th Corps and removed them from Culp's Hill on July 2, leaving only a brigade there to defend the entire right flank.

Challenge: What was the mix-up in the command structure?

Devil's Den seen from Little Round Top (photograph by Lloyd W. Klein).

Challenge #IX-15

On day two, Confederate major general John Bell Hood launched an attack against the Union army's left flank. At Devil's Den, a private in the First Texas Infantry climbed on top of a rock outcrop and began to shoot retreating Union army soldiers. Despite being wounded several times, causing him to fall off the rock, he repeatedly returned to this position. Finally,

Vermont 13th Infantry Regiment Monument (courtesy Ramona I. Lyman, https://rilynam.blogspot.com).

he was wounded so severely that he could not return to this position. He was honored with the Confederate version of the Medal of Honor, the Southern Cross of Honor.

Challenge: Name this Southern hero of the battle.

Challenge #IX-16

The monuments at Gettysburg are intended to share the story of their regiment on the field. A good deal of thought went into their design. One of the most interesting is this one to the 13th Vermont Infantry. If you look carefully, you will see by the figure's right foot an object protruding over the edge of the base on which the statue of Second Lieutenant Stephen F. Brown of Company K stands.

Aerial view of base of Vermont 13th Regiment Monument (courtesy Tim Fulmer, http://gettysburgsculptures.com/).

The regiment had spent most of its nine-month enlistment in the forts surrounding Washington. The enlistment period was almost over when the regiment was ordered to make a forced march, joining the First Corps at Gettysburg on the evening of July 1.

On July 2, the regiment made a charge to Emmitsburg Road that turned back the Confederate attack and captured guns and prisoners. The next day, during Pickett's Charge on July 3, his men moved forward from their position on Cemetery Ridge. They attacked the flank of the Confederate attack, stopping its advance and capturing hundreds from Kemper's Virginia brigade.

The monument to the 13th Vermont Volunteer Infantry Regiment is south of Gettysburg on Hancock Avenue, at its position on July 3.

Challenge: What is this object, and why is it depicted on this statue?

4. July 3

Challenge #IX-17

On July 3, Pickett led his division across the open field along with those of Pettigrew and Trimble. Only men from Pickett's division made it to the Angle. His division of course started from the more southern areas; the main forces of Pettigrew and Trimble never crossed the Emmitsburg Pike, although members of the 26th North Carolina and 11th Mississippi did make it to the wall just north of the Angle. Although traditionally the Copse of Trees near the Angle has been cited since Bachelder as the visual landmark of the attack, it is probably not true.

Challenges: (1) Why did Lee order Pickett's Charge, a desperate charge across 0.8 mile of open farmland into the center of a well-armed foe? (2) Which landmark was used for the focus of the attack? What was its objective? (3) Why didn't anyone get there?

Challenge #IX-18

James Longstreet's reluctance to order Pickett's Charge is one of the most renowned anecdotes of the Civil War. His memoirs say that he was planning an attack around the Federal left flank to the rear of Big Round Top but that Lee did not approve of that plan. Lee ordered Longstreet to attack Cemetery Ridge, the center of the Union position. The distance to be covered during the charge was just short of one mile. Longstreet famously told Lee, "It is my opinion that no 15,000 men ever arrayed for battle can take that position."

In fact, although Longstreet is typically portrayed as favoring the defensive, and in contradistinction Jackson the audacious offensive, Longstreet led four of the largest charges across open fields during the war, plus another massive charge from a railroad cut. Longstreet commanded these charges: four of the five led to victories.

Challenge: Name the five large-scale attacks led by General Longstreet.

Challenge #IX-19

Pickett's Charge was undoubtedly the single iconic moment of the battle and perhaps the entire Civil War. Whether Longstreet was to blame for not putting enough men into the battle or whether it was hopeless has remained controversial for 160 years and undoubtedly will continue to be.

Challenge: The attack was made by about 12,000 men. How many would have been needed to carry the position?

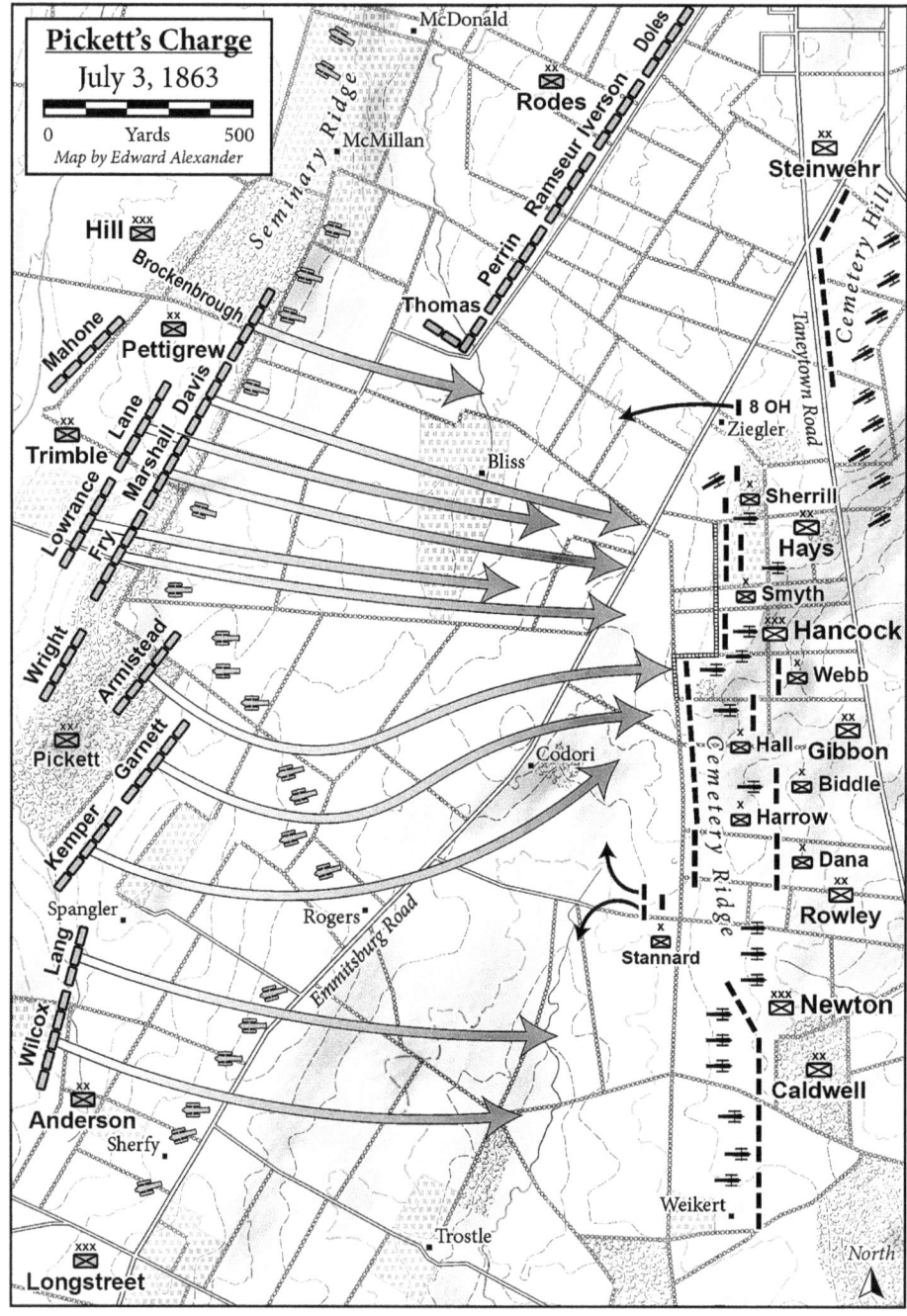

Map showing Pickett's Charge. Trimble and Pettigrew led the north end of the field while Pickett led the south end.

Challenge #IX-20

The July 3 bombardment prior to Pickett's Charge was the largest of the war, with hundreds of cannons from both sides firing along the lines for one hour, starting around 1:00 p.m. The number of active Confederate guns was between 150 and 170, fired from distance of over two miles long, starting in the south at the Peach Orchard and running roughly parallel to the Emmitsburg Road.

Despite its ferocity, the fire was mostly ineffectual. Confederate shells overshot the Union front lines which the smoke covering the battlefield concealed. Union artillery chief Brigadier General Henry J. Hunt had about 80 guns available to conduct counterbattery fire because the geographic features of the Union line had limited areas for effective gun emplacement.

The day was hot, 87°F and humid, and the Confederates suffered under the hot sun and from the Union counterbattery fire as they awaited the order to advance. When the Union artillery died down, General Alexander believed that the time to charge had arrived.

Challenges: (1) Why was the Confederate artillery so inaccurate? (2) Why was the decrease in artillery fire not a good sign that severe casualties had been inflicted?

Challenge #IX-21

This officer received the Medal of Honor 151 years after his heroic act in the war. Who is he and what did he do?

Challenge #IX-22

Photography existed during the war, as Brady's and Gardner's work shows, but could not be used on the battlefield, as photographic equipment was too cumbersome and exposure times were too slow. And there was no way to transfer a photograph to a printing

See Answers for details.

General Armitage leading Pickett's Charge. See Answers for details.

plate since this was well before the advent of the halftone process for printing photographs. Thus, the photos could not be put in a newspaper.

An artist would do detailed sketches in the field, which were then rushed by courier back to the main office of the newspaper they were working for. There, a staff of engravers would use the sketches to create engravings on blocks of boxwood. Since the blocks were about four inches across, they would have to be composited together to make one large illustration. The wood engraving was then copied via the electrotype process which produced a metal printing plate for publication.

This illustrator was the best of the best. He attended every battle of the Army of the Potomac between the First Battle of Bull Run in 1861 and the siege of Petersburg in 1865. He was one of only two artists present at the Battle of Gettysburg.

The illustration above (also on the cover of this book) shows one of his most well-known sketches. The illustration is his famous drawing of Pickett's Charge, with General Armistead leading the charge. You have surely seen others like it, but all are based on this sketch: this depiction is thought to be the only visual account by an eyewitness.

Challenge: Name this amazing artist who became even more famous after the war.

5. Aftermath

Challenge #IX-23

Lincoln and Stanton insisted that Meade pursue Lee during the retreat. During the night of July 4, General Robert E. Lee's battered Confederate army began its retreat from Gettysburg, moving southwest on the Fairfield Road, screened by Major General J.E.B. Stuart's cavalry. The Union infantry followed cautiously on July 5, converging on Middletown, Maryland. Lee's infantry reached the rain-swollen Potomac River but was not able to cross because the pontoon bridge had been destroyed by a cavalry raid. On July 11, Lee entrenched in a line protecting the river crossing and waited for Meade to advance. Meade chose not to attack. The river crested, a bridge was built, and Lee escaped.

Despite having won the bloodiest battle of the Civil War, Meade immediately came under harsh criticism—in particular from President Abraham Lincoln—for what was seen as his failure to destroy Lee's battered army, which had escaped across the Potomac River.

Challenges: (1) Why didn't Meade attack? (2) Where did these events take place?

Challenge #IX-24

Cornelia Hancock was a resident of Hancock's Bridge, New Jersey, and 23 years old in 1863 when the Battle of Gettysburg occurred. Hancock, intent on serving as a nurse in the aftermath of the battle, was too late to smell the flowering peach blossoms and the saltpeter of expended gunpowder but was in plenty of time to smell the dead. She wrote home, "A sickening, overpowering, awful stench announced the presence of the unburied dead upon which the July sun was mercilessly shining and at every step the air grew heavier and fouler until it seemed to possess a palpable horrible density that could be seen and felt and cut with a knife."

Hancock was so overcome by the smell that she viewed it as an oppressive, malignant force, capable of killing the wounded men who were forced to lie amid the corpses until the medical corps could reach them. Hancock's account, vivid in its horror, proves the limitations of the visual record of war. No photograph of the aftermath of the battle, writes Smith, could "capture the sounds, the groans or the rustle of twitching bodies"—and no image could ever capture that smell.

Challenge: How many Union and Confederate soldiers were buried on the battlefield during the 12 days after the battle?

Answers

Answers #IX-1

1. Gettysburg can't be understood as a stand-alone campaign. It was a final try to win on the battlefield. Lee wanted to bring on a huge battle in the North that might be decisive. The idea was to take attention away from the events out west and to precipitate a battle in the east that might change the trajectory of the war.

2. (a) It would give war-torn Virginia a much needed respite and would allow the Army of Northern Virginia to provision itself from its enemy's resources. (b) The invasion into Pennsylvania might cause the federal government to shift troops from the west possibly loosening the grip of General Ulysses S. Grant's siege on Vicksburg. (c) Probably foremost was General Lee's confidence in his army and that if he could find and prepare ground that was to his advantage, the Army of Northern Virginia could defeat the Union army on its own soil. This, Lee reasoned might possibly have caused the war-weary North to sue for peace. (d) It might also have been the military stroke needed to demonstrate to Great Britain and France the strength of the Southern will for independence.

3. Lee didn't want the Union commander to know exactly where he was and he wanted to create confusion in occupied areas to demonstrate to the people of the North that he had the upper hand and they should lose spirit for the fight. Splitting up was also crucial for them to find supplies, which his train was inadequate for, and to keep his corps from having traffic jams.

4. Lee's army was not designed to leave the confines of Virginia. First, unlike the North, Lee had no intelligence operations. Lee obtained his information from three sources: (a) the civilians of Virginia, (b) Stuart's cavalry, and (c) Lee's staff itself. In Lee's campaigns north, he left behind his greatest intelligence source he had, the civilians of Virginia themselves. This could be why J.E.B. Stuart was retained as cavalry commander and not promoted to corps command; he was the intelligence arm. Second, Lee's supply support was primitive. He had no railroads and no rivers, and his wagon train had to traverse a huge distance. Finally, his staff was too small to plan a foray into unknown territory.

Lee thought Hooker was his opponent. Lee expected that he'd freeze again when confronted with an unexpected enemy tactic, like at Chancellorsville. When Lee learned that Hooker was out, he had to pivot and change tactics quickly. He knew General Meade was a careful and methodical engineer warrior. The first step was to collect his army in one place. He chose a central location, a crossroads town close to his forces to gather.

5. When Meade took command three days before the battle, he had no clue where Lee's army was, what his plan was, or any sense of what his own deployments should be. His communication and rail transportation had been cut, and he had staff who didn't support him. Yet a battle was imminent; he decided to prepare for it by building a defensive perimeter. The Pipe Creek Line was a defense against any threat to attack Baltimore and D.C.

Answers #IX-2

#IX-2a

Brigadier General Beverly Robertson. He covered Lee's retreat after the battle, sustaining heavy losses. Lee then banished him to Charleston, South Carolina, for the remainder of the war.

#IX-2b

On June 30, Jubal Early, who would go on to blame every other Confederate general at Gettysburg for its loss and was one of Stuart's most vociferous critics after the war, heard the sound of the battle at Hanover. Yet, he did nothing to discover who was fighting despite knowing that Stuart was supposed to be finding him. Eric J. Wittenberg and David Petruzzi in *Plenty of Blame to Go Around* believe that Early was within five miles of the battle and that had contact been made, Stuart could have been present at Gettysburg July 1.

Bonus: Skirmishes: Thoroughfare Gap, June 25; Fairfax Courthouse, June 27; Rockville, June 28; and Westminster, June 29; Battles at Hanover, June 30, Huntersville, July 2, and Carlisle, July 2.

FURTHER READING
- Wittenberg, Eric J., and J. David Petruzzi. *Plenty of Blame to Go Around*. Savas Beatie, 2006.

Answer IX-3

1. Herman Haupt. He also supervised the rebuilding of the line from Rectortown to Piedmont, with Union forces in pursuit of Jackson.

While under the outstanding management of Haupt, the railroad was utilized by Union forces in the Maryland (1862) and Gettysburg (1863) Campaigns, although it faced continuous threats from Confederates until the war's end.

2. Pipe Creek. Meade was preparing a defensive line in northern Maryland. This remained his primary plan until the early morning of July 2.

Further Reading

- Brown, Kent Masterson. *Meade at Gettysburg: A Study in Command*. University of North Carolina Press, 2021.

Answers #IX-4

Corporal Cyrus James of the Ninth New York Cavalry was killed on vidette duty at daybreak on the Hunterstown Road—east of the town. Obviously, this is the opposite direction of the actual attack, so it's been ignored. He was killed in a skirmish with the Virginia 14th Cavalry. We know the time for a fact since his horse dragged his body back into the town, creating a commotion.

Bonus: John L. Burns, who is seen in the photo at age 69, was the constable of Gettysburg. After being arrested by Early in his first pass through town, he was released, then arrested Confederate stragglers. At daybreak on July 1, he stopped the horse dragging Corporal James's body in the street. Angered at the kerfuffle brewing in his quiet town, he volunteered his services to General Buford, intending to fight at McPherson Woods with the Iron Brigade. He received wounds in the arm and leg and minor chest wounds after falling in with the 24th Michigan. He escaped capture by hiding his weapon and telling the Confederates he had been caught in the cross fire. He became a national hero. He met Lincoln on the day of the cemetery dedication, and he became the subject of a poem by Bret Harte.

Answers #IX-5

1. Pettigrew was killed several weeks later, so we don't know for sure what he said he saw. Clearly, his leadership blundered in not taking his report seriously. Heth and Hill were both new to their jobs and had reputations for rashness. Pettigrew wasn't a West Pointer and had no military experience before the war. He was born to a wealthy family and was an author, linguist, and lawyer. He had been severely wounded at Seven Pines, captured and exchanged, and had just joined

Hill's corps prior to the campaign. His men were newly uniformed with new rifles, and his staff was composed of aristocrats. Likely, his lack of prior connection to Hill, his lack of war experience, and the appearance of his staff and men without the grime of battle led to his interpretation being discounted by Hill.

On July 1, Pettigrew deployed his men without cavalry in front; the first enemy he ran into were Union vedettes. The front of the line was Pegram's artillery, followed by Archer's and Davis's infantry brigades.

 2. Heth's division had 7,600 men versus Buford with 2,748, about 2.75:1 disadvantage.

 3. A hat stuffed with paper. He had purchased a hat that was a size too large the day before in Cashtown, so he placed cardboard and other paper inside the brim so it would fit.

Answers #IX-6

 a. This myth was propounded by Shelby Foote in his trilogy, and cited by several historians since, to explain the high rate of fire by Buford's troops. It is false because the Spencer carbine did not go into mass production until September 1863. The cavalry at Gettysburg was armed with breech-loading single-shot carbines. This weapon was capable of five to seven rounds per minute but had a shorter range than muzzle-loaded weapons (~3 shots/min).

 b. Correct answer. Buford traded three ridges for enough time for Reynolds and the First Corps to come up. His defense has since been copied and in modern warfare is practiced the same way, just with tanks and armored vehicles instead of horses. The U.S. Army teaches it on a staff ride to this day.

 c. Colonel Gamble may or may not have led his brigade in a cavalry charge—he might only have threatened it. Lane's brigade may or may not have formed squares. There are eyewitnesses who said it happened and others who never saw it happen. Buford's report does not say, nor does Lane's. This myth began just a few years after the war. No doubt, Gamble did something that saved the retreating flank, but no one knows for sure what. Harry Pfanz in *The First Day* does as good a job sorting this out as anyone probably can ever do.

 d. This is probably the single most persistent myth of the battle. Sears wrote an entire chapter propounding this inaccuracy. General Pettigrew was very clear that he was facing more than militia on June 30; it's just that A.P. Hill didn't believe him. Heth advanced that day in order of battle, although he erred in putting Archer's brigade at the front and his artillery in the rear. Buford also knew what he was facing and told General Reynolds so the night of June 30. The idea that shoes was the cause of the battle is nothing more than a story based on a single exaggerated statement of Heth.

    e. While Reynolds was alive, he did send his corps into the battle as they arrived. Thereafter, Buford (and Doubleday to some extent) managed the positions entirely. Howard never even came onto the field of battle.

Further Reading

- Wittenberg, Eric J. *The Devil's to Pay: John Buford at Gettysburg.* Savas Beatie, 2014.

Answers #IX-7

#IX-7a

    1. Abner Doubleday. The movement of the 1st and 11th Corps to Gettysburg was a covering force action/advance guard operation to draw out and consolidate Lee's forces and lure them back to the Pipe Creek Line.

    2. The Union counterattack flanked the Confederate position across the eastern end of the railroad bed to the northern edge of the cut and enfiladed the Confederate positions. About 300 Confederates surrendered, while the remainder of the brigade retreated out of the west of the cut. A similar result was seen at the Crater and at Vicksburg. This linear landmark also cuts off one side of the field from another so communication is disastrous; this was exactly the problem with the original Confederate attack: Wadsworth had ordered a withdrawal, but the 147th New York was on the north side and didn't get the order, resulting in severe casualties.

#IX-7b

He saw his men fall and thought they were lying down because they were cowards, but they had been killed. His appointment was politically motivated, and his military ineptitude was exacerbated by a drinking problem. Very likely, he was intoxicated on the field. He was shuffled off to Williamsport, Maryland, after this battle, to the chagrin of the survivors of his regiment. During Sherman's campaign in Georgia, Iverson and his men captured Federal major general Stoneman and hundreds of his men.

Further Reading

- https://gettysburgcompiler.org/tag/alfred-iverson/

Answers #IX-8

1. (a) His men had been through a huge firefight after marching many hours and were fatigued. (b) Making an assault on the hill through the streets of Gettysburg was not an easy task since the narrow passageways prevented massing the troops for an attack. (c) Lee's ambiguous order resonates through history. The orders were contradictory, and Ewell had no idea what Lee actually wanted. In brief, the order read to "carry the hill occupied by the enemy, if practicable, but to avoid a general engagement until the arrival of the other divisions of the army." Any dispassionate reading of that phrase in the context of battle is more confusing than anything else. And it should be noted that Early himself was reluctant at that moment. (d) Ewell requested assistance from A.P. Hill, who declined due to the condition of his own corps, which had taken the brunt of the first day. (e) There was intelligence that Union troops were approaching from the east on the Hanover Road. This was the front of the 12th Corps under Slocum. If those troops had arrived at the wrong time, Ewell's flank would have been turned. (f) This was Ewell's first corps command. He was hesitant given these issues. Ewell was never the same after the loss of his leg and marriage.

2. They encountered the Seventh Indiana Infantry of the First Corps, part of Brigadier General James S. Wadsworth's division, linked up with the Iron Brigade, digging in following their fierce battle on Seminary Ridge.

3. Although General Lee certainly wanted General Ewell to take Cemetery Hill, his phrase "if practicable" was open to the interpretation and discretion of General Ewell. It means "if able to be done or put into practice successfully." In this instance, General Lee lacked communication with the front, knowledge of the obstacles, the status of the troops, or of the mindset of his general. Thus, the lack of clarity of instruction probably reflects that even though he expected Ewell to try, he gave him an option if there was something important that he didn't know in that rapidly changing situation. If Lee wanted Ewell to attack, he should have said so.

4. 12th Corps in George Greene's brigade of John Geary's division.

Bonus: Geary had been the first mayor of San Francisco, and a street is named after him. He had also been governor of Territorial Kansas. During the war, he was the military governor of Savannah after Sherman's march. After the war, he was governor of Pennsylvania.

Answer #IX-9

1. Captain Samuel R. Johnston. He later wrote that he was joined by Longstreet's chief engineer, Major John C. Clarke.

2. Johnston claimed he took a route very close to Longstreet's countermarch and made it to the top of Little Round Top. If so, there were Union troops all over that area. At Gettysburg on July 2, General Lee planned an attack based on information that couldn't possibly have been accurate. Furthermore, once Sickles moved to the Peach Orchard, the whole plan was obsolete, yet Longstreet had orders to attack.

Buford's cavalry and Geary's division were bivouacked in front of Little Round Top. Two regiments were posted on Little Round Top with skirmishers. Geary later wrote that he was relieved by Third Corps troops at 5:00 a.m. Major General David B. Birney, Third Corps, relieved Geary at 7:00 a.m. It has been estimated there were 18,000 Union troops between the Emmitsburg Road and the Taneytown Road and between Little Round Top and the George Weikert farm at the time Johnston claimed to have been on Little Round Top. It seems highly improbable that Johnston could have made this scouting without discovery. Further, Captain Lemuel B. Norton, the chief signal officer of the Army of the Potomac, reported that a signal station was established on Little Round Top by 11:00 p.m. July 1 and remained there until July 6. Thus, Johnston could not have been there and reported the hilltop empty. https://scienceviews.com/parks/johnston.html.

3. It has been long thought that Johnston might have been on Big Round Top. *http://npshistory.com/series/symposia/gettysburg_seminars/11/essay4.pdf.*

Pfanz, Coddington, and Tucker have suggested that he might have been at Little Round Top but mixed up either the time or some other key factor. Wittenberg hypothesized that he may have been on Bushman Hill, which is located southwest of Big Round Top. https://militaryimages.atavist.com/fallout-from-the.

Answer #IX-10

Longstreet's attack was supposed to go north, up the Emmitsburg Turnpike. But the occupation of the Peach Orchard, located on the turnpike, required the direction of the attack to be altered. Consequently, Longstreet's attack direction was east, across the turnpike, on the left flank. But Lee had intended an attack on the Union center, not its left flank. McPherson summarized, "Sickles's unwise move may have unwittingly foiled Lee's hopes."

Sickles's unauthorized move was based on his similar experience at Chancellorsville, where Hooker had ordered him off high ground at Hazel Grove. That hill was then occupied by Stuart's troops on day two and used as an artillery base to defeat the Union army. He was not going to be ordered off such a position again. His assessment of the situation was that the ground he was ordered to occupy, between Little Round Top and Cemetery Ridge, was lower than that at the Peach Orchard. Modern observation shows he was correct, that there is a 12-foot drop. Normally, the high ground is preferable but only when it fits in with the total positioning with other corps of the army, so it was a tactical mistake. He created a salient that was susceptible to enfilading fire. The creation of a salient diluted the concentrated defensive posture of his corps by stretching it too thin, and it created a target that could be bombarded and attacked from multiple sides. He didn't have enough infantry to cover his ground, leaving large gaps in his position. And he disregarded a direct order by his commanding general. This controversy continues, just as Sickles would have wished.

FURTHER READING

- Frassanito, William A. *Gettysburg: A Journey in Time*. Scribner, 1975.
- Petruzzi, J. David. *The Complete Gettysburg Guide*. Savas Beatie, 2009.
- Reardon, Carol, and Tom Vossler. *A Field Guide to Gettysburg, Second Edition: Experiencing the Battlefield through Its History, Places, and People*. University of North Carolina Press, 2017.
- Sears, Stephen W. *Gettysburg*. Houghton Mifflin, 2004.
- Shaara, Michael. *The Killer Angels: The Classic Novel of the Civil War* (Civil War Trilogy). Modern Library, 2004.

Answers #IX-11

(1) Colonel Patrick O'Rorke

His action on July 2 probably saved Little Round Top. His gallantry is among the most influential of the entire Civil War, and many respected military historians have commented that O'Rorke's heroism and selflessness at such critical time in the battle is unsurpassed.

On July 2, 1863, the 140th New York arrived by forced march at Gettysburg on the battle's second day. As part of the Third Brigade, the regiment was immediately ordered to the Wheatfield, with the 140th the last regiment in line. Brigadier General Gouverneur Warren recognized that Little Round Top dominated the Union position and had been left undefended. Warren knew O'Rorke from West Point, having been his mathematics instructor. Warren rode up to O'Rorke and ordered him to reinforce Little Round Top; "Never mind [your brigade orders], Paddy. Bring them up on the double-quick and don't stop for aligning. I'll take the responsibility."

O'Rorke did not hesitate. Warren's aide was Washington Roebling, who would later build the Brooklyn Bridge. He guided O'Rorke and his men to the correct position on the hill. Reaching the top, O'Rorke saw the line of 16th Michigan holding tentatively. O'Rorke drew his sword, shouting, "Down this way, boys!" The 140th "follow[ed] their Colonel [and were] met with a devastating volley ... O'Rorke grabbed the regimental flag and turned to urge his men forward ... [A] bullet ripped through his neck. Patrick O'Rorke was dead before he hit the ground." The monument to the 140th New York has his name and likeness on the front.

(2) The chief engineer of the Army of the Potomac, Brigadier General Gouverneur K. Warren, was considered the "Savior of Little Round Top" for his quick reaction to get troops to the summit before the approaching Confederates arrived on the afternoon of July 2. His statue on what is now known as Warren Rock immortalizes the moment that he saw the long line of rebel soldiers approaching from the south.

FURTHER READING

- https://aoh.com/2019/03/25/patrick-ororke-a-forgotten-hero-of-gettysburg/
- https://killedatgettysburg.org/patrick-ororke-140th-new-york/

Answers #IX-12

#IX-12a

1. He received a promotion to brigadier general by General Meade before he died. Little Round Top could not have been held without his leadership.

2. One of Vincent's regiments, the 20th Maine, led by Colonel Joshua Lawrence Chamberlain, received great fame for the defense of Little Round Top. Vincent made clear to Chamberlain the importance of his position on the brigade's left flank while he attended to the

brigade's right flank. In fact, Chamberlain was the very end of the line; if he failed, the entire Union position might fall.

#IX-12b

1. When he expressed his desire to serve, the administration at Bowdoin prevented him from doing so. Undoubtedly experienced in recalcitrance dealing with college students, he did not let this stop him. In 1862, he asked for and received permission for a sabbatical to travel to Europe to study languages. Instead, he immediately volunteered.

2. The strategic significance of this position was such that the entire Union line was at jeopardy if he did not hold it. The 15th Regiment Alabama Infantry, commanded by Colonel William C. Oates, charged up the hill multiple times attempting to flank the Union position. The line of the 20th Maine was doubled back upon itself, with a squad well off to the left. Having sustained multiple casualties and with ammunition running low, Chamberlain recognized the dire circumstance and ordered his left wing to initiate a bayonet charge. The resulting action, with the left wing wheeling to make the charging line swing like a hinge, created a simultaneous frontal assault and flanking maneuver. One hundred one of the Confederate soldiers were captured, and the charge saved the flank. Chamberlain sustained one slight wound in the battle when a shot hit his sword scabbard and bruised his thigh. After initiating the maneuver, a Confederate officer wielding a revolver fired, narrowly missing his face. Chamberlain put his saber at the officer's throat and accepted the man's surrender. He received the Medal of Honor for this action.

3. Chamberlain was wounded six times during the war. The most severe was at Petersburg, where he was shot through the right hip and groin, the bullet exiting his left hip. Two surgeons performed surgery to extract the bullet and repair his damaged bladder and urinary tract, an operation that was unusual at that time. It is believed that the wound caused him to be incontinent and perhaps impotent for the remainder of his life. He required multiple surgeries over the ensuing years. He died of urosepsis as a consequence of a bladder infection in 1914. He might have been the final soldier to die of his Civil War wounds.

Further Reading

- Schmidt, Jim. "The Medical Department: A Thorn in the Lion of the Union." *Civil War News*, October 2000.
- https://www.civilwarmed.org/chamberlain/

Answer #IX-13

William J. Colville, Jr.

His wife was a direct descendent of William Brewster (of the Pilgrims). His regiment was the First Minnesota, an iconic regiment that suffered perhaps the greatest losses of any at Gettysburg. Seeing a Confederate brigade advancing up the southern section of the Cemetery Ridge and with no defensive line, Hancock ordered them to a suicidal bayonet charge to save the position. Colville ordered the charge without hesitating and, despite very heavy losses, bought enough time for more troops to be brought up, saving Cemetery Ridge. It's a great story, and he was a true American hero.

Further Reading

- Moe, Richard. *The Last Full Measure: The Life and Death of the First Minnesota Volunteers.* HarperCollins, 1994.

Answer #IX-14

Major General Henry Slocum thought he was in command of the right wing, 11th and 12th Corps, and Williams was only the temporary corps commander of the 12th. Slocum held the Union right from Culp's Hill to across the Baltimore Pike. His successful defense of Culp's Hill was crucial to the Union victory at Gettysburg. Williams convinced Meade to leave a brigade on Culp's Hill instead of moving them. This saved the position that evening when the Confederate left wing attacked. Williams led two days of hard fighting on the Union extreme right but received no official credit. Since Slocum was late turning in his report, Meade already submitted his report to the War Department.

The allegations that Slocum failed to come to assist General Howard's 11th Corps on day one are now understood to be wrong. Slocum dispatched the First Division of his corps to Gettysburg immediately upon hearing the first report of the fighting. Contrary to older interpretations, Slocum's actions in fact showed initiative, as he was never ordered to make these arrangements and acted despite an order (known as the Pipe Creek Circular) issued by General Meade that morning, received by Slocum at 1:30 p.m., to "halt your command where this order reaches you." In fact, Slocum arrived at the battlefield marching from Two Taverns on the Baltimore Pike, about five miles southeast of the battlefield, late in the afternoon on July 1. As the ranking general on the field, Slocum commanded the Union army for about six hours until Meade arrived after midnight. However, Howard and Hancock had made the correct arrangements in the interim.

FURTHER READING
- Harman, Troy D. "In Defense of Henry Slocum on July 1." http://npshistory.com/series/symposia/gettysburg_seminars/9/essay3.pdf
- Himmer, Robert. "New Light on Maj. Gen. Henry W. Slocum's Conduct on the First Day at Gettysburg." *Gettysburg Magazine* 43 (July 2010).

Answer #IX-15

Private Wilson J. Barbee from the First Texas Infantry.

Here is a brief summary of his actions during the storming of the Devil's Den during the late afternoon of July 2, 1863, as narrated in his recommendation:

> Although detailed as a courier to the division commander, Pvt. Barbee joined his regiment near Devil's Den during the hottest part of the engagement. Eager for action, Pvt. Barbee climbed a high prominent rock and with wounded compatriots passing him loaded muskets, opened fire on the enemy. Although dangerously exposed to a storm of enemy fire by his defiant, erect stance on the rock, Pvt. Barbee continued to discharge his weapons until knocked from his position by a bullet to the right leg. Despite his wound, he promptly reclimbed the rock and continued to fire at the enemy. Moments later, a bullet to his left leg tumbled him from his perch, but again he climbed to the top of the rock and fought on. After having fired more than two dozen rounds, a third, serious wound to the body knocked Pvt. Barbee into a crevice where, despite his cries for aid so that he might continue the fight, he lay trapped on his back until freed at battle's end. His reckless example of brazen valor solidified the battle line during the height of the fighting and remained an inspiration to his fellow soldiers during the engagement.

Private Barbee was later killed in action at Knoxville in 1864.

Answer #IX-16

The object is a hatchet.

While en route to Gettysburg, Brown violated a "no straggling" order. He intentionally disobeyed a security detail guarding a well to refill the canteens of several soldiers in his company who were succumbing to the effects of the summer heat. Brown was placed under arrest; his sword and pistol were taken away.

Once he arrived at Gettysburg on July 2, Brown was determined to take part in the fight. He was finally allowed to leave confinement and rejoin his regiment. His men were far away at the front making the attack across Emmitsburg Road. Brown had no weapons, so he picked up a camp hatchet and ran to the front line, rushed into the fray, and singled out a rebel officer 50 yards away. He then penetrated the rebel ranks and collared the officer, seizing from him his sword and pistol. Then he dropped the hatchet, while his men cheered him amid the bullets and smoke.

Brown suffered head trauma from the concussion of an artillery shell that exploded near him as he rendered aid to a member of the regiment. Despite hearing loss and dizziness, Brown refused to leave the field, telling the regimental surgeon that he would continue to fight unless the entire regiment was ordered to retreat. He took part in the repulse of Pickett's Charge the next day as part of the Stannard flank movement. Brown continued to wear the captured sword and pistol until the end of his service. The charges against him for violating the "no straggling" order were not pursued.

Brown reenlisted as a member of the 17th Vermont Infantry. Promoted to captain, he was commander of the regiment's Company A. Brown was wounded at the Battle of the Wilderness, when a bullet struck his left shoulder. His left arm was amputated, and Brown was discharged in August 1864. After the war, Brown went to law school and became a successful lawyer and real estate investor in Chicago. He was very active in veteran reunions.

When the design for the 13th Vermont monument was first drawn, it was the desire of the committee to have the statue represent Captain Brown, hatchet in hand. Accordingly, a model was produced, but the federal government would not permit its erection because of concern that it appeared to be a Native American attack. A modification was approved showing Captain Brown holding a saber and belt in his hand and the hatchet lying at his feet as though he had just dropped it. The saber depicted in the statue reproduces the details of the one captured.

Further Reading

- https://gettysburg.stonesentinels.com/union-monuments/massachusetts/9th-massachusetts-battery/
- http://npshistory.com/series/symposia/gettysburg_seminars/5/essay4.htm

Answers #IX-17

1. Pickett's Charge was the only rational decision Lee could have made under the circumstances. He was there for a decisive battle and as he famously said, "the enemy is there and I am going to strike them there." He had tried the left and right flanks, he could not retreat when the course of the war depended on a decisive victory, and he could not advance farther on the right flank because he had minimal supplies, a fragile supply line, and he had to protect his escape route.

Inexperience at the command level also took its toll. Lee took 28 brigades into Chancellorsville. Nine of those brigades lost their commanders, and of those, three brigades lost multiple commanders. Lee had also lost 64 of 130 regimental commanders and of course the most important corps commander. As a result of those losses, many of Lee's brigades went into battle at Gettysburg with inexperienced unit commanders.

2. Lee wouldn't have planned an attack on the Angle because a breakthrough there doesn't change the military situation. As General Lee stated in his official report, "the general plan was unchanged." The commanding position on the battlefield was Cemetery Hill, the Union center. That's why a coordinated attack at Culp's Hill was so important. This combined with a simultaneous pincer move on Culp's Hill by General Edward "Allegheny" Johnson's division from Richard S. Ewell's Second Corps was the plan.

This is a highly controversial subject, but modern scholarship favors Ziegler's Grove, in front of Cemetery Hill, as the likely focus. It was much more strategically significant than the open area where the Copse of Trees was, and it would command Baltimore Turnpike, the direct route to Washington, D.C. Taking this hill would force Meade to withdraw; it was the key to the fishhook. The idea that the copse was the focus was Batchelder's misleading attempt to bring attention to the area on the field where the attack went.

3. So once you realize the copse wasn't the focus, then you have to ask why the attack went awry. The artillery fire that devastated the charge also forced a shift to the center of the Union line, where the copse was, due to cross fire from the flanks; in addition, the Eighth Ohio flanked the left of the Confederates, further pushing them to the center. Also, the fences on both sides of the turnpike remained present on the north end, which prevented any of those divisions from getting through. Most of the men from Pettigrew and Trimble who did not retreat were caught on the road. Pickett's men faced a road in which

Enlargement of photograph by Mathew Brady taken 10 days after the battle from Little Round Top. The Copse of Trees is on the left and Ziegler's Grove is on the right. This is the only known photograph of this area before 1876. Note that the copse is inconspicuous by comparison (enlargement and annotation by Greg Ainsworth, used with permission).

the fences had been removed on July 2. Their mission was moving left under artillery fire and ended up at the Angle when they reached the convergence of the flank cross fires. The fences on both sides of the turnpike remained present on the north end, which prevented those divisions from getting through. Most of the men from Pettigrew and Trimble who did not retreat were caught on the road. Clusters of the 11th Mississippi made it to the wall as did elements of Fry's brigade.

The modern argument favoring the copse is this: With Pettigrew's division, only the left-hand brigades of Davis and Brockenbrough would have included the grove in their forward advance. Brockenbrough's brigade broke long before it ever made it there. Marshall's and Fry's brigades on the right-hand side of the division led to the north end of the Angle. Trimble's two brigades (Lane and Gordon) aligned themselves behind the center of Pettigrew's line and not its northern (left) flank opposite the grove. Pickett, as ranking officer, and his three brigades were posted very far south; to unite with Pettigrew's command, a series of leftward shifts (based on Garnett's brigade) had to be accomplished during the advance.

FURTHER READING

- Harman, Troy D. *Lee's Real Plan*. Stackpole Books, 2003.
- Hess, Earl J. *Pickett's Charge—The Last Attack at Gettysburg*. University of North Carolina Press, 2001.
- Reardon, Carol. *Pickett's Charge in History and Memory*. University of North Carolina Press, 2003.

Answer #IX-18

Malvern Hill: 30,000. Battle victory but the attack itself not successful.
Second Bull Run: 25,000–30,000. Successful.
Gettysburg: 13,000. Not successful.
Chickamauga: 10,000–12,500. Successful.
Wilderness: 16,000, via an unfinished railroad cut. Successful.

The truth of Longstreet's defensive views was that the four successful actions were an offensive action as part of a defensive position, which is a more exact formulation of Longstreet's philosophy. Labeling Longstreet a "defensive commander" is a terrible simplification about his thoughts regarding offensive operations.

The other factor is that Longstreet appreciated the high attrition rates the Army of Northern Virginia was experiencing and that its tactical battle victories were not sustainable.

Answer #IX-19

Mathematical modeling based on the Lanchester equations developed during World War I to determine the numbers necessary for successful assaults demonstrates that, with the commitment of one to three more infantry brigades to the nine brigades in the initial force, Pickett's Charge would probably have taken the Union position and altered the battle's outcome. However, the Confederates would likely have been unable to exploit such a success without the commitment of still more troops.

Lee ordered nine infantry brigades to make the charge on July 3. Five more brigades were held in reserve, which Longstreet never ordered to advance. If he had put most of those reserves into the charge, the model estimated it would have captured the Union position. However, assuming the same rate of casualties, there would have been insufficient fresh troops left to take advantage of that success or to defend against the inevitable counterattack. And what about the next hill and the next one?

The authors do not include Wilcox's and Lang's brigades in the initial force. If these troops and Anderson's entire division had attacked with the initial force, this would have supplied five additional brigades and around 5,000 more men, making the attack force 14 brigades and from 15,000 to 18,000 men. These numbers would have guaranteed a lodgment at the Angle. Rollins has identified another five brigades and one regiment scheduled for the second wave of Pickett's Charge from Pender's and Rodes's divisions, as well as at least another brigade from McLaws's division, all of which would have brought the attack column still nearer the 30,000 Longstreet thought necessary. Thus, Longstreet's guess that "thirty thousand men was the minimum of force necessary for the work" was pretty much on target.

Applying mathematical equations derived from World War I to the Civil War isn't as complicated as it might seem. Differing rates of firing and distances of armament efficiency merely require tweaking a few constants in the formula.

Further Reading

- Armstrong, Michael J., and Steven E. Soderbergh. "Refighting Pickett's Charge: Mathematical Modeling of the Civil War Battlefield." *Social Science Quarterly* 96, no. 4 (May 14, 2015): 1153–1168.
- Rollins, Richard. "The Second Wave of Pickett's Charge." *Gettysburg Magazine* 18 (July 1998): 104–110.
- https://theconversation.com/picketts-charge-what-modern-mathematics-teaches-us-about-civil-war-battle-78982

Answers #IX-20

1. The Confederate artillery was purposefully aimed to explode above the heads of the Union line to inflict more casualties. Because of

Section IX. Gettysburg 213

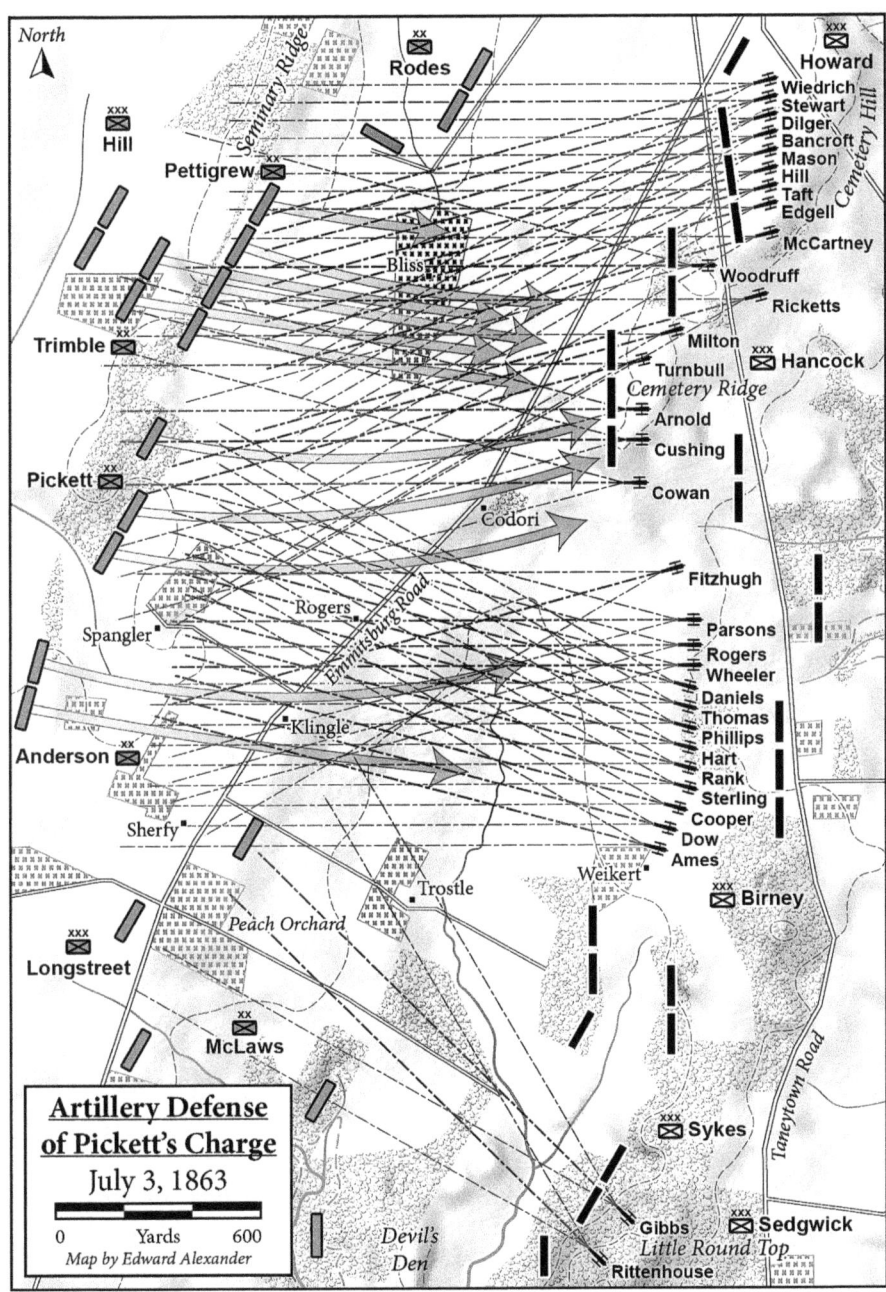

Map showing placement of the Union artillery by General Hunt and the cross fire created by the lines of fire. These enfilading lines of fire may explain why the apex of the Confederate attack ended up at the Angle.

inferior shell fuses that delayed detonation by one or two seconds, the ordnance instead overshot, exploding behind the line. The crews were used to "cutting" their fuses to a certain length to explode overhead. The Bormann fuse was a slower burning fuse, so the expected time of detonation was 1 to 1.5 seconds longer.

The Brown's Island disaster in Richmond on March 13, 1863, resulted in an interruption of the supply of fuses. Fuses from the Augusta Powder Works, called Bormann fuses, were used instead. The fuse lengths had to be cut individually. They contained a resin filler that would soften and mix with the powder in humid warm weather such as that in the first days of July. The filler mixing with the powder was the cause for the longer burning fuses and non-detonating shells. The different burn rates were not accounted for, and this resulted in overshooting. *https://richmond.com/news/local/browns-island-munitions-explosion-was-worst-wartime-disaster-in-richmond/article_9683aac6-847f-11e2-b033-0019bb30f31a.html.*

A combination of additional factors were also involved including crude sights, smoke obscuration of the target area, lack of range finders, and that the large guns had to be manhandled back into battery after each shot. Taken together with the elevated trajectory and the relatively narrow ridgeline, these factors caused the systematic misses.

2. General Hunt ordered his artillery to cease fire slowly to create the illusion that they were being destroyed one by one. When all of Hunt's cannons ceased fire and still blinded by the smoke from battle, Alexander fell for Hunt's deception and believed that many of the Union batteries had been destroyed and unable to respond effectively to Pickett's charge.

Answer #IX-21

Alonzo Cushing.

On July 3, 1863, during Pickett's Charge at the Battle of Gettysburg, a hole opened in the Union line. Rebel troops charged through the gap at the Angle. Union lieutenant of artillery Alonzo Cushing stood directly in their way. But he would lose his life in the struggle. His artillery battery was positioned on Cemetery Ridge just north of the Copse of Trees. He was wounded first in the shoulder but continued commanding his battery. Then he was grievously wounded in the abdomen, exposing his intestines. Despite severe pain, he continued leading and refused to leave the field. Finally, he was mortally wounded. He received the Medal of Honor from President Barack Obama after a decades-long campaign by a woman who had researched him in Wisconsin.

Answer #IX-22

Alfred Rudolph Waud.

He was highly acclaimed in his time. He was responsible for making *Harper's Weekly* a famous publication for decades.

Answer #IX-23

The Battle of Falling Waters, also called the Battle of Williamsport, was fought as part of the Gettysburg Campaign. It was an inconclusive battle. Meade didn't attack because General John Imboden had constructed an outstanding defensive position next to the Potomac River at Falling Waters. An attack would have resulted in huge Union losses.

On July 6, Brigadier General Judson Kilpatrick's cavalry drove two Confederate cavalry brigades through Hagerstown before being forced to retire by the arrival of the rest of Stuart's command. By July 7, Brigadier General John D. Imboden stopped Buford's cavalry from occupying Williamsport. On July 14, Kilpatrick attacked the rearguard division of Major General Henry Heth, taking more than 500 prisoners. Confederate Brigadier General J. Johnston Pettigrew was mortally wounded in the fight. Lee and the ANV were able to escape over the Potomac River into Virginia.

Further Reading

- Brown, Kent Masterson. *Retreat from Gettysburg: Lee, Logistics, and the Pennsylvania Campaign.* University of North Carolina Press, 2005.
- Wittenberg, Eric J., J. David Petruzzi, and Michael F. Nugent. *One Continuous Fight: The Retreat from Gettysburg and the Pursuit of Lee's Army of Northern Virginia, July 4–14, 1863.* New York: Savas Beatie, 2008.

Answer #IX-24

Over the first 12 days, 3,903 Confederate and 3,155 Union soldiers were buried. Except in a few individual cases, the Confederate army didn't bury the dead when it controlled the field, being concerned with winning the battle. After the Confederate retreat, the level of decomposition of the bodies was substantial, as they had been exposed to the elements and foraging animals. Most of the burials were in trenches, many quite shallow. It has also been estimated that there were several thousand dead horses.

FURTHER READING

- https://gettysburgcompiler.org/2012/08/02/burying-the-dead-by-allie-ward-54463

Section X

1864 Battles and Campaigns

Challenges

1. East

The Overland Campaign

Challenge #X-1

The Battle of the Wilderness took place in an area of Virginia that was (and remains) almost impossible to see through; the forest was composed of multiple trees and secondary growths, and the dirt roads were awful. These conditions made command and control and large troop movement almost impossible to coordinate.

In crossing the Rapidan River, Grant knew Lee was waiting for his invasion. To maintain flexibility, the Army of Northern Virginia was dispersed widely west of the wilderness so he could cover both the Shenandoah and the area toward Fredericksburg. Lee expected Grant to use the Germanna and Ely Fords, and that is exactly what Grant did. Lee was prepared for the movement, and it did not help that some Union units moved slowly, creating gaps.

After two days of heavy fighting and despite huge casualties, Grant decided neither to attack again nor to retreat but rather to proceed as quickly as possible to Spotsylvania Court House, putting himself between Richmond and Lee's army.

Challenges: (1) Because of the lack of maneuverability, the crossroads of the two main roads became the center of the Union line. What was this intersection? (2) On the second day, had this Union general moved rapidly

The Wilderness in afternoon (photograph by Lloyd W. Klein).

when ordered (or even at all), A.P. Hill's corps might have been destroyed. But once again, he was too slow to recognize the potential. (3) On the second day, a Confederate general appeared just in the nick of time and attacked Hancock's corps. But just as the attack seems as if it needs just one more push, he is wounded severely by his own men. Who? (4) Later in the day, another Confederate commander is given permission finally to attack on the other side of the line. Had he been given permission earlier, as he insisted, the Union army might have been trapped. Which general led this attack, and which generals delayed it? (5) Who won the battle?

Challenge #X-2

The Battle of Spotsylvania Courthouse was the second major battle in the Overland Campaign. Following the inconclusive Battle of the Wilderness, Grant's army disengaged and moved to the southeast, moving by its left flank, in order to lure Lee into battle under more favorable conditions. However, due to delay in the Union movement and the building of a road by the Confederates, Lee reached the critical crossroads of Spotsylvania Court House minutes before Grant. The Confederate army began

Section X. 1864 Battles and Campaigns

Grant meeting with his staff during the Overland Campaign. He is seen smoking a cigar between the two trees. May 21, 1864, by Timothy O'Sullivan, from a window on the balcony of Massaponax Church (Library of Congress).

entrenching, a strategy that began in earnest in this battle and continued well into the 20th century. Fighting occurred from May 8 through May 21, 1864, as Grant tried various lines of attack to break the Confederate line. The fighting at Spotsylvania was perhaps the most brutal of the war, with hand-to-hand combat of vicious severity on both sides, especially at the Mule Shoe.

Challenges: (1) What was the Mule Shoe? (2) Who devised a method to attack it and why did so many die trying to carry it? (3) What was the strategic result of this battle? (4) Estimate the ratio of dead and total casualties on the Union and Confederate sides. (5) Explain why this is surprising but shouldn't be.

Challenge #X-3

If you wanted to find the moment in 1864 when General Lee had a real opportunity to defeat Grant, the Battle of North Anna would be that instant. Having left Spotsylvania, Grant once again turned left (south and east) hoping to catch Lee unentrenched but once again lost the race, this time to a position south of the North Anna River. Attacks by A.P. Hill on Warrens's Fifth Corps and on Hancock's Second Corps on a bridge did not result in a conclusive result. Lee created an unusual-shaped earthworks to defend, which split the Union into two wings and a center, which could not reinforce each other because of the location of the river. After a repulsed attack, an opportunity presented itself which would never come again.

Challenges: (1) What was the shape of the entrenched line and why was it such a clever position for an army outnumbered 2:1 (100,000 to 53,000)? (2) Why didn't Lee attack at the critical moment?

Challenge #X-4

Philip Sheridan was only 5 feet 5 inches tall (Little Phil), but he was sure one tough dude. When Ulysses S. Grant was promoted to general-in-chief of the Union armies, he promoted Sheridan to commander of the Army of the Potomac's cavalry corps. Sheridan took command on April 5, 1864, less than a month before the start of the Overland Campaign.

At first, Sheridan's corps was used for reconnaissance. He fought with mixed success in Grant's 1864 Overland Campaign, failing in his reconnaissance role. He and General Meade engaged in a running feud. Sheridan suggested he could take on Stuart's cavalry. His men were sent on a strategic raiding mission toward Richmond in May 1864, defeating the Confederate cavalry at Yellow Tavern.

The Shenandoah Valley was vital for its food and supplies to the Confederacy and was also an important transportation route. Grant sent Sheridan to the Shenandoah Valley to destroy its warehouses and supplies. In September 1864, Sheridan defeated Jubal Early at Third Winchester and at Fisher's Hill. The Union army burned all of the buildings and farms; over 400 square miles of the valley was rendered uninhabitable and prevented supplies from reaching Lee's army.

In October, Jubal Early caught Sheridan off guard. Early launched a surprise attack at Cedar Creek on October 19. Sheridan was 10 miles away in Winchester. Hearing the sound of artillery, Sheridan quickly rejoined his forces and arrived in time to rally his troops. Sheridan received many honors for these victories. The personal meaning to him was summed up in changing the name of his horse.

Challenges: (1) Who suggested to Meade that Sheridan be given the chance to take on Stuart directly? (2) What was the name of Sheridan's horse (both before and after the name change)?

Challenge #X-5

The Battle of Yellow Tavern resulted in the mortal wounding of J.E.B. Stuart. On May 9, Sheridan began the raid, and Stuart followed with the advantage of the interior lines. Splitting his command, Sheridan held off Stuart's pursuit while striking the Virginia Central Railroad at Beaver Dam Station. After damaging the railroad, Sheridan continued southward toward Richmond. Dividing his men to have several units to follow Sheridan's trail, Stuart led most of his command on a forced march to get between Sheridan and Richmond. On May 11, Stuart encountered Sheridan at Yellow Tavern. The outnumbered Confederate cavalry was routed, and Stuart himself mortally wounded. Too weak to attack the defenses of Richmond, Sheridan reached Federal lines at Haxall's Landing on May 14.

Overall, the casualty rates were low, as in most cavalry fights, and few of Sheridan's strategic objectives were met. Meanwhile, Sheridan was not present at Spotsylvania where he might have been decisive.

Challenges: (1) How many Union cavalry did it take to finally kill Stuart? (2) Who killed General Stuart? (3) Who took over command of the Confederate cavalry and with what success?

Challenge #X-6

Grant's biggest mistake of the war, as he acknowledged in his autobiography, was June 3 at Cold Harbor. Several thousand Union soldiers were killed or wounded in a hopeless frontal assault against fortified positions. He wrote, "I have always regretted that the last assault at Cold Harbor was ever made.... At Cold Harbor no advantage whatever was gained to compensate for the heavy loss we sustained." There are various estimates of the losses of the battle but generally, approximately 7,000 total Union casualties versus 1,500 Confederates, although Gordon Rhea's estimate is somewhat less.

Although this was one of the most lopsided battles of the war, Grant's losses were still less than Lee's daily losses at Antietam and Chancellorsville and is comparable to Pickett's Charge and Malvern Hill. Nevertheless, its emotional impact was substantial then and remains the centerpiece of our "memory" of Grant as a general. The battle led to marked antiwar sentiment in the North; Lincoln was concerned he would lose the election. Grant became known as the "butcher" for his poor decisions and apparent disregard for his men. The unnecessary casualties also lowered the morale of his remaining troops.

Still, the result was favorable to Grant. Lee had lost the initiative and was forced to defend Richmond and Petersburg. He beat Grant to Petersburg, barely, but spent the remainder of the war behind a fortified trench line. Southerners realized their situation was desperate, but they hoped that Lee's defense causing a stalemate would lead to Lincoln's defeat in the election.

Bad as June 3 was, the attacks on June 1 and 2 that preceded it were also failures. Numerous faults have been alleged, which Grant never did acknowledge.

Challenges: (1) Name at least five factors that the Union army leadership failed to consider at Cold Harbor. (2) Why did Grant consider only the last charge a mistake and not the other costly charges as well?

Challenge #X-7a,b

#X-7a

The many postwar years of downplaying General Grant's strategic military genius has led to miscomprehension of his skills. Grant's operation to extricate his Union army from Cold Harbor in mid–June 1864 displays Grant's genius. Grant transformed a position that Lee thought boxed Grant up into the strategy that won the war.

General Grant was just two miles from where McClellan was after Malvern Hill. Lee's army was in his front. Every move so far had been south and east. But Lee was already at the next crossroads, waiting. In almost the precise position two years before, McClellan retreated and ended the Peninsula Campaign.

After Cold Harbor, Grant realized that Lee's defensive position was too strong to defeat by further attacks. Therefore, he knew he had to maneuver again. As the map shows, he is east and a bit north of Richmond, the Chickahominy River is south of him, and Lee has already sent his men to cover all approaches to Richmond.

Challenges: (1) What was the strategic value to Grant of going so far south, far beyond Richmond? (2) To accomplish this plan, Grant had to cross not one but two rivers (the James and the Chickahominy Rivers) and do it faster than Lee can catch up. There were terrible roads in this area and no bridges. The James River is about 4/10ths of a mile wide, which is a formidable obstacle to moving a 100,000-man army with an enemy in one's front. What military and engineering strategy was employed to cross this river? How quickly was it done?

#X-7b

Suggesting Grant was no better than a butcher conveys a deep flaw in understanding. Grant was a shrewd military leader, and he respected General

Section X. 1864 Battles and Campaigns

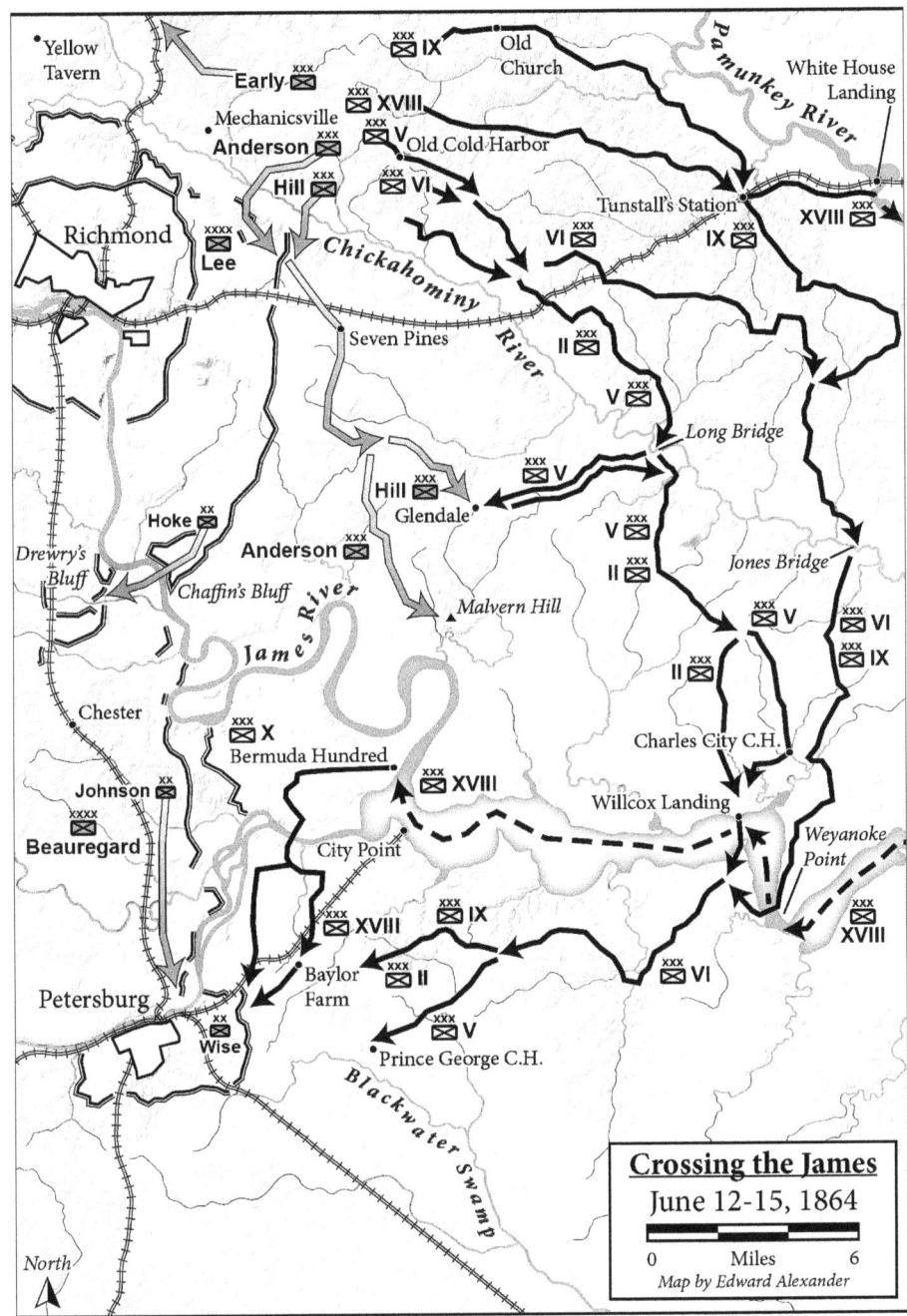

Grant's Crossing of the James. Note the troop locations are similar to the Peninsula Campaign two years previously.

Lee greatly. He realized that in crossing the James River, he was making a huge gamble that his outstanding rival would not suspect what he was doing.

Grant, of course, was a master of deception, as he showed at Vicksburg. And he did it again at this moment.

Challenge: What deceptions did Grant employ and how successful were they?

Challenge #X-8

The Battle of the Crater occurred during the siege of Petersburg. A mine was exploded beneath the Confederate works, achieving a complete surprise. Despite weeks of preparation and strategy, Union soldiers incorrectly charged into the crater, where they were sitting ducks for Confederate counterfire.

The idea was originated by Lieutenant Colonel Henry Pleasants, commanding the 48th Pennsylvania Infantry. He was a mining engineer before the war, and many of his men had been miners. They dug a mine shaft under the Confederate lines, then planted explosive charges directly underneath. With the subsequent surprise and confusion, perhaps an advance could be made to break the lines and enter Richmond.

Challenges: (1) Who was the leader of the Union assault? (2) Who was the leader of the Confederate response? (3) What went wrong?

Challenge #X-9

Robert Gould Shaw was born into a prominent abolitionist family in Boston. He served as a private with the Seventh New York Militia before becoming an officer in the Second Massachusetts Infantry. He saw action at Winchester, Cedar Mountain, and Antietam.

Shaw is most famous as the white commander of the 54th Massachusetts, the first all–African American regiment in the Northeast. Colonel Shaw was killed leading the 54th against the Confederate Fort Wagner near Charleston, South Carolina. Colonel Shaw was killed in the assault, as were many of his troops.

Only one regiment at a time could attack because the beachfront was just 60 yards wide. The 54th Massachusetts was the first regiment in line to make the assault. The 54th attacked the west side while the white regiments followed, attacking the center and east. Despite casualties from cannon and musket fire, the 54th continued to march onto the parapet and fought in hand-to-hand combat. Union forces were pushed back by a counterattack, and within two hours the battle was over with 1,500 Union casualties scattered across the field. The Confederates suffered only 174 casualties.

Within the Union casualties was one brigadier general and three colonels leading their regiments, including Colonel Shaw. Lewis Douglass, the son of Frederick Douglass, was also killed. The 54th Massachusetts suffered 40 percent casualties, but their sacrifice would be honored throughout the Union and would greatly improve the image of African Americans being brave capable soldiers.

Challenge: Where is Colonel Shaw buried?

THE 1864 VALLEY CAMPAIGN

Challenge #X-10a,b

#X-10a

In late 1864 as General Lee was entrenched at Petersburg and Richmond, a force of the Confederate army approached Washington, D.C. Only a smaller force of inexperienced 100-day men of Union infantry led by a disgraced general was in the path. He chose to defend making a stand by a river despite being outnumbered 16,000 to 4,500. A cavalry attack did not dislodge the Union despite outflanking them. Then the Confederate infantry engaged in a double envelopment which led to the Union army retreating across a stone bridge after having survived five attacks by the best division commander in the Confederate army at the time. Finally, after 24 hours, the Union army fell back. The disgraced general, despite making a heroic stand, was blamed for yet another mistake.

Although a small battle, its impact was huge. As a consequence of the Union defeat, the Union commander was briefly demoted until it was recognized that despite overwhelming odds, he had bought critical time that saved Washington, D.C.

Challenges: (1) Name the battle and the heroic but disgraced general. (2) Name three reasons why this battle was a strategic victory for the Union. (3) Name the Confederate division commander.

#X-10b

The Confederate army in the valley was weakened after threatening Washington, D.C. The Union commander was convinced it couldn't sustain further attack. He was convinced by trickery that Longstreet was about to join forces, and so he needed to attack. A brilliant Confederate major general found a vulnerability in the Union line from a Signal Corps position and planned a surprise attack. The bold attack against superior forces found the Union commander in a different town. The attack succeeded brilliantly, and the Union army was defeated. The Confederates unwisely began to plunder, and the Confederate commander halted the attack. The Union commander galloped to the field and rallied his forces, leading a counterattack that retook the field and resulted in a crushing defeat.

Challenge: Name the battle, the brilliant Confederate general, and the Union commander who galvanized his troops from defeat to victory.

3. WEST

THE ATLANTA CAMPAIGN

Challenge #X-11

With the fall of Chattanooga, Sherman was prepared to march to Atlanta. Sherman had 110,000 men in three armies around Chattanooga. General Joseph E. Johnston had 53,800 troops initially at Dalton, 80 miles north of Atlanta. He also received 15,000 reinforcements within the month. Although the 69,000-man army was the South's largest, it was still markedly outnumbered. Consequently, Johnston's defense was to take strong defensive positions and wait for the enemy to attack him.

From May 1 to June 22, there were five battles and skirmishes more days than not. Those battles under Johnston were Dalton, Resaca, Adairburg, New Hope Church/Pickett's Mill, and Kennesaw Mountain.

Challenges: (1) How did Sherman respond to Johnston's strategy? (2) Davis came to disrespect Johnston for not fighting a battle. Johnston planned a large battle at Resaca, but it never came off. Why not? (3) Sherman did attack Johnston at Kennesaw Mountain, which held, but Johnston nevertheless retreated again. Why? (4) It is intriguing that Johnston became friends with Grant and Sherman, who both praised him in their memoirs, and was remembered well by Longstreet. What did these men say about Johnston after the war? (5) How did Johnston die?

Challenge #X-12

The Battle of Atlanta undoubtedly was the last chance the Confederate army had to stop Sherman in the west. The fall of Atlanta not only

Section X. 1864 Battles and Campaigns

General William T. Sherman on horseback at Federal Fort No. 7, Atlanta, Georgia (Library of Congress).

ended any plausible chance of Confederate military victory but also ensured Lincoln's reelection. Atlanta was a critical industrial center and railroad hub, and although not the sophisticated, large population center it is today, everyone recognized its military importance to the future of the war. Few buffs make the connection that the battle, which occurred on July 22, 1864, was separated from the actual fall of the city, on September 2. That finality required a siege and battles over supply lines and railroads.

After the battles at Resaca, Marietta, and Kennesaw Mountain, General Johnston was relieved of command because of his perceived lack of aggressiveness. John Bell Hood took his place just as the Battle of Peachtree Creek was forming. Hood attacked Sherman at that battle on July 20 despite being outnumbered, with 2,500 casualties to his army. The Peachtree battlefield is now an area called Colonial Homes and includes the grounds of the current Piedmont Hospital, centered on Collier Avenue, but then was merely a river crossing. Buckhead, where the Union army was located, is now a beautiful and stylish area of shops and restaurants.

Two days later, the Union army was now on the east side of town. Hood thought there was a weakness on the Union left flank. However, Hardee was delayed in his deployment, and James B. McPherson recognized the threat and moved his reserve in place. The Confederate attack was repulsed, but the Union line began to retreat. A Union and a Confederate general were killed at this time.

With the lines of both armies shaped as an *L*, a severe hand-to-hand battle raged at a hill east of the city. General Logan was the hero of this battle. At the end of the day, the Union held the hill, but the Confederates held the city.

Challenges: (1) Which generals were killed in this battle? (2) What was the name of the hill that was the focus of the fight? (3) What was the ratio of Union to Confederate casualties?

Challenge #X-13

One of the most interesting Confederate generals was John Bell Hood, an outstanding and brave brigade and division commander who became an unsuccessful army commander, in part because of a lack of resources and manpower in the last year of the war but also in part because of his over-aggressiveness and lack of planning in many battles despite being outnumbered.

A clear example was a battle during the Atlanta Campaign. Hood planned to intercept the Union army and catch them completely by surprise on the west side of the city, expecting that Sherman would maneuver from the north of the city (Peachtree). The Union strategy was to surround Hood by capturing the railroad to Macon. Although outnumbered in terms of the total armies, Hood calculated that a surprise attack against an isolated portion of the enemy could succeed.

Unfortunately for Hood, there was no surprise at all. In fact, the tables were turned: the Union army had already reached the road and had dug in! Union troops were waiting in their trenches when Hood reached them. The Confederate army had not performed a sufficient reconnaissance prior to the attack. Further, they underestimated the number of Union troops present and made an uncoordinated attack. The Union army had improvised a breastwork of logs and rails to support its defense.

The rebels were defeated, although they did manage to stop the line from reaching the railroad temporarily. The casualties for this mistake: 3,000 on the Confederate side and 642 on the Union side.

Section X. 1864 Battles and Campaigns

Challenge: Name the battle; the outstanding corps commander who led the attack; and the reason why the surprise was on the Confederates, not the Union army.

Challenge #X-14

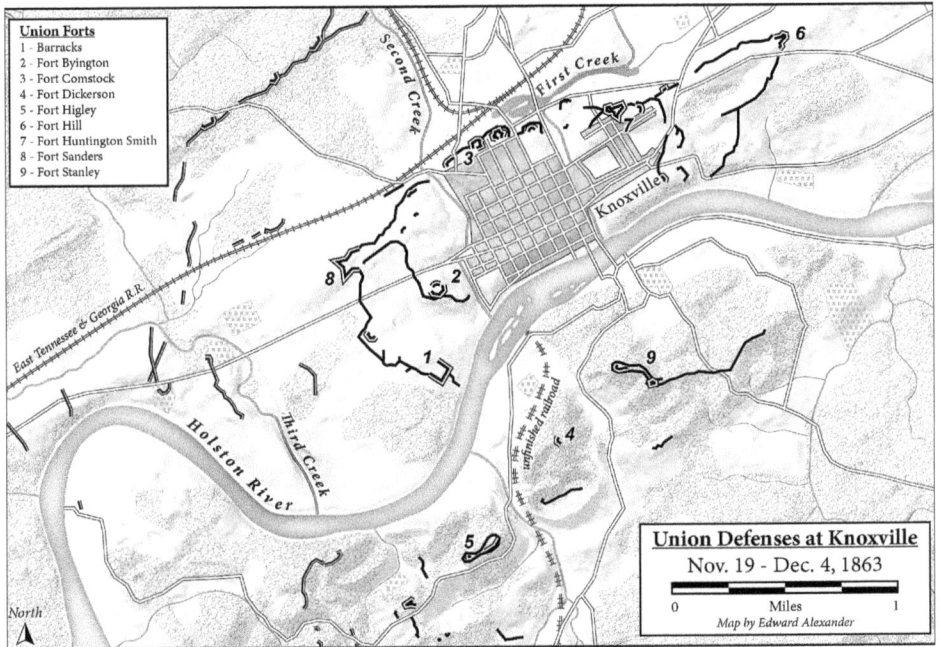

Defenses at Knoxville, November–December 1863. The various forts are interconnected, making the position almost unassailable.

General Longstreet wanted a chance at independent command, which he thought he had earned. When he didn't get it, he was depressed again, particularly after Bragg refused to press Rosecrans after Chickamauga. He was given the assignment to take Knoxville in an independent command, but this assignment really was intended to get him away from Bragg and closer to returning to General Lee in the spring.

The strategic intent of the Knoxville Campaign was to prevent Burnside's reinforcement of the besieged Federal forces at Chattanooga. Longstreet's movement forced Burnside back into the defensive works in Knoxville. Longstreet then began a siege, but it wasn't very effective. After the first week, Longstreet learned of Bragg's defeat at Chattanooga. Longstreet realized that time was not on his side, so he ordered an assault a few days later, but it failed miserably.

Longstreet's siege ended when Major General William Tecumseh Sherman led the Army of Tennessee to Knoxville, entered the city, and relieved Burnside. Longstreet withdrew his men and later rejoined General Robert E. Lee's command in Virginia.

Challenges: (1) Why was it impossible for Longstreet to succeed at Knoxville? (2) What was the result of the campaign?

Challenge #X-15

Major General William Tecumseh Sherman led the March to the Sea in the late fall of 1864. The march began with Sherman's troops leaving the captured city of Atlanta on November 15 and ended with the capture of the port of Savannah on December 21. The myth that has followed suggests an uncivilized band of out-of-control soldiers on the rampage. This is an outrageous falsehood. In fact, General Sherman planned this march to every detail to match his military strategy.

His forces followed a policy of destroying military targets as well as industry, infrastructure, and civilian property, disrupting the Confederacy's economy and transportation networks. The entire idea was to inflict "total war" and operate deep in enemy territory without a supply line.

His orders were specifically to control, not destroy, infrastructure in areas where there was no resistance but a scorched earth policy where the local population fought. He understood that foraging would destroy the morale of the civilian population, and that was an intentional objective of his movement. Foragers were specifically identified to seize food—crops and livestock—from local farms. Horses, mules, and wagons, which might have military value, could be freely "appropriated."

Challenges: (1) What was the name given to the foragers? (2) What were the precedents for an army moving without a supply line? (3) How did Sherman know that where his march was going would be able to sustain an army of its size? (4) What was the point?

Challenge #X-16

Sherman's march of about 300 miles through Georgia was accomplished in just 36 days, of which there were 25 days of actual marching.

It is often incorrectly stated that this phenomenal achievement was the result of having no enemy to oppose the movement, but in fact, several excellent cavalry units opposed him and there were skirmishes. General Hardee was also in his front, albeit with a small force. Still, it was

Section X. 1864 Battles and Campaigns

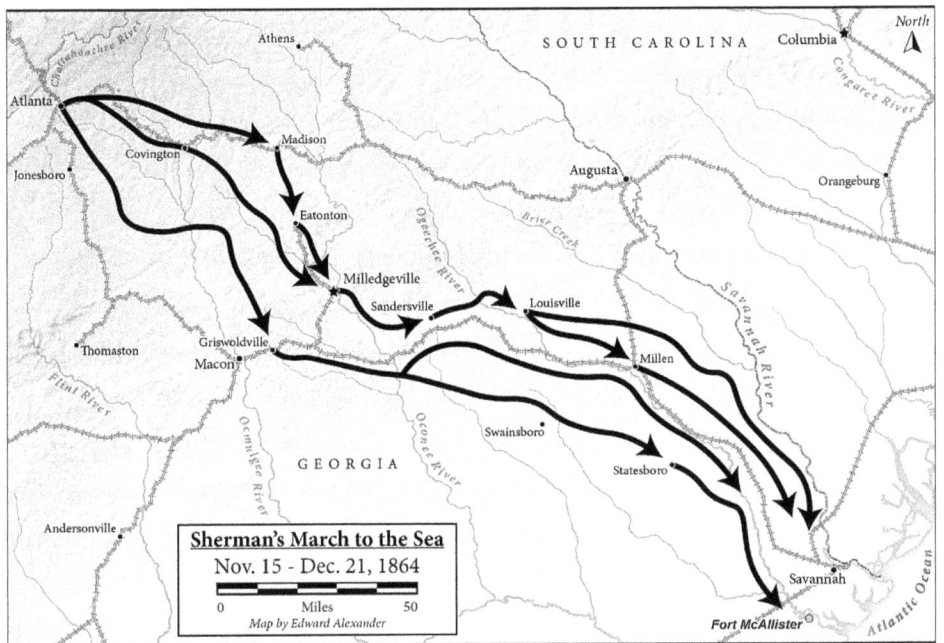

Sherman's March to the Sea. Note the three columns of advance.

necessary to camouflage exactly where he was heading and how he was planning to get there.

The method he used was to divide his army into two "wings," and the army followed four separate but parallel routes 20–60 miles apart. The right wing, or the southern column, was composed of the Army of Tennessee, which marched along the Macon and Western Railroad. The left wing, or the northern column, was composed of the Army of Georgia, which marched following the Georgia Railroad.

Challenges: (1) Under what generals did Sherman organize his army? (2) Why did the left wing take a more southerly route to get to Savannah? (3) Why did Sherman select Savannah as his destination? (4) What cavalry units opposed his movement, and how were they kept from causing significant delays?

Challenge #X-17

Nathan Bedford Forrest was an outstanding cavalry leader and probably the most controversial personality of the entire war. Today's challenge focuses on his incredible victory at Brice's Cross Roads.

The biggest threat to General Sherman's advance toward Atlanta in

1864 did not come from General Joseph Johnston's army but from the cavalry that threatened his supply lines. These were vulnerable, going back to Chattanooga. One of the most effective of those cavalry forces was the one led by Nathan Bedford Forrest. After the massacre at Fort Pillow, Sherman became concerned that his lines back to Chattanooga might be threatened and thus ordered pursuit.

At Brice's, Union general Samuel Sturgis, outnumbering Forrest 8,500 to 3,500, attacked Forrest at a crossroads. Federal cavalry led by Grierson confronted Confederate cavalry. Sturgis then made a strategically unsound move.

Challenges: (1) What was Sturgis's order? Why was it a huge mistake? (2) Everyone knows the story that Forrest ordered a double envelopment despite never having had any formal military training. What was it that Forrest saw that led him to that strategy? (3) What happened one month later in Tupelo?

Challenge #X-18

Today, Franklin, Tennessee, is a beautiful small town and suburb of Nashville. Alas, it was the scene of a huge Confederate disaster that plainly signified final defeat. The Confederate commander John Bell Hood has often been described as ordering this attack to teach his men discipline; although probably inaccurate, no doubt it was ill advised. However, it may be true that General Hood ordered the futile attacks in anger toward his subordinates. He ordered the forced march and attack at Franklin that morning after verbally blaming them for letting General Schofield slip through. Hood's inability to defeat Sherman and prevent him from taking Atlanta that summer certainly weighed on him heavily as well.

Schofield had been trapped by Hood but then marched the entire night before the battle to escape. They came close to annihilation at Columbia and Spring Hill. In retrospect, it's often not appreciated how close Hood came to destroying Schofield's corps.

Hood's battle strategy was simply a series of frontal attacks. Six infantry divisions (18 brigades with 100 regiments numbering) repeatedly charged the entrenched Union army. The battle resulted in devastating losses to the Army of Tennessee, which at that stage of the war were unreplaceable. Despite an equal number of men on both sides, about 27,000, the South had 6,200 casualties (1,750 killed) versus 2,300 Union casualties (just 189 killed). Even more devastating, 12 Confederate generals and 55 regimental commanders were casualties: five generals were killed on the battlefield, one died of his wounds, one was captured, and six were wounded.

Section X. 1864 Battles and Campaigns

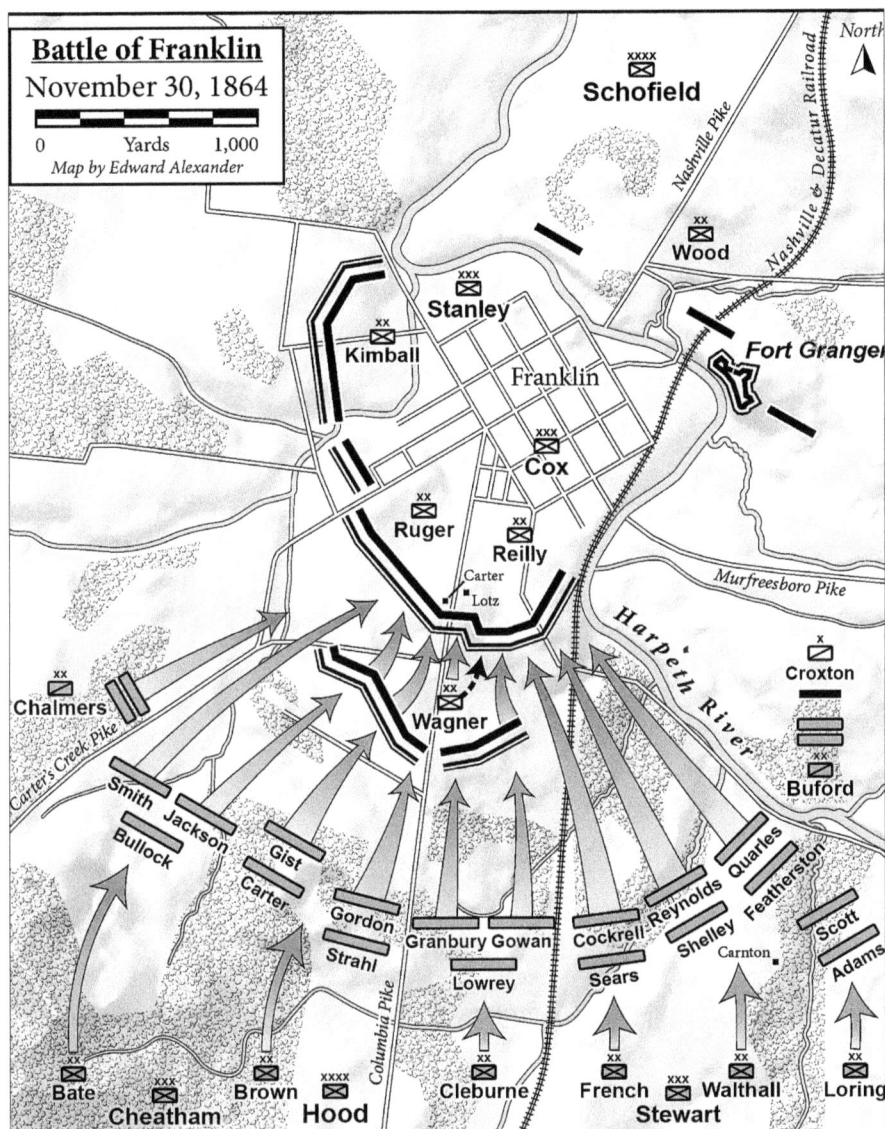

Battle of Franklin. Note the attack required a convergence of the Confederate line due to the rivers on either side of the front. This made the invasion force an easy target to defend against.

Much of the fighting took place on the Carter family grounds; one of the Confederate soldiers was a member of that family and had grown up there. Tod Carter died in the battle close to his family home.

After being defeated by General Thomas at the subsequent Battle of

Nashville, Hood's Army of Tennessee retreated with half the men with which it had begun.

Challenges: (1) At least three generals told Hood that the Union defense was formidable. Who? (2) See the map. What critical geographic reality made this attack doomed to failure? (3) There was also a discrepancy in terms of armaments. Describe. (4) Which mansion became the Confederate hospital after the battle? (5) Name at least five Confederate generals killed during the battle.

Answers

Answers #X-1

1. The intersection of Orange Plank Road and Brock Road.
2. Burnside didn't attack when it could have changed the game.
3. Longstreet was wounded in the shoulder. He had ridden into an area of contention and had been warned not to proceed. He advised Lee to continue the attack, but Lee delayed.
4. John B. Gordon insisted that a flank attack would have wrapped up the Union right flank. Early and Ewell delayed because of incorrect intelligence that the Union Ninth Corps was reinforcing the zone and did not want to attack with an outnumbered force.
5. This question is essentially unanswerable. Neither side left the battlefield in retreat. Both armies had a very high rate of casualties: Union 15.0 percent with 17,666 (2,246 killed) of 118,00 engaged; Confederate 16.7 percent with 11,033 (1,477 killed) of 66,140 engaged. Tactically, it was probably a draw. Strategically, Grant was able to advance, but Lee had prevented him from reaching Richmond. Indecisive is probably the best descriptor.

Further Reading

- https://www.battlefields.org/learn/civil-war/battles/wilderness
- Rhea, Gordon C. *The Battle of the Wilderness, May 5–6, 1864.* Louisiana State University Press, 2004.

Answers #X-2

1. A salient on the right side of the Confederate line. The Mule Shoe was a weak point in Lee's Spotsylvania defenses that stuck out beyond the rest of the trenches like a bulge. The western edge of the Mule Shoe became known as the "Bloody Angle." The attack on May 12 involved almost 24 hours of desperate hand-to-hand fighting, some of the most intense of the Civil War. This attack was repeated on the 13th with several corps against a better prepared (yet still somewhat surprised) Army of Northern Virginia. It breached the lines again and took thousands of rebel prisoners, but reinforcements were able to come up and prevent further

progress. It turned the battle into a bloody stalemate, and the fighting did not stop for almost 24 hours. Fighting was at extremely close quarters. This fight turned Spotsylvania into a stalemate.

 2. Colonel Emory Upton became renowned for leading infantry in attacking entrenched positions successfully at the Battle of Spotsylvania Court House. He developed a new tactic to attack the Confederate entrenchments, an innovation that foreshadowed the trench warfare of World War I. The standard infantry assault method at the time employed a wide battle line advancing slowly, firing at the enemy as it moved forward. Rather than attack in rows or lines, Upton prepared columns of massed infantry. The idea was to overwhelm the defenders in a concentrated sector with large numbers of troops advancing rapidly and without stopping to load and fire. Called the "stacking method of attack," the attackers would not fire a shot. Upton had his men storm a weak point in the enemy's position and use hand-to-hand (bayonet and rifle butt) tactics rather than taking the time to fire.

On May 10, 1864, Upton led 12 regiments in this assault against the Confederate's Mule Shoe salient. His men attacked in lines of columns with rifles unloaded, bayonets fixed, and marching at the double quick. Initially, the attack penetrated the center of the Mule Shoe, but holding it led to severe fighting. The attack would have been completely successful had the supporting regiments also attacked to carry the salient. However, Upton was forced to withdraw due to enemy artillery and increasing reinforcements.

Upton was wounded in the attack. He was promoted to brigadier general to rank from May 12. On that same day, Major General Winfield S. Hancock modified Upton's columnar assault concept to the entire Second Corps, which succeeded in breaking through the Mule Shoe defense.

 3. The battle was tactically inconclusive despite two weeks of brutal fighting. Both sides declared victory. The Confederacy thought they had won because they were able to hold their defenses. The Union thought it was their victory because their offensive continued and Lee's army suffered losses that could not be replaced.

 4. Union: 100,000–110,000 total

Casualties and losses: Total: 18,399 (2,725 killed, 13,416 wounded, 2,258 captured or missing)

Confederates: 50,000–63,000 total

Casualties and losses: Total: 12,687 (1,515 killed, 5,414 wounded, 5,758 captured or missing)

 5. By percentages, the battle appears to be a draw, although by absolute numbers, clearly the Union paid dearly. The early phases of the

Section X. 1864 Battles and Campaigns

battle went poorly for the Union. Laurel Hill was a disaster, and the May 9 attacks were delayed and not well supported. The Mule Shoe attacks did the most damage to the Confederates and many were lost as prisoners. With the prisoner exchange suspended, those men would never rejoin the fight.

Further Reading

- Ambrose, Stephen E. *Upton and the Army.* Louisiana State University Press, 1993.
- Rhea, Gordon C. *The Battles for Spotsylvania Court House and the Road to Yellow Tavern May 7–12, 1864.* Louisiana State University Press, 1997.

Answers #X-3

1. Lee took an inverted-V-shaped line in which the left flank, defended by A.P. Hill, had its flanks covered by a river, the front was on the North Anna, and the right flank was similarly covered by rivers. Once the Union army crossed the North Anna, there is no way for the

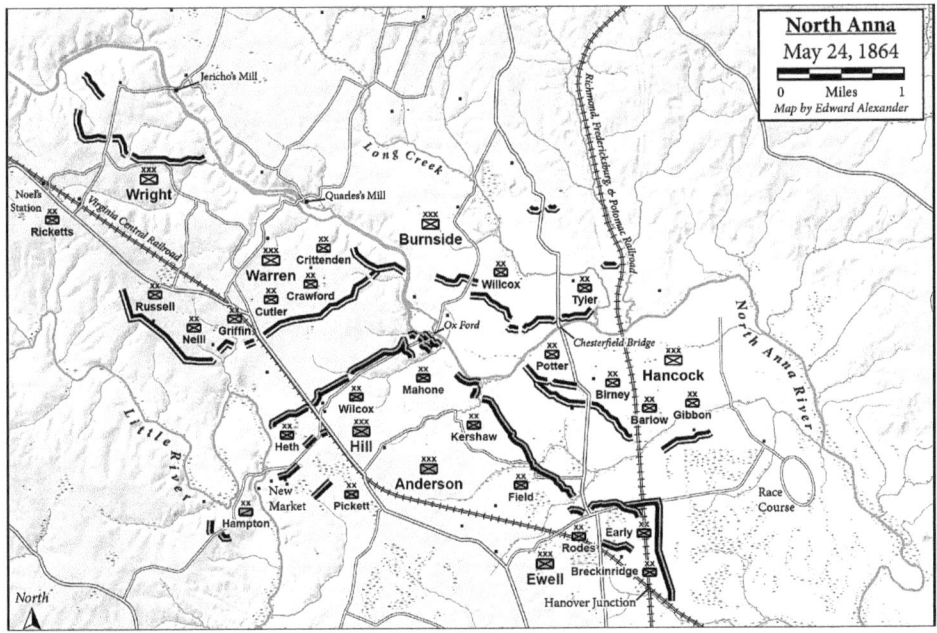

Battle of North Anna. The inverted V-shape of the Confederate defense allowed a smaller force to defend against a much larger enemy.

flanks to cover the other without recrossing it. The Union army was consequently divided into three parts. The fight to control the Ox Ford bridge was therefore a critical aspect of this battle. Other smaller fights composed the overall battle. For this reason and as shown on the map, exactly how many Union troops took part depends on proximity to the various skirmishes. The number of Union troops actually involved may actually have been only 67,000, while Lee's strength was 53,000.

2. Lee could have launched an attack against one of these three isolated positions. However, Lee was too ill with dysentery to lead an attack and take advantage. With Longstreet wounded, he had no one to coordinate an attack. Hill was sick again, Stuart had been killed, Ewell was exhausted, and Anderson was inexperienced.

In *Lee's Lieutenants*, Freeman wrote of Lee's "intestinal ailment that had the usual effect of sharpening his temper and shaking his control of it." He dramatized a scene in which Lee rebuked his Third Corps commander, A.P. Hill: "Why did you not do as Jackson would have done—thrown your whole force upon those people and driven them back?"

Modern historians disagree that Lee's health affected the battle. The traditional story was based on the postwar remarks of Lieutenant Colonel Charles S. Venable, his aide-de-camp, but modern military strategists doubt any such attack would have succeeded. Some historians also dispute whether Lee was really going to attack because there is no other corroborating evidence. Grimsley concludes that Lee never planned to attack the Federal Second Corps, given how well they were dug in.

Further Reading

- Grimsley, Mark. *And Keep Moving On: The Virginia Campaign, May–June 1864*. Lincoln: University of Nebraska Press, 2002.
- Luebke, Peter. "North Anna, Battle of." February 12, 2021. https://encyclopediavirginia.org/entries/north-anna-battle-of/
- Rhea, Gordon C. *To the North Anna River: Grant and Lee, May 13–25, 1864*. Louisiana State University Press, 2000.

Answers #X-4

1. Grant told Meade that if Sheridan thought he could succeed, he was generally right.

2. His horse's original name was Rienzi, named after a town in Mississippi in which he was stationed.

After the Battle of Winchester, the general enjoyed Thomas Buchanan Read's poem "Sheridan's Ride"—and he renamed his horse "Winchester." Sheridan's horse was 16 hands high, much taller than Sheridan. The horse was stuffed and is displayed in the Smithsonian Institution.

Further Reading

- https://www.battlefields.org/learn/biographies/philip-sheridan
- https://www.smithsonianmag.com/history/union-colonel-phil-sheridans-valiant-horse-124899830/

Answers #X-5

1. The Union force of three divisions included 10,000 troopers, and 32 artillery pieces were arrayed against the Confederate force of two brigades, about 4,500 men.
2. Stuart was killed via a shot from a revolver at close range by a dismounted Union private in retreat named John A. Huff. Huff was killed a few weeks later.
3. Fitzhugh Lee temporarily, then Wade Hampton thereafter.

Further Reading

- Rhea, Gordon C. *The Battles for Spotsylvania Court House and the Road to Yellow Tavern May 7–12, 1864.* Louisiana State University Press, 1997.
- https://www.minecreek.info/federal-army-2/sheridans-raids-may-9-24-and-june-7-28-1864.html
- https://www.thoughtco.com/battle-of-yellow-tavern-2360264

Answers #X-6

1. Essentially all facets were flawed, including communications, reconnaissance, coordination, delays, and planning.

    a. Warren's division commanded by Lockwood got lost and couldn't participate in the June 1 charge.

    b. The army had made a long march to get to the battlefield, causing the planned morning attack of June 1 to be delayed to 6:30 p.m.

 c. A proper reconnaissance of the area was never performed, so there was no idea what the topography of the area they were attacking looked like.

 d. On June 2, a right flank attack was planned by Meade, but again, Hancock's men had marched all night, delaying the attack until June 3.

 e. There was no plan of coordination of the attack, nor was the Confederate position studied.

 f. The delays allowed Lee to fortify his position, which the Union army did not anticipate. The defense not only included barricades of earth and logs but also artillery posted with converging fields of fire.

2. Although the battle and its flawed attacks are often blamed on overconfidence that the Confederate army had weakened morale, I do not think this explains the mistakes. Grant and his army by this point in the war knew very well how to plan an attack and were professional killers. Foote describes that orders for corps commanders gave them the responsibility for reconnaissance but that merely convinced them that there was no overall plan.

Much more likely is that Grant was in a bind. His way to victory was to keep fighting and keep the calculus of war moving. Lee was fighting behind entrenchments, not out in the open. Grant's only way forward was to attack prepared positions, regardless of casualties. That's why he thought only the last attack was a mistake: because the others had to be done. The last attack was a mistake because by then, he knew, or should have known, that it wouldn't work. But at that point, he probably hadn't planned the next exceptionally complex move.

Grant at Cold Harbor made an error for very similar reasons that Lee ordered Pickett's Charge. They were staking everything on a battlefield victory, yet in the positions they were in, there was no good alternative tactics to move them closer to their goal. They did what was consistent with their goal: attack.

Further Reading

- Rhea, Gordon C. *Cold Harbor: Grant and Lee, May 26–June 3, 1864*. Louisiana State University Press, 2002.
- https://www.battlefields.org/learn/articles/they-called-grant-butcher-can-butcher-have-regrets
- https://emergingcivilwar.com/2020/06/03/cold-harbor-guest-post/

Section X. 1864 Battles and Campaigns

Answers #X-7

X-7a

1. Grant's plan was to seize Petersburg, the rail hub supplying Richmond. The strategic value to Grant of going so far south, far beyond Richmond, is to both extend Lee's defense lines and to threaten his supply lines. Since Lee has to protect Richmond with inferior numbers, his lines and Beauregard's must merge, forcing him to entrench. Without the railroads entering Petersburg, Richmond could not be supplied with food, clothes, or military matériel.

2. Union engineers worked rapidly to assemble a 2,170-foot pontoon bridge on June 14, 1864. The distance bridged is the longest to be covered by a temporary span in modern military history. Its rapid construction allowed Grant to rapidly shift operations south of the James River and threaten Petersburg from the east. At 4:00 p.m. on June 15, Union engineers began work on the pontoon bridge on the James between Windmill Point and Fort Powhatan; they completed it in just seven hours! Grant then crossed his army over the James during the next two days with Lee still unsure as to his intentions in one of the most daring and successful maneuvers of the war. In Grant's autobiography, he states that he fully recognized the immense risks of such a movement but believed it had to be done and thought that his proximity to Richmond would keep Lee in a position to protect it.

#X-7b

To divert Lee's attention, he sent Sheridan and most of his cavalry on a raid to the west, where they fought Hampton again at Trevilian Station. Despite outnumbering Hampton, Major General David Hunter fought a draw but incurred casualties of almost 2:1. Still, Hampton was screened from learning Grant's plan, so it was a strategic success.

Grant began the construction of an entrenchment line behind his Cold Harbor position to make Lee believe his plan was to dig in. Hancock's and Wright's corps withdrew to the new entrenchments. Warren's corps crossed the Chickahominy River and headed south. Burnside's corps followed with Hancock's and Wright's corps taking up the rear. Smith's corps marched to White House on the Pamunkey River and was shipped by the navy to Bermuda Hundred.

Further Reading

- https://www.beyondthecrater.com/news-and-notes/siege-of-

- petersburg-sesquicentennial/150-years-ago-today/150-18640614-crossing-james-river/
- https://almostchosenpeople.wordpress.com/2014/06/12/june-12-1864-grants-crossing-of-the-james-begins/
- Wittenberg, Eric J. *Glory Enough for All: Sheridan's Second Raid and the Battle of Trevilian Station*. University of Nebraska Press, 2007.

Answers #X-8

1. General Ambrose Burnside was the corps leader of the Union assault. He was relieved of command for the final time for this failure. Brigadier General Edward Ferrero's division of black soldiers sustained very high casualties, perhaps because the Confederates refused to accept them as prisoners when they tried to surrender. He and General James H. Ledlie were drinking rum throughout the battle in a bunker behind the lines. Ledlie was forced to resign by Meade and Grant.

2. General William Mahone was the Confederate general on the scene. He rallied troops to reinforce the stunned soldiers who were present. He became celebrated as a rising star at the end of the war.

3. A division of U.S. Colored Troops under Ferrero trained to lead the assault. The plan was for one brigade to go left of the crater and the other to the right. A regiment from both brigades was to rush perpendicular to the crater. Then the remaining force was to seize the Jerusalem Plank Road just 1,600 feet behind the line.

But the day before, Meade ordered Burnside not to use the black troops in the lead assault. Instead, Ledlie's division was chosen, but no one told them what to do once the explosion occurred. Meade did not let them charge because he thought if it failed, then it would receive political backlash in the North and only prove Lincoln's message as false. He was aligning military goals with political ones. The U.S. Colored Troops instead charged behind the lead troops.

Tactically, Union troops entered the crater instead of going around it. There, they were trapped in a hole with no support on the flanks. The Army of Northern Virginia began shooting surrendering troops, perhaps due to racial animus.

Union casualties were 3,798 (504 killed, 1,881 wounded, 1,413 missing or captured), many of them the black troops. Confederate casualties were 1,491 (361 killed, 727 wounded, 403 missing or captured). Burnside was dismissed and court of inquiry censored him, but Meade was just as much to blame. The Congressional Joint Committee on the Conduct of the

War later exonerated Burnside and blamed Meade for changing the plan of attack.

Answer #X-9

Confederate general Johnson Hagood refused to return Shaw's body to the Union army. To show contempt for the officer who led black troops, Hagood had Shaw's body buried in a common trench with his men. Shaw's father proclaimed, "We would not have his body removed from where it lies surrounded by his brave and devoted soldiers.... We can imagine no holier place than that in which he lies, among his brave and devoted followers, nor wish for him better company—what a bodyguard he has!"

Answers #X-10

X-10a

1. Battle of Monocacy; General Lew Wallace (later, the author of *Ben-Hur*)
2. The results were that the fight (a) stalled General Early for enough time to buy Washington a to prepare time enough to get reinforcements, (b) the delay cost Early the initiative that he could never really recover and (c) that not taking Washington influenced the course of the war and Lincoln's reelection.
3. General John B. Gordon

#X-10b

(1) Battle of Cedar Creek, (2) John B. Gordon, (3) Philip Sheridan. Gordon's memoirs give substantial detail about his role in this battle.

Answers #X-11

1. Sherman eschewed frontal attacks of the kind Grant was employing against Lee. In broad terms, Sherman used Thomas's Army of the Cumberland and Schofield's Army of the Ohio to demonstrate against the rebel lines, while he sent McPherson's Army of Tennessee to maneuver around Johnston's left flank and threaten the Western & Atlantic Railroad, which was the supply line.

In basically every case, Johnston set up defenses along the main road, then Sherman demonstrated frontally while flanking him. Johnston kept his army together to fight another day.

Several engagements were fought during this four-week period, called the Battle of Marietta, during which Sherman flanked Johnston and threatened his supply lines and, in one case, made a direct assault. Sherman forced Johnston to withdraw after a month of small battles and maneuvers. Later, the town that was protected by the entrenchments was burned. Today, Marietta is a suburb of Atlanta.

2. While the two armies traded short, sharp attacks at Resaca May 14–15, McPherson crossed the Oostanaula River, flanking the prepared defensive line and forcing Johnston to retreat again.

3. Sherman flanked Johnston again. Approaching the Chattahoochee River, Sherman feinted right and moved troops across upstream. Davis relieved Johnston of command soon after.

Sherman described him as a "dangerous and wily opponent." Johnston's strategy of falling back and stalling further Federal advances threatened to stall the Federal war effort. It worked far better than Hood's direct attacks. After Hood's reckless aggression, he was down to 30,000 versus 81,000.

4. Sherman and Johnston became good friends after the war, corresponding and often meeting for dinner in Washington.

Grant wrote about the Atlanta Campaign: "For my own part, I think that Johnston's tactics were right. Anything that could have prolonged the war a year beyond the time that it finally did close, would probably have exhausted the North to such an extent that they might then have abandoned the contest and agreed to a settlement."

Said James Longstreet to a reporter years after the war: "General Johnston was one of the ablest generals the war produced. He could handle a large army with ease. But his usefulness to the South was greatly impaired by the personal opposition of the President. He dared take no risks on account of this 'fire in the rear,' fearing that he would not be sustained, perhaps discredited before the world. A menace like that will paralyze the best efforts of any commander in the field. General Johnston never had a fair trial."

5. Johnston died of pneumonia 10 days after standing in the rain and serving as a pallbearer at Sherman's funeral. Despite concerns for his health at the funeral, he said, "If I were in his place, and he were standing here in mine, he would not put on his hat."

Answers #X-12

1. Major General James B. McPherson was the second highest ranking Union general killed in the war and had been a classmate of

General Hood. He was considered a man of huge potential. Confederate Major General William H.T. Walker was killed by a Union picket. A monument at the site of McPherson's death is today located at the end of Monument Avenue where it intersects McPherson Avenue, not far from Interstate-20, in a residential area. The monument to Walker is in ill repair on a corner of a street in front of a gas station. The preservation of these sites is woeful.

2. Bald Hill was the site of the main struggle on the center of the line. Today, Interstate-20 and Moreland Avenue intersect in the remaining wooded area of the battleground.

3. The Union had 3,600 casualties of 35,000 troops engaged versus the Confederates' 5,500 casualties of 40,000 engaged. The Confederate losses were staggering relative to their available manpower.

Answer #X-13

The battle occurred on July 28, 1864, near a chapel called Ezra Church. Lieutenant General Stephen D. Lee was the corps commander who led the Confederate attack. The Union commander was Oliver Otis Howard, who was a West Point classmate of Hood and used that familiarity to anticipate Hood's move.

Answer #X-14

Longstreet strongly objected to being given this assignment. Knoxville was a tall order for anyone with the forces he had. Burnside was well defended and well supplied. Remember that the railroad ran to Knoxville, which is why it was a target. Moreover, he was significantly outnumbered. Longstreet had 10,000 men in two infantry divisions (under Major General Lafayette McLaws and Brigadier General Micah Jenkins) and 5,000 cavalrymen under Major General Joseph Wheeler versus Burnside's 12,000 infantry and 8,500 cavalry in entrenched positions.

Furthermore, he knew that reinforcements were arriving for Grant's army, which would way outnumber the 40,000 Confederates around Chattanooga. Longstreet argued that by separating the Confederate forces, "we just expose both to failure, and really take no chance to ourselves of great results." The trains he took to get his troops to Knoxville were days late, and no supplies were sent to him.

At the Battle of Campbell Station, he attempted a double envelopment, but Burnside's defense held. Burnside's entrenchments were strong, and he had more men, on defense, than the attacking force.

On November 25, Bragg had been defeated at Chattanooga, and Longstreet was ordered to return to Lee. Longstreet told Bragg the order was a very bad idea, as then Burnside could unite with Grant and well outnumber Bragg as Longstreet returned to Virginia. Longstreet made a final attempt to take Knoxville on November 29 at Fort Sanders. There, he led a charge that resulted in high casualties due to a deep ditch.

(2) Sherman brought 25,000 men to Burnside and relieved the siege. There was minimal strategic impact of the campaign, but it did deprive Bragg of troops he needed, just as Longstreet had predicted. However, Longstreet's one trial in independent command was a failure, and his self-confidence was damaged. His emotional response to the failure of the campaign was not productive, as he himself admitted in his memoirs, Instead, he blamed others, just as he had done at the Battle of Seven Pines in the Peninsula Campaign the previous year. He relieved Lafayette McLaws from command and requested the courts-martial of Brigadier Generals Jerome B. Robertson and Evander M. Law. He submitted a letter of resignation to Adjutant General Samuel Cooper on December 30, 1863, but his request was denied.

Further Reading

- https://www.history.com/this-day-in-history/siege-of-knoxville-tennessee-begins

Answers #X-15

1. Bummers. Contrary to usual accounts, this was not a chaotic rabble, but in fact, there was clear military organization: each brigade assigned 50 enlisted men and 1 officer to a foraging team responsible for supplying food for all. Approximately 3,000 infantrymen were engaged in foraging on any day, or 5 percent of the army.

2. The most modern previous example was Winfield Scott's inland march to Mexico City during the Mexican War had no formal supply lines. In the Civil War, Grant's innovative and successful Vicksburg Campaign is usually cited as the first modern military campaign of living off the land with no viable supply line. However, Grant's operations landing south of Vicksburg did in fact have supply wagons after crossing the river, which continued to arrive after the Black River Bridge fight. But it was Sherman's Meridian Campaign,

which took place from February 3–March 6, 1864, from Vicksburg, Mississippi, to Meridian, Mississippi, that was the real proof that it could be done.

3. Sherman cautiously studied livestock and crop production data from the 1860 census to ensure that his troops marched through areas where forage would be available. He planned his march routes extremely carefully, and in fact, the campaign was one of the best planned in all of military history. It was scrutinized by everyone in the War Department in agonizing detail from Lincoln and Stanton on down.

4. The Civil War was the first industrialized war. This meant that large armies could be amassed and kept in the field almost indefinitely so long as the civilian economy could support them. To win, one side must attack the supporting civilian economy. That is what Sherman's March to the Sea Campaign was all about.

Further Reading

- Doctorow, E.L. *The March: A Novel.* Random House, 2005.
- Klein, L.W. "Sherman's March to the Sea." https://www.rebellionresearch.com/shermans-march-to-the-sea
- https://www.battlefields.org/learn/articles/shermans-march-sea
- https://www.georgiaencyclopedia.org/articles/history-archaeology/shermans-march-to-the-sea/
- https://www.history.com/topics/american-civil-war/shermans-march

Answers #X-16

1. General Henry Slocum was in command of the left wing, composed of the newly created Army of Georgia (14th and 20th Corps) and the Army of the Cumberland. General Oliver O. Howard commanded the right wing, consisting of the 15th and 17th Corps of the Army of Tennessee. Brigadier General Judson Kilpatrick commanded the cavalry. It is astonishing that three of the most disappointing, if not incompetent, eastern generals became so successful in the west (as did Hooker).

Sherman also detached two armies under Major General George H. Thomas to battle Hood in the Franklin-Nashville Campaign.

2. The idea was to suggest the possibility of moving to Augusta or Macon instead.

3. The Union navy controlled the coast, and thus the South would be entirely divided in half (or quarters, as Vicksburg had divided it previously).

4. Although Hardee's infantry put up minimal resistance, it was Joseph Wheeler's cavalry that did the best it could. However, the discipline was lax, and the behavior of his men often led to worse complaints by civilians than those lodged against Union men.

Answers #X-17

1. He ordered his infantry to attack the Confederate cavalry, despite their not being up in the line of battle and having to march on the double for five miles to get there.

2. Forrest improvised it on the fly. When the infantry took over for the cavalry, both flanks were uncovered, and the road crossed swampy ground. Forrest merely spent hours trying to get around both flanks which took about five hours.

3. After Brice's Cross Roads, Forrest was regarded as a potential mortal threat to Sherman's supply lines. A second Union expedition was soon sent out against him, defeating him just over one month later at Tupelo (July 14, 1864). Major General Andrew C. Smith accomplished his goal of stopping Forrest from raiding into Tennessee and became a member of the exclusive and minute club of Union commanders who defeated Forrest in battle.

Answers #X-18

1. Patrick Cleburne (killed in action); his commander, Frank Cheatham; and Nathan Bedford Forrest, who asked to lead infantry with which to flank the position.

2. Franklin sits in a curve of the Harpeth River. Trenches were constructed from bank to bank, making it essentially an unflankable position unless preparations were made to attack across the river, as Forrest suggested. The Confederates were gathered in a wide field, but the river on either side funneled the attack into a narrow front. The attack was made across open and clear terrain with no cover. It is unknown why Hood did not consider other strategies.

3. Some Union troops were armed with Spencer and Henry repeating rifles. Near the Carter House, located at the center of the Union position, 350 men of the 12th Kentucky and 65th Illinois fired

16-shot lever-action Henry rifles, the predecessors to the Winchester repeating rifle. These rifles were capable of at least 10 shots per minute, which gave these men several times more firepower than infantrymen with the more common muzzle-loading rifle muskets.

There was also a lack of artillery coverage for the Confederate attacks; Hood had earlier detached all of the artillery to move with Stephen Lee's corps so that Stewart and Cheatham could move as quickly as possible.

    4. The Carnton Plantation. Many of the dead remain buried there, and the floors still have the blood stains from severed limbs. Cleburne's body was laid out on the back porch.

    5. Pat Cleburne
Otho Strahl
John Adams
Hiram Grandbury
States Rights Gist
John Carter (wounded mortally, died on December 10)

Further Reading

- https://amp.en.google-info.in/423215/1/battle-of-franklin-1864.html
- Sword, Wiley. *The Confederacy's Last Hurrah: Spring Hill, Franklin, and Nashville.* Blue and Grey Publishers, 1995.

SECTION XI

Spies and Secret Organizations

Challenges

Challenge #XI-1

This woman was a prominent member of Richmond, Virginia, society. A 43-year-old quiet, genteel lady, she lived with her widowed mother in a three-story mansion on Church Hill. Her family was very prominent in the town and owned many slaves. She was proud of being from Richmond and lived a Southern lady's life. She showed no interest in the war or politics and was certain that Virginia would preserve the country.

Her behavior was noticeably odd. She wore dirty clothes and mumbled to herself on the street. She went to ladies' society gatherings but otherwise kept to herself and had no close friends. Her neighbors called her "Crazy Bet."

Challenge: What was her most singular accomplishment?

Challenge #XI-2

At the start of the war, a woman in Washington, D.C., received information that the Union army was planning to advance on Manassas in mid-July. She was a socialite in Washington, D.C., before the war, married a physician, and was friends with Dolley Madison. Her sister married Dolley's nephew, and their daughter married Stephen Douglas.

She moved in significant political circles and cultivated friendships with important political and military personalities, including John C. Calhoun and James Buchanan. She used these connections to gather key military information and communicated secret information to the

Confederacy at the start of the war. She was the leader of a pro-Southern spy network in Washington, D.C. The spy network had active members in several states and included 48 women and 2 men. Her source for the information was a very highly placed government official.

The network was started by Captain Thomas Jordan, who left D.C. to become a Confederate army captain. This lady is known to have sent at least eight ciphers to General P.G.T. Beauregard regarding the defenses around Washington, D.C. One was a message that the Union army would be advancing. A major reason that General Beauregard defeated Irvin McDowell at First Bull Run was that he had been "tipped off" as to where and when the Union was moving by this lady.

See Challenge #XI-1 answer for details (Virginia Museum of History & Culture).

She found a courier for the message. A Washington socialite from a wealthy family in Maryland tucked the coded message into her hair and traveled south dressed as a simple farm girl. Her mission was to make sure the message reached General Beauregard. One of Beauregard's officers wrote, "Upon my announcing that I would have it [the note] faithfully forwarded at once, she took out her tucking comb and let fall the longest and most beautiful roll of hair I have ever seen. She took then from the back of her head, where it had been safely tied, a small package, not larger than a silver dollar, sewed up in silk."

Challenges: (1) Who was this intrepid spy and what became of her? (2) Who was the spy's source of information? (3) Who was the lady who served as courier? (4) How accurate was the message? (5) How was the message recognized by Beauregard to be authentic? (6) How was she caught?

Challenge #XI-3

Belle Boyd was perhaps the most famous Confederate spy of all and in many ways prefigures Mata Hari. Known by various nicknames, "Cleopatra

Belle Boyd by Mathew Brady (Library of Congress).

of the Secession," "Siren of the Shenandoah," and "La Belle Rebelle," she was highly effective in her chosen craft.

Despite suggestions that she was a "lady of the night," in fact she was well educated, strongly motivated, highly intelligent, and from a prosperous family. Her father owned and operated a store in Martinsburg, Virginia. Both of her parents were from affluent and socially prominent Virginia families, and the Boyds possessed several slaves. At age 12, she entered Mount Washington Female College near Baltimore, where she pursued an academic curriculum with emphasis on languages and literature. Following her education, Boyd spent the winter of 1860–1861 as a Washington debutante in a season that was "preeminently brilliant," perhaps stimulated by the atmosphere of intense political crisis. There, she met eminent political and military figures, which she later turned to her advantage.

Most everyone knows that the information she gave Stonewall Jackson was a major benefit in the Shenandoah Campaign; in particular, she sent him accurate information about Union army troop movements and dispositions. Fewer know that that she was arrested eight times for espionage activities but jailed only twice. After the war, she was married three times, had a daughter, became an actress on the London stage, wrote a two-volume memoir, and went on a national lecture tour speaking about life as a spy. She was one tough lady!

Challenges: (1) How did Boyd first come to the attention of Union soldiers in her town? (2) As a consequence of this action, sentries were posted around her home. How did she use having enemy soldiers surrounding her to her own advantage? (3) Probably her most well-known exploit was to let Stonewall Jackson know about the Union army position at Front Royal in May 1862. How did she obtain this information?

Challenge #XI-4

A "scout" (meaning "spy") for J.E.B. Stuart and Robert E. Lee, this man was considered the "most dangerous man in the Confederacy." There was a $10,000 bounty on his head. Posing as a dental assistant in Alexandria, he gathered intelligence on multiple missions. After the war, he married his sweetheart whom he had repeatedly risked his life to court—Emma Green—who assisted him in his espionage, and he became an Episcopal minister. The rumors that he assisted in Lincoln's assassination are likely not true.

Challenge: Who was he?

Challenge #XI-5

A secret society was founded in 1854 by a con man named George Bickley. The objective was to create a new country where slavery would be legal. The country would have been centered on Havana and would have consisted of the Southern United States and territories in Mexico (which was to be divided into 25 new slave states), Central America, northern parts of South America, and Cuba, Haiti, Dominican Republic, and most other islands in the Caribbean, about 2,400 miles (3,900 km) in diameter.

Originally, the group advocated that the new territories should be annexed by the United States in order to vastly increase the number of slave states and thus the power of the slave-holding Southern upper classes. In response to the increased anti-slavery agitation that followed the Dred Scott decision (1857), the group changed their position: the Southern United States should secede, forming their own confederation, and then invade and annex the international areas to vastly expand the power of the South.

Challenges: (1) What was the name of this organization and why? (2) What activities did Bickley and his group participate in during the war? (3) What became of his society?

Challenge #XI-6

A Canadian woman, this hero ran away from home at age 15 to escape an unwanted marriage and assumed the identity of a man, which allowed her to live independently. As Thompson, she enlisted in 1861 in Company F of the Second Michigan Infantry. She participated as a male nurse in the battles of both Bull Runs, Antietam, the Peninsula Campaign, and Fredericksburg.

When a Union spy in Richmond, Virginia, was discovered and put before a firing squad, she took advantage of the open spot. She applied for the position under the name Franklin Thompson. She traveled into enemy territory undercover to gather information. One disguise obliged her to use silver nitrate to dye her skin black, wear a black wig, and enter Confederate territory posing as a black man by the name of Cuff. After a few days in the military camp, she learned that the Confederate army was building "Quaker guns," or cannons that looked real from a distance but were just wooden logs in reality. Then she escaped and returned to Union lines where she told her leadership about the deception. Another time, she entered enemy territory as an Irish woman named Bridget O'Shea, claiming she was a sutler selling apples and soap to the soldiers. Once, while posing as a black laundress working for the Confederates, a packet of official papers fell out of an officer's jacket. She returned to Union lines with the papers, and the generals used the information to plan an attack. In another mission, she worked as a detective in Kentucky named Charles Mayberry to uncover a Confederate agent. She took part in 11 spy missions during the war. At the end of the war, she worked as a female nurse, perhaps because "Franklin Thompson" was listed as a deserter.

Challenge: Fascinating story and completely true. *Or was it?* Who was she?

Challenge #XI-7

An unemployed actor, in large part due to small stature, with no military training, this man played an outsized role in the 1863 Confederate Pennsylvania Campaign.

Challenge: Who was he and what was his contribution?

Challenge #XI-8

Information gathering at the start of the war was amateurish, often wrong, and suggests the Keystone Cops. Allan Pinkerton had worked for Lincoln and was a friend of McClellan's, so even though he was a private citizen, he was hired to gather info for the Union as a "secret service." Meanwhile, Lincoln had also hired a detective, as did General Winfield Scott, and Colonel Charles Pomeroy Stone had hired several. All of these detectives were civilians attempting to make a profit rather than soldiers working for the country, so it became a competition and squabble ending in a lot of hilarious gaffes, such as the various detectives sometimes arrested each other!

Pinkerton was an immigrant from Scotland who settled in what is now a suburb of Chicago, Dundee, Illinois, He found a group of counterfeiters in a forest, leading to their arrest. This was his major success before he became sheriff of his county and then was hired as the first police detective in Chicago, which developed into the Pinkerton National Detective Agency. He solved a series of train robberies in the 1850s by hiring agents to act as passengers and spy on its workers.

Pinkerton was the head of the Union Intelligence Service in 1861–1862. He identified the assassination plot against Lincoln on the president-elect's way to take office in Washington, D.C. His main job was identifying the number of troops in the Army of Northern Virginia. We are all familiar with the inflated estimates of the army McClellan reported, but we do not know if Pinkerton was responsible. His men worked undercover as Confederate soldiers, and he himself went undercover using an alias.

The intelligence service he started was the predecessor of the U.S. Secret Service. His work led to the establishment of the Federal Bureau of Investigation many years later. At his death, he was working on a system to federalize all criminal identification records so that a crime committed in one state would be searchable in another, now a computerized database of the Federal Bureau of Investigation.

Challenges: (1) How did he come to know Lincoln and McClellan? (2) What was his undercover alias, what was his mission, and how did he fare?

Challenges #XI-9a–d

#XI-9a

After Antietam, Lincoln had grown tired of the intelligence antics and the inflated numbers of troops McClellan had claimed. Ultimately, he placed General Joseph Hooker in charge. His disaster at Chancellorsville aside, Hooker was actually a very good administrator whose leadership showed a high aptitude for organization. He improved sanitation, diets, and introduced a better furlough system. He doesn't get credit for it, but his efforts led to the start of the Bureau of Military Information (BMI). By federalizing an intelligence system, the military could better control the nature and quality of the collected information. The BMI consisted of nearly 70 spies, 10 of whom were killed while in service.

Hooker arranged the reporting so that his chief of staff, General Daniel Butterfield, was the middleman through whom the intelligence was filtered. That way, he could not influence what was being reported and would receive unaltered information.

But the real cleverness Hooker displayed is whom he chose to run it. This man had served as a lawyer and diplomat. He established working groups, interrogation policies and procedures, and interviewed and hired his own scouts. He determined the missions, rather than the cavalry. Once he had agents, the Signal Corps, cryptanalysts, and other varied sources working for him as well, the bureau became a full-fledged organized operation.

Like himself, his spies were well chosen. He chose a captain, John McEntee, to lead the rest of the spies. They were recruited from enlisted men and local citizens. One convinced the Confederates to give him a 120-mile tour of their front and rear lines by the order of Richmond authorities, and he maintained his ruse for 10 days.

Challenge: Who was this man whose contributions are underemphasized?

#XI-9b

General Lee had no separate intelligence organization, and his staff was composed of just four officers. He primarily used individual undercover agents to provide intelligence, usually assigned to one of his subordinate generals. Lee strongly depended on his cavalry scouts and never trusted in actual intelligence from other sources. This deficit was an advantage for Meade and Grant.

Two examples of where BMI provided critical information to his enemies that made a real difference were Gettysburg and the Overland Campaign.

Challenge: What crucial intelligence did the BMI bring to Meade at Gettysburg and Grant in the Overland Campaign that strongly influenced their decisions leading to Union victories?

#XI-9c

Today, Chancellorsville is recognized as General Lee's greatest battle victory and Hooker's greatest disaster as a general. You might question the value of his intelligence service when, after all, he lost the very battle he was preparing for.

Prior to the battle, the BMI prepared evaluations of the Confederate army's strength and activities based on sources that included infiltrations of the Confederacy's War and Navy Departments. Sharpe deployed scouts and enlisted civilians to report on the Army of Northern Virginia's activities from behind enemy lines. He and his assistants interrogated prisoners, deserters, and refugees and analyzed documents. Sharpe also obtained reports from cavalry reconnaissance, Balloon Corps observation, Signal Corps observation, and flag signal intercepts for his analysis.

Section XI. Spies and Secret Organizations

The BMI performed remarkably well in providing the Federal army commander the intelligence he needed to be successful during the Chancellorsville Campaign. Sharpe provided relevant information in the months leading up to the battle as well as during the battle. One of his crucial intelligence findings was that although the Union army had broken the Confederate semaphore code, theirs had also been broken. This allowed Hooker (and his chief of staff, Butterfield) to create a ruse that allowed General Stoneman to begin his raid.

Challenge: So, if the BMI was so smart, why didn't they tell Hooker that Stonewall Jackson was marching on his flank?

#XI-9d

Another one operatives in the spy circle noted in Challenge #XI-1 was a Southern gentleman named Samuel Ruth. As superintendent of the Richmond, Fredericksburg, and Potomac Railroad, Ruth was in an excellent position for a spy.

Challenge: What information was Ruth privy to, whom did he give the information to, and how else did he assist the Union cause?

Challenge #XI-10

Pauline Cushman was the stage name of Harriet Wood. Pauline was one of the most successful Union spies in the war. She was born in New Orleans to a Spanish merchant and a French lady. The family moved to Grand Rapids, Michigan, when she was young to run a Native American trading post. In 1862, she made her stage debut and then traveled to the Broadway stage.

While a successful actress, she went undercover as a rebel sympathizer but was well known to the Union side as a spy. She used her acting skills to dress as both a man and a woman in undercover work. She prevented the poisoning of soldiers in a boarding house posing as a Southern belle. Dressed as a man, Cushman convinced a Southern woman that "he" was an undercover Confederate official with important information. The woman, who was smuggling medical supplies and documents to the South, invited Cushman to join her. Instead, Cushman had the woman arrested and her contraband confiscated. Her biggest mission was posing as a distraught woman "searching for a lost brother"; she gained access to Confederate camps in Tennessee. Her mission was to determine the size of the Confederate forces, how well they were supplied, and whether they were entrenching. General Rosecrans used this information in planning the Tullahoma Campaign.

She was caught at least twice. She was caught in 1864 with battle plans and drawings in her shoes. She escaped but was recaptured and sentenced to hang by General Bragg. After getting out of that little brouhaha, she returned to the South dressed in male uniform to continue her spying. General Garfield made her a brevet major. At the end of the war, she toured the country giving lectures about being a spy, at one point with P.T. Barnum. A friend wrote a book collecting her activities and publishing them. Unfortunately, she was married three times and died of a morphine overdose at the age of 60, penniless and ill in San Francisco. Major Cushman is buried in the officers' circle of the Presidio in San Francisco under her third husband's name of Fryer.

Challenges: (1) How did she get into the spying business from her acting career? (2) How was she able to get out of her sentence to hang? (3) What nickname was she given by P.T. Barnum?

Challenge #XI-11

The difficulty of the Confederate economy and the huge inflationary rate it experienced during the war led to rising prices, loss of wealth and credit, and nearly a collapse of the government. The essential reason was that paper money was being printed with insufficient gold and silver specie to back it up.

A subsidiary reason, though, was that a very clever con man/gold prospector/journalist decided to go into the counterfeiting business. Looking for a way to make money from the war, he began by printing patriotic items, one of which was a card with the head of Jefferson Davis on the body of a jackass. Finding that novelty not sufficiently wealth producing, he decided to use his printing press to make pretend Confederate notes. He purchased an electroplate that produced almost-perfect copies of Confederate $5 bills. At first, he produced 3,000 $5 notes and sold them for 1 cent each. The original version had the fact that these were fake printed on the bottom, but this print was cut off by smugglers and passed as real in the South.

Realizing that he was onto something big, he started buying genuine Confederate notes and stamps and duplicating them. He sold the currency notes for 5 cents each and the stamps at face value. Then he really went for it: he started using high-quality banknote paper and stopped pretending he was producing novelties. Eventually, his product became indistinguishable from real money.

Challenges: (1) Who was this clever swindler? (2) How much counterfeit Confederate money did this man produce? (3) The U.S. government didn't try to stop him. Why wasn't he charged with a crime?

Challenge #XI-12

You can't run a rebellion without arms, and you can't purchase arms without money. And if your country doesn't produce weapons, then how can you get them through a blockade? So where did the Confederacy get financial support to carry out a war? And how did European armaments make it to the South despite a blockade when they had no navy? The answer was two business agents who were actually foreign agents. Both were based in Liverpool.

One was a South Carolina cotton merchant who was the senior partner of a private firm, and the business acted as the European banker for the Confederate States of America. As such, this firm purchased military armaments, transported them to the United States through the blockade, and extended the Confederate States of America's credit when it couldn't meet its obligations.

The other, who was the Confederacy's chief foreign agent in Great Britain, led the effort to obtain Confederate ships in Liverpool. He worked with John Laird Sons & Co. in Birkenhead, across the Mersey River estuary from Liverpool, as an agent of Fraser, Trenholm and Company, to build blockade runners.

Challenges: (1) Who were these men? (2) What was the name of the firm? (3) Who was their managing partner? (Hint: He became Confederate States of America secretary of the Treasury.) (4) How did this company get so much credit extended to it without international recognition of its client and get military supplies delivered despite the blockade?

Answers

Answer #XI-1

Elizabeth Van Lew, known as "Crazy Bet," is today considered the most successful Union spy of the Civil War. She feigned her madness and was purposeful in appearing eccentric. She reported directly to General Butler and, through him, to General Sharpe. She provided accurate reports of troop and prisoner movements, food and supply shipments, and other developments in the Confederate capital.

Van Lew ran a spy ring with at least 12 operatives in Richmond, many of them in administrative positions in the Confederate government. She used her family's slaves and friends to manage the network without discovery for four years. She sent frequent dispatches of intelligence in a special cipher code written in a colorless liquid that turned black when exposed to milk.

When horses were being confiscated for use by the army, Van Lew rode her horse up the stairs to her home and quartered him in her library so she could ride to pass her secret messages. She carried books with notes folded into the spines and food trays with false bottoms to Union prisoners.

She also helped Union prisoners of war plan their escapes. One especially successful example occurred on February 14, 1864, when 100 Union officers escaped from Libby Prison by digging a tunnel underneath the building; 50 found their way back to Union lines with her help. She worked secretly with other Richmond Unionists to hide escaped Union prisoners. She also secretly found Ulric Dahlgren's hidden grave and had his body reburied elsewhere until after the war.

Her most famous exploit was that she convinced Varina Davis, the president's wife, to hire her family slave, Mary Elizabeth Bowser, as a household servant. This post enabled Mary to spy in the White House of the Confederacy. Although Mary appeared uneducated and simple, this too was an act, as she in fact had a photographic memory. Inside Jefferson Davis's office, under cover of dusting his desk, she could read his letters and dispatches. Supposedly, the communication was so smooth that she'd send a report to Van Lew in the morning and Grant would have it in the afternoon.

Van Lew gathered information on Confederate troop strength and movements, which she passed on via couriers to General Grant and his intelligence officer, Colonel George H. Sharpe. The officers later acknowledged both the quantity and quality of the information she provided to them. Grant personally thanked Van Lew and told her she had provided the most accurate information he received during the war.

Van Lew was a Virginian, but she fervently opposed slavery and secession. Her education was at the Quaker School in Philadelphia, where she was taught that slavery was immoral.

Despite the scorn she received after the war from her friends, President Grant appointed her postmaster of Richmond. She had spent the family's fortune maintaining the spy network, and this post relieved her expenses. Also, Paul Revere's grandson had been one of those she had helped, and after the war, the Revere family helped support her.

No one ever knew that she kept a diary buried in her garden. She revealed its existence only on her deathbed. It remains available commercially. The diary revealed that she used her entire cash inheritance to purchase and free her slaves' relatives. Elizabeth's brother frequented the Richmond slave market, where he would purchase an entire family to prevent them being split up and then issue papers of manumission.

Further Reading

- https://ehistory.osu.edu/biographies/elizabeth-van-lew
- https://www.mentalfloss.com/article/75414/female-spies-changed-course-civil-war
- https://www.smithsonianmag.com/history/elizabeth-van-lew-an-unlikely-union-spy-158755584/?fbclid=IwAR1RCvUHY8Z4KkKVoGX0Z1nkd2uAFkXqiwClv_I_2Ks2rFt4G-dqERgGJh8
- Van Lew, Elizabeth. *A Yankee Spy in Richmond. The Civil War Diary of "Crazy Bet" Van Lew.* Stackpole Books, 1996.

Answers #XI-2

1. Rose O'Neal Greenhow
2. She had become a widow in 1854 and was romantically involved with abolitionist Republican U.S. senator Henry Wilson from Massachusetts (married at the time), the chairperson of the Senate Military Affairs Committee. She considered him her best source. He later became vice president serving under Ulysses Grant in his second term.
3. Betty Duvall
4. Jefferson Davis credited the message she sent and delivered by

Betty Duvall as ensuring the South's victory at the First Battle of Bull Run in late July 1861. In fact, McDowell did depart Washington on July 16. Beauregard was prepared for the invasion, positioned near Manassas Junction. He placed his men along the south bank of the Bull Run river with his left guarding a stone bridge.

5. When Beauregard received the coded message, he was able to determine it was authentic and how to read it from the package. The outer package was a black purse made of "mourning" silk, proof it came from the "lady in mourning." The key to the cipher was on the envelope; the six symbols spelled out "Jordan," her handler, in cipher. Deciphered, the message said, "McDowell has certainly been ordered to advance on the sixteenth. ROG"

When this information reached Jefferson Davis, he was initially concerned about its authenticity. He sent Lieutenant George Donnellan, an engineer in the Provisional Army Confederate States, to call on Greenhow for confirmation. Dressed in civilian clothes, Donnellan confirmed the information and placed it in a hollowed-out part of his boot. Beauregard had the dispatch by nighttime. The encoded letter written by Greenhow is in the Library of Congress.

6. The U.S. government realized that there was a leak and the trail led to Rose Greenhow's residence. On August 22, 1861, Allan Pinkerton was on surveillance outside Greenhow's house. He noticed a young Union officer entering. Standing on the shoulders of another officer, he looked into the front parlor through a window, observing the officer and Greenhow whispering and looking over a map. When the officer left the residence, Pinkerton tried to stop him, but the officer ran. Pinkerton followed the officer to the provost marshal station and, there, was arrested by Union soldiers. Pinkerton was able to send a message to Winfield Scott (by bribing a guard) about what he witnessed. Scott brought Pinkerton to the War Department and had the officer arrested.

Rose O'Neal Greenhow by Mathew Brady (Library of Congress).

As Rose was returning from a walk the next day, she was arrested by Union soldiers. When her house was searched, the map of the Union fortifications that the officer had brought the day before was found, along with other incriminating materials.

In 1862, she and her daughter, "Little Rose," were imprisoned for five months. Using her contacts (including Senator Wilson), she convinced Secretary Stanton to release her. Deported to the Confederate States, she traveled to Richmond, Virginia, for further activities. She ran the blockade, sailing to Europe to represent the Confederacy in a diplomatic mission to France and Britain from 1863 to 1864. She wrote a book about her being a spy that was well received in Europe. Her returning ship ran aground off the coast of Wilmington, North Carolina, carrying a huge weight in gold intended for the Confederacy in 1864. As she tried to escape a Union gunboat, her rowboat overturned, and she drowned. She was ultimately honored with a Confederate military funeral.

Further Reading

- https://www.battlefields.org/learn/biographies/rose-onealgreenhow
- https://www.history.com/this-day-in-history/rose-greenhow-dies
- https://sites.psu.edu/slavoffpassion/2017/02/05/rose-onealgreenhow/

Answers #XI-3

1. On July 4, 1861, Union soldiers confronted Boyd and her mother after being told Belle had decorated her room with rebel flags. When the men raised a Union flag over the house, Boyd's mother objected. One of the soldiers responded with a curse, and Belle Boyd drew a hidden pistol and shot him. An investigation exonerated her of murder.

2. One of the officers sent to guard her became her friend, whom she thanked in her memoirs "for some very remarkable effusions, some withered flowers, and a great deal of important information." She conveyed those secrets to Confederate officers via her slave Eliza Hopewell, who carried them in a hollowed-out watch case.

3. General James Shields and his staff gathered in the parlor of the local hotel in mid–May 1862. Boyd hid in the closet in the room, eavesdropping through a knothole that she enlarged in the door. She learned that Shields had been ordered east from Front Royal, Virginia.

That night, she rode through Union lines, using false papers to bluff her way past the sentries, and reported the news to Colonel Turner Ashby, who was scouting for the Confederates. She then returned to town. When the Confederates advanced on Front Royal on May 23, Boyd ran to greet Stonewall Jackson's men, avoiding enemy fire that put bullet holes in her skirt. She urged an officer to inform Jackson "the Yankee force is very small.... Tell him to charge right down and he will catch them all." And he did. She was awarded the Southern Cross of Honor, and Jackson made her a captain.

The veracity of her memoirs, *Belle Boyd in Camp and Prison*, has often been challenged. Despite skepticism, most of these stories, told on stage to appreciative male audiences, are probably true. A careful examination of Boyd's text by historian Louis A. Sigaud in 1944 confirmed its fundamental accuracy using eyewitness accounts.

Answer #XI-4

Benjamin Franklin "Frank" Stringfellow.
A high school Latin teacher in Mississippi, he tried to enlist in the Confederate army immediately after secession but was repeatedly rejected due to his diminutive size (5 foot 8 inches but weighing only 100 pounds). To prove his worth, he staked out a Confederate encampment and captured three guards; he then returned them to their commanding officer as his prisoners. Impressed, J.E.B. Stuart asked him to be his personal scout. Originally a graduate of the high school in Alexandria, Virginia, he returned to his hometown using disguises that ranged from posing as a dentist's assistant to dressing as a woman. There, he was able to learn about troop movements and plans. His repeated narrow escapes are the stuff of legend.

Further Reading

- https://military.wikia.org/wiki/Benjamin_Franklin_Stringfellow_(1840%E2%80%931913)
- PBS ran a series called *Mercy Street* about him. http://www.pbs.org/mercy-street/uncover-history/real-people-places/frank-stringfellow/

Answers #XI-5

1. The Knights of the Golden Circle (KGC) (El circulo dorado). The idea was that a map of the geography described above forms a large

circle. Albert Pike (1809–1891) is thought to be the genius behind the influence and power of the KGC, while Bickley was the organization's president and leading promoter. KGC lodges were called Temples. There were three classes or levels of military readiness.

 2. This group composed a powerful spy network during the war. When the Civil War started, they resorted to drastic measures and went underground to oppose the North and the Union army with secretive and bold actions, including sabotage, infiltration of the government, and a very efficient spy network. Many top politicians, officials, and men of importance were members. They were so effective that President Lincoln once referred to them as a "Fifth Column," which might have been the original use of the term.

 3. In 1934, two boys in Baltimore found 5,000 gold coins under a house that was believed to be a treasury of this group. John Surratt after the war described being inducted in a ceremony in 1860 in this "temple." John Surratt was a KGC member and later said that he met John Wilkes Booth at the Baltimore Castle. He claimed that at his induction, an elaborate affair, cabinet members, congressmen, judges, actors, and other politicians were in attendance. He also notes that kidnapping Abraham Lincoln was planned at that time, and we may reflect on this as the predecessor of the assassination. The original plan was to then inaugurate John Breckinridge as president.

Pike is believed to have met with Cherokee chief Stand Watie and helped him to join the Confederate army. Quantrill's Raiders were an offshoot of a Kansas Castle. The James Gang could be thought of as another offshoot.

An invasion of Texas was organized, but his expedition failed. There were many other planned bizarre secret expeditions, none of which ever happened. A plot to annex the northwestern United States failed but made headlines at the time.

It changed names many times, including the Order of American Knights, then the Order of the Sons of Liberty, which affiliated with the Copperheads. Congressman Vallindingham from Ohio was a Copperhead and a member of the KGC. It may well have also served as a model for the Ku Klux Klan after the war.

Further Reading

- https://knightsofthegoldencircle.webs.com
- https://www.tshaonline.org/handbook/entries/knights-of-the-golden-circle

Answer #XI-6

Sarah Emma Edmonds.

In 1864, Boston publisher DeWolfe, Fiske, & Co. published her account of her military experiences as *The Female Spy of the Union Army*.

In 1867, she married Linus H. Seelye, a mechanic and a childhood friend. She had three children, all of whom died young, and she and her husband adopted two others.

She may have made it all up. Some historians are skeptical, but no one really knows.

Answer #XI-7

Henry Thomas Harrison—at most, he was 5 foot 1 inches tall. He was often drunk and gambled. When he arrived at 10:00 p.m. in the Confederate camp, Moxley Sorrel described him thus: "Harrison straggled into the lines filthy and ragged, showing some rough work and exposure."

Harrison told Moxley Sorrel, James Longstreet, and General Lee (i) that General Hooker had been replaced, (ii) that Meade was now in charge, and (iii) that the Union army was located near Frederick, Maryland. When Lee received this information directly from this spy, he ordered his dispersed army to converge around a central crossroads named Gettysburg.

Moxley Sorrel in his book *Recollections of a Confederate Staff Officer* describes Harrison's activity in March 1863:

> While Longstreet was holding this brief independent command, a scout, more properly a spy, was placed at his service by the War Department. He was a man of about thirty years, calling himself a Mississippian, and was altogether an extra-ordinary character. He was paid in United States greenbacks. I approved requisition on the quarter master every month for $150 for him. His time seemed to be passed about equally within our lines and the enemy's. Harrison (such was his name) always brought us true information. There was invariable confirmation of his reports afterwards.

He was briefly detained in April 1863 for appearing to be spying, but there was a lack of evidence, so he was released. Longstreet then contacted him to go to Washington and to report on information prior to a Northern invasion.

Further Reading

- https://www.civilwarprofiles.com/henry-harrison-secret-agent-man/

Answers #XI-8

1. The train robberies he solved was for the railroad in Chicago, which brought him to the attention of the Illinois Central Railroad and its chief engineer and vice president, one George McClellan, and its young attorney, a fellow named Abraham Lincoln.

2. Major E.J. Allen. He worked undercover in summer of 1861. His interest was focused on fortifications and Confederate plans. He sent agents into Kentucky and West Virginia and performed espionage in Tennessee, Georgia, and Mississippi. He also detected several counterespionage plots. He was discovered in Memphis, almost caught, and barely escaped with his life.

Answers #XI-9

#XI-9a

Colonel George Henry Sharpe was appointed by General Hooker and remained in that capacity until the end of the war. He studied law at Yale and was secretary of the U.S. legation to Austria before the war.

BMI was essential to Union success in the Eastern Theater. Sharpe's estimates of the size and location of the Army of Northern Virginia were invariably accurate. He was able to accomplish this mission even when the cavalry was not able to make these discoveries.

In April 1865, after Lee's surrender at Appomattox Court House, Sharpe, as deputy provost marshal general, paroled 28,000 Confederate army soldiers, among them General Lee.

FURTHER READING
- Tsouras, Peter G. *Major General George H. Sharpe and the Creation of American Military Intelligence in the Civil War.* Casemate, 2018.

#XI-9b

1. Gettysburg: Sharpe's BMI assistant, John Babcock, developed and brought Meade detailed charts revealing enemy troop strength. From this, the BMI deduced that Pickett's division was the only unit remaining to attack on the last day of Gettysburg, and that fact convinced Meade to not retreat. This intelligence brought Meade and his commanders crucial information that allowed them to plan

a defense against a force that they might anticipate. Remember, it was precisely the lack of this sort of information of strength and deployment of the Union army that led to Lee's defeat. This story is well described in Brown's *Meade at Gettysburg*.

2. Overland Campaign: the interrogation of Confederate soldiers contained valuable information, not in what they were telling the interrogators but the fact that none of Jubal Early's division was in those captured soldiers. From this, it was determined that Early's division had left Lee's forces and presumed to be heading toward Washington and the Potomac. Grant therefore had time to send forces to stop him and to know that Lee's army was that much smaller. Earlier, Sharpe kept Grant updated on the size of Lee's forces and the location of Longstreet's corps: Longstreet had returned to Charlottesville from Tennessee.

#XI-9c

They did! Hooker was informed that only two of Longstreet's divisions was in his front and that where Jackson was unknown. In fact, the lessons learned from how Hooker didn't use his information changed how intelligence is handled in the U.S. military ever since.

Sharpe knew that none of his interrogated prisoners were from Jackson's corps and kept telling Hooker that they didn't know where Jackson was. Prisoners told them that Jackson was coming up, yet none of the prisoners were from Hood's or Pickett's divisions. A secret agent at Guinea Station knew that Jackson had already moved north but was unable to report it until too late.

Other agents strongly suspected that Longstreet was not on the front; this was reported to Sharpe and Hooker but couldn't be confirmed. Longstreet and most of his corps were involved in the Suffolk Campaign at that time. His divisions present at Chancellorsville were those of Major Generals Lafayette McLaws and Richard H. Anderson.

Hooker was ineffective in the use of this intelligence; he was inundated with information and was unable to discern fact from rumor. This miscalculation of accurate intelligence, plus Hooker's insistence that Lee was in retreat, was largely responsible for the Confederate victory at Chancellorsville.

There were numerous reports of Jackson's movement reported to Hooker besides Sharpe. Hooker believed that Lee was retreating and not looking to flank him. After all, his army was divided and a portion was in Fredericksburg, and Hooker did not even consider that Lee was daring enough to divide his army a third time. So Hooker sent Sickles to chase the backend of Jackson's troops. Consequently, Sickles was out of position to help Howard. Howard's corps had been warned, but that threat was thought to be false, and Howard put up no real defense. The fact is that Hooker blamed Howard and Pleasonton for the failure of the battle and the concussion he sustained; but a significant problem was that he was overconfident and interpreted facts he was given in the most favorable way.

Another factor was that Hooker had limited cavalry for reconnaissance during the campaign because he sent most of them on Stoneman's raid on the Richmond-Fredericksburg Railroad, holding back only 1,300 troopers to support infantry operations. Cavalry would have been useful in detecting the true location of Jackson's flank march and the departure of Lee's divisions to Salem Church.

#XI-9d

Ruth was responsible for the rail movement of troops and supplies for the Confederate forces in Virginia. Besides being able to delay rail movements, Ruth was able to provide valuable information to Colonel Sharpe about Confederate plans gleaned from troop movements, supplies, and the condition of rail network for which he was responsible. This was a crucial supply line for the Army of Northern Virginia.

Despite appearing loyal to the rebellion, he masterminded slow troop trains, fewer railroad employees, certain bridges waiting too long for repairs, and nonmilitary trains being given priority. Lee noticed and complained, but Ruth would straighten up and fly right for a bit to avoid detection, only to later slip back into his inefficient ways.

Another thing Sharpe did, and this was revolutionary at the time, was he correlated all his information to synthesize a bigger picture. For example, if Ruth reported he ran trains with 100,000 pounds of bacon and 100,000 pounds of flour three times a week, Sharpe would remember interviews with deserters that they were only getting half a pound of bacon and flour each day instead of their full ration of 1 pound of each. Sharpe could then put the two pieces of information together and calculate Lee's troop strength fairly accurately.

FURTHER READING

- http://www.civilwarsignals.org/pages/spy/pages/grantintel.html

Answers #XI-10

1. Two paroled Confederate sympathizers offered her $300 if during a stage performance in Louisville, Kentucky (the troubled

border state then under Union control) she would make a toast to the Confederacy while on stage. The play's manager refused to allow it. She went to the local provost marshal's office, Colonel Moore, who told her to accept and see who came to the event. When she did and reported back, she was fired from the play but officially offered a position as a spy. She began an undercover effort among Southern troops that secured information valuable to Federal forces.

2. She was an actress, remember? That is why she was so great at undercover work. So, after her sentencing, she actually developed a mild case of typhoid fever, but she acted as if she was severely ill. This bought her time to be liberated by the advancing Union army. The timely arrival of Union troops rescued Cushman from being hanged. She later received an honorary major's commission from President Lincoln. You might say that this role saved her life.

3. "'The Spy of the Cumberland,' the Greatest Heroine of the Age." https://www.battlefields.org/learn/biographies/pauline-cushman.

Answers #XI-11

1. Samuel Curtis Upham, known as "Honest Sam"
2. Upham claimed to have produced 1,564,000 counterfeit notes, with values ranging from 5 cents to $100, probably totaling $15 million. Modern estimates are that his fake bills composed between 1 percent and 3 percent of the Confederacy's money supply. He claimed to have made more than $50,000 from the scheme.
3. The legal problem was that since the Federal government didn't recognize the Confederacy, it wasn't clear exactly what laws he was violating. He might have gone to trial anyway on false charges, but Secretary of War Stanton intervened personally in the case. This has given rise to speculation that the source of the genuine banknote paper was Stanton himself, who was deliberately engaging in subterfuge.

Further Reading

- Weidenmier, Marc D. "Bogus Money Matters: Sam Upham and His Confederate Counterfeiting Business." *Business and Economic History* 28 no. 2 (1999): 313–324.
- https://www.crimemuseum.org/crime-library/silent-crimes/samuel-curtis-upham/
- https://prescottenews.com/index.php/2021/09/26/holy-cow-history-the-man-who-conned-the-confederacy/

Answers #XI-12

1 and 2. (a) Charles Kuhn Prioleau, perhaps the most influential Confederate agent in Britain. He was the sole British partner and representative of Fraser, Trenholm, & Co., the unofficial bankers of the Confederacy in Europe, and helped supply the South with arms throughout the war. (b) James Dunwoody Bulloch. The CSS *Alabama* was his highest success. All of these men and their English collaborators were in a group called the Southern Club, a pro–Confederate business alliance with their residences in Abercromby Square, Liverpool.

3. George Alfred Trenholm

4. Trenholm ultimately operated 60 commercial ships running the blockade, including the CSS *Alabama*, which was the most successful. Prioleau was a partner in Trenholm's business and worked directly with the Confederate military, through Brigadier General Josiah Gorgas, chief of ordinance, to supply their military needs. He had moved to Liverpool in the early 1850s to establish a steamship line from England to Charleston. With his connections to Fraser, Trenholm, he became very well respected in Europe. When the war broke out, the Confederate States of America deposited large amounts of funds with this firm. Prioleau purchased armaments on Confederate States of America credit, earned fees by shipping them on Trenholm's blockade runners, then collected profits on transactions involving sales of cotton, tobacco, and turpentine on the return voyage.

FURTHER READING

- Klein, L.W. *The Financing and Construction of the Confederate War Supply Network*. North and South issue II-4-2 (Series II, volume 4, issue 2).
- Wilson, Walter E., and Gary L. McKay. *James D. Bulloch: Secret Agent and Mastermind of the Confederate Navy*. McFarland, 2012.

Section XII

Civil War Medicine

Challenges

Challenge #XII-1

Six hundred twenty thousand American soldiers died in the Civil War; two-thirds died from diseases, not war wounds. Medical science in 1860 incorrectly thought disease was caused by pollution or "bad air" (miasma). The concept of bacteria and sterile wound care did not widely develop for another 5 or 10 years. The need to drink only pure water, to keep latrines away from campsites, and not to eat spoiled food was not known. The necessity of strict sanitation was one of the few good things that came out of these experiences.

Challenges: (1) What were the most common diseases that caused illness and death among soldiers in the Civil War? (2) When did a French scientist first strongly argue that bacteria caused human diseases? (3) When did a British surgeon first insist that sterile surgery and wound dressings protected from infection?

Challenge #XII-2

Amputations were the most common surgical procedure of the Civil War. Many lives were saved by removing unsalvageable limbs despite widespread criticism for performing too many. Amputations were the chief operation during the Civil War. Of the 174,000 extremity wounds recorded in the Union, about 30,000 resulted in amputations. A rough rule of thumb is that of all battle wounds, one-third were mortal, one-third were permanently disabled (e.g., amputation), and one-third returned to the ranks.

Section XII. Civil War Medicine

Surgeons depicted as butchers with blood all over their clothes are a misleading cliché. Medical education in 1850s required at least two years of study. Combat surgeons had to be certified by their peers. Certainly, they weren't well liked by the soldiers, who gave them names like "sawbones." Another incorrect impression is that there wasn't anesthesia for these procedures and that "biting the bullet" was common. In fact, over 95 percent of operations in the war employed ether or chloroform. Surgeons could remove a limb in five minutes.

Later, scientific studies showed that wounded soldiers treated by Union or Confederate surgeons had lower mortality in all situations, including amputations, than the British and French in the Crimean War.

Challenge: Why did amputation of injured limbs save soldiers' lives?

Challenge XII-3

Gangrene as a consequence of surgical wound infections caused many deaths and prolonged recovery for months, even years. Without antibiotics, treating deep tissue infection was usually unsuccessful. Many gangrene prevention techniques and treatments were tried, most of which would obviously not be effective against bacterial infections: whiskey, cathartics, balanced diets, and poultices of mud, flaxseed, slippery elm, or charcoal. Still other ideas were toxic and likely harmful: concentrated sodium hypochlorite solutions, nitric acid, and tinctures of iron and turpentine were applied.

Middleton Goldsmith was a surgeon in the Union army working in Louisville, Kentucky. During the war, Dr. Goldsmith found himself treating a large volume of gangrene, so he focused on the problem. He made a brilliant observation that led to a major discovery. In an era when hospital gangrene mortality was 45 percent, Goldsmith's method, tested in over 330 cases, yielded mortality under 3 percent.

Challenge: What was Dr. Goldsmith's insight?

Challenge #XII-4

When a chloroform-soaked cloth was placed over Stonewall Jackson's face to relieve the pain during amputation, he murmured, "What an infinite blessing."

The Confederate army had difficulty acquiring anesthetics because of the Northern blockade. Typically, chloroform was administered by placing drops of the solution onto a cloth which was then placed over the patient's nose and mouth. The standard method of soaking a handkerchief with chloroform was a waste because much of it evaporated into the air. In addition, the vapor often left everyone in the operating room slightly affected by the drug.

A brilliant Confederate surgeon solved the problem. Dr. Julian John Chisolm received his MD from the Medical College of South Carolina in 1850 and continued his training in Paris with an emphasis on eye surgery. In 1859, he returned to Europe to observe the treatment of the wounded from European battles of that time. In South Carolina, he treated the wounded from the Battle of Fort Sumter and then as Confederate surgeon in Virginia. After the war, he became dean of the university medical schools in South Carolina and Maryland and performed surgery on the eye and ear. He was highly renowned for referring Helen Keller to Alexander Graham Bell.

Challenge: The device he invented to solve the Civil War anesthesia problem is shown. How did it work and how effective was it?

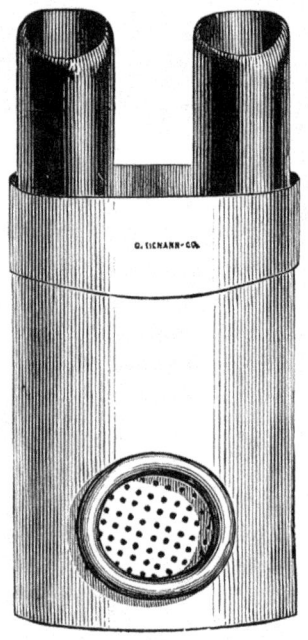

The Chisolm Inhaler (from George A. Otis, *The Medical and Surgical History of the War of the Rebellion*, Vol. 2, Part 3 [Washington, D.C.: Government Printing Office, 1883], 889; National Library of Medicine).

Challenge #XII-5

Lieutenant General Thomas J. "Stonewall" Jackson was shot at night during the Battle of Chancellorsville on May 2, 1863. That day, he had led his corps in a surprise attack on a 12-mile roundabout route using a primitive road that wasn't on maps. The road led to the right flank of the Union army, which had neither entrenched nor was protected by a natural defense.

Jackson had ventured out in front of his lines along the Plank Road to see what defensive arrangements the Union army was preparing. A night attack was a serious possibility given the disorganization the Union army was experiencing after the surprise attack. Members of his staff joined him. He had decided that A.P. Hill would continue the attack that evening. When his party turned around, they left the main road in a very dark area. His party instead rode into an ambush. Two of his staff was killed, and Jackson was shot in the back of the

Section XII. Civil War Medicine

Location of Stonewall Jackson's wounding. The path taken by Jackson and Hill returning from their reconnaissance is demonstrated (photograph by Lloyd W. Klein).

left arm as well as his right hand. The wound bled profusely, and a handkerchief was used as a tourniquet. Jackson told A.P. Hill it was very painful and that his arm was undoubtedly broken.

Because Jackson was severely fatigued, likely due to blood loss, he could not walk. He was transported by stretcher carried by men who, in the dark and uneven ground and under fire from Union units, tripped or dropped the stretcher, resulting in Jackson falling from that height, on at least two occasions.

Dr. Hunter Holmes McGuire, Jackson's medical director, rendered General Jackson appropriate care. He controlled the bleeding, amputated the badly injured left arm, and diligently cared for him until the general's death on May 10, 1863.

Challenge: A skilled surgeon amputated the arm, the bleeding stopped, and there was no infection. So why did Stonewall Jackson die?

Challenge #XII-6

When we read about Civil War battles, the cries of anguish of the wounded never fail to be mentioned. Battle-related casualties of Civil War battles included 20 percent dead and 80 percent wounded. Of the soldiers who were wounded, about one out of seven died.

When the war began, there were no systems to bring the wounded to receive appropriate treatment; either you were one of the lucky "walking wounded" or some of your friends risked their lives to drag you behind your lines. Unless carried by a comrade, a wounded soldier might suffer for days in distress from exposure and thirst. The inefficient treatment of casualties impacted morale and military command and control.

A brilliant Union medical officer made the observation that wounded troops are saved not only by early treatment of their wounds but also by expedited travel to appropriate levels of medical facilities behind the lines. The greatest proof of his system was after Gettysburg, when 14,000 Union and 6,800 Confederate wounded were treated in a vast medical encampment near Gettysburg named after him. Every soldier had any necessary surgery performed within 24 hours of the injury, and the mortality rate was just 2 percent, down from 33 percent at the start of the war.

The concept of triage was then instituted. After transfer behind the battleline, those who were mortally wounded would not be transported farther; those who had minimal injuries were bandaged and sent back; those who could be saved by urgent surgery were transported to hospitals well behind for immediate care. Then those who survived were further transported to large facilities away from the battlefield for definitive surgery and postoperative care. The concept of "ambulances" to rapidly transport the acutely wounded was also his idea.

Challenge: Who is the physician who devised this system? His essential system continues today, albeit improved with contemporary methods (helicopters, etc.) in modern warfare. The MASH (Mobile Army Surgical Hospitals) unit is a direct descendant of this system.

Challenge #XII-7

The wounds produced by artillery and large bore bullets and minié balls were ghastly. Having survived, the soldier had to live with wounds of frightening mutilation. One doctor, Gurdon Buck, began performing facial reconstruction surgeries during the Civil War. His specialty was repairing facial wounds that left disfigured men suffering from the results of being shot or hit with shrapnel in the face. One of his first patients was a Union soldier suffering from deformity after the removal of one cheekbone. Buck crafted dental and facial pieces, today called prosthetics, to replace the bone, reshaping the patient's face. By doing the needed repair over the course of several separate operations, the best effect possible was created. He is also the first doctor to incorporate pre- and post-operative photographs into his publications. He was renowned for helping many regain a semblance of normality in their everyday lives.

Challenge: What branch of surgery did he create?

Challenge #XII-8

The Civil War featured numerous types of weapons and ballistics. These included artillery (e.g., shell, grape/canister, solid shot) and hand-held weapons (e.g., minié ball, musket ball, pistol/buckshot). The minié ball caused 76.0 percent—over 108,000—of all treated wounds, far exceeding the second-place ballistic (round or musket ball).

Challenge: Why was the minié ball such a damaging ballistic? The two minié bullets, for example, that struck John Bell Hood's leg at Chickamauga destroyed five inches of his upper thigh bone. This left surgeons no choice but to amputate the shattered limb.

Challenge #XII-9

At age 40, Clarissa Harlowe "Clara" Barton embarked on a completely new career. A teacher who later became a clerk at the U.S. Patent Office, she began collecting supplies at the outset of the war. Concerned that these were not getting to the soldiers, she became involved in obstacles to supply. She gathered bandages and other much-needed provisions, but she realized that she could best support the troops by going in person to the battlefields. She nursed, comforted, and cooked for the wounded in many major battles of the war. She was called the "Angel of the Battlefield" for her amazing service.

Her assistance of wounded soldiers went beyond tending to their wounds; she actively collected both food and medical supplies, organizing "Ladies' Aid" societies to distribute these materials within the army, ultimately gaining permission from the quartermaster to work on the front lines. She was appointed by General Benjamin Butler as the "lady in charge" of the hospitals at the front of the Army of the James in 1864. Perhaps her most stressful experience was an incident in which a bullet tore through the sleeve of her dress without striking her but instead killed a man to whom she was tending.

After the war, she became friends with Susan B. Anthony and became an ardent supporter of the woman's suffrage movement and, with Frederick Douglass, was an early supporter of civil rights. Exhausted by her work, in 1869 she traveled to Europe to rest from her responsibilities. Instead, she became involved in organizing French and German military hospitals during the Franco-Prussian War, assisting an organization she later brought home to the United States, becoming its founder and first president.

Challenge: Which organization?

Challenge #XII-10

Robert E. Lee died in 1870 at the age of 63 after a stroke two weeks earlier. He had been suffering from heart failure and had severe angina for some time. Obviously, in the mid–19th century, no one had any idea what a heart attack was, let alone how to diagnose or treat cardiovascular disease, and there was no medication to prevent it.

We know a good deal about Lee's health because of investigations of Lee's medical history and death from *Lee–The Last Years* by C.B. Flood, including accounts by his physicians, Drs. H.T. Barton and R.L. Madison; close friend Colonel W.P. Johnston; and family. In the autumn of 1870, while serving as president of Washington College, Lee regularly experienced fatigue, shortness of breath with exertion, and chest pains. Undoubtedly, he was suffering from heart failure due to multiple prior heart attacks and perhaps a recent one.

On September 28, Lee stood to say grace over supper, "opened his mouth but no words came out." Sitting back in his chair, he "bowed down, looking very strange and speaking incoherently." In the following days, he never uttered a word but communicated with nodding or shaking his head. His famous last words about A.P. Hill and striking the tent is most unlikely from a medical perspective.

The constant stress from defending Southern independence undoubtedly contributed to anxiety and stress-related medical disorders, including heart and vascular disease. In fact, his chest pains as described are classic for angina pectoris.

In 1869, doctors diagnosed Lee with pericarditis due to severe chest pain, but more modern clinical evaluations of his symptoms conclude that his condition was more likely attributed to stress-induced ischemic heart disease. Pericarditis was well known at the time, but today, we know it can be due to a large heart attack.

Challenge: When during the war had Lee been diagnosed with pericarditis? At what battles did he experience frequent chest pain and a heart attack? Could that have affected his military judgment?

Challenge XII-11a–d

#XII-11a

Dr. Hunter Holmes McGuire was a highly skilled Confederate physician and surgeon. After the war, he founded several hospitals around Richmond, which became the Medical College of Virginia and where he became chairman of surgery. He also contributed to the Geneva Conventions, thus creating humane rules of war. He was also president of the American Medical Association. He was recognized in his day as a brilliant physician, teacher, and lecturer.

Challenge: During the war, he amputated the limbs of three Confederate generals. Name the generals, the battles at which the injuries occurred, and the limbs he removed.

#XII-11b

Alexander Thomas Augusta was the highest ranking black officer in the Union army during the Civil War.

Challenge: What was his extraordinary pathway to attain that position? Bonus: What was his most remarkable achievement *after* the war?

#XII-11c

She developed over 300 military hospitals during the war as part of the U.S. Sanitary Commission, including overseeing nursing, physicians, food, cleaning, and construction. Later, she served as a lawyer assisting veterans and their families with obtaining pensions after the war. She followed the Union forces and cared for the wounded on 19 battlefields, including Shiloh, Vicksburg, Chattanooga, and Atlanta. She acted as General Grant's, then later Sherman's, chief of nursing.

Challenge: Who was she?

#XII-11d

Born to alcoholic parents and perhaps an abusive father, she was raised by her grandmother in Boston, where she was a schoolteacher but was often sick. She went to Europe and met a group of reformers interested in how the mentally ill were treated. On her return to the United States, she began touring hospitals and suggesting to politicians how to make reforms, which they were not inclined to do. Despite this resistance, she established asylums in several states. Her successes in lobbying Congress led to lobbyists as a profession.

When the Civil War started, she became the superintendent of army nurses. She set extremely high standards. In an era when physicians were skeptical of women nurses, this leader changed nursing forever. After the war, she continued her work, founding hospitals for the insane and leading other social reforms.

Challenges: (1) Who was this woman? (2) What were her standards for a nurse?

Challenge #XII-12

James Longstreet was wounded by friendly fire at the Battle of the Wilderness. Eerily, the event occurred just four miles from where Stonewall Jackson was wounded a year before. The episode is an interesting medical story with significant historical implications.

On May 5, 1864, the Union corps under General Winfield Scott Hancock were driving A.P. Hill's men back, and there was a threat to the rear, including General Lee's headquarters. Longstreet arrived after a 28-mile march in one day, and his counterattack saved the day for the Confederate army. The nature of the movement was a flank attack on Hancock's left through an unfinished railroad bed in the heavily wooded forest that was not on local maps. Longstreet and Micah Jenkins, one of his division commanders, were planning another attack.

Mahone's 12th Virginia was returning to the Orange Plank Road, but a brush fire caused them to take a different route that led them across the road in a different location than other members of their brigade. Longstreet and his staff unknowingly passed in the middle of Mahone's men. One section, who were either prone or kneeling, saw indistinct forms and opened fire. Jenkins was struck in head and later died. Two others were also killed.

In his memoirs, Longstreet describes the bullet as passing through his throat and right shoulder and that his right arm immediately dropped to his side. He reportedly gave orders and spoke with a whispery voice while blood arose in his mouth and throat. Surgeons found no bone injuries and no bullet, which was thought to be a .58 caliber minié ball.

Historians (Steere, Freeman, and Foote) say the bullet entered his shoulder in the front, as he was riding toward his men. The description given traditionally is that the minié ball struck him in the shoulder and tore his throat. Moxley Sorrel witnessed the event and described that Longstreet was actually lifted straight up off his saddle (hint: remember he was a large and heavy man who was 6 feet 2 inches tall weighing 220 pounds). For the remainder of his life, Longstreet's right arm was paralyzed, although there was preserved sensation, and he spoke with a weak voice.

Challenge: The descriptions of the event and his medical symptoms, both at the time of his wounding and later in life, simply cannot be explained by a shoulder wound from his front.

The permanent disability can only be explained by questioning certain aspects of the traditional story. Using modern knowledge of human neural and cervical anatomy, reconstruct what must have happened.

Challenge #XII-13

John Stith Pemberton was an American physician, pharmacist, and Confederate States Army veteran. Pemberton went to medical school at the Reform Medical College of Georgia in Macon, Georgia. He graduated in 1850, at the age of 19. His main talent was chemistry, which today is called pharmacology. After initially practicing medicine and surgery, Dr. Pemberton opened a drugstore in Columbus, Georgia.

During the Civil War, Pemberton served in the Georgia State Guard, which was an element of the Confederate Army. Pemberton was a first lieutenant of the Third Georgia Cavalry Battalion, rising to the rank of lieutenant colonel. During the last major battle of the war, the Battle of Columbus in April 1865, Pemberton received a saber wound to the chest.

Like many soldiers wounded in the war, he lived with pain forever after. But Pemberton, a talented chemist, realized that his addiction to morphine was what was truly incapacitating. He decided to work on finding a cure for soldiers who were addicted to morphine to relieve their chronic pain syndrome.

Challenge: What was the cure he created?

Answers

Answers #XII-1

1. Dysentery was the most common illness, mostly due to shigella but also to other microbes. Typhoid and malaria ran rampant in camps. Yellow fever, smallpox, and measles were also significant illnesses. The germ theory of disease had not yet been advanced, so no one understood the causes.

2. Louis Pasteur's work was conducted concurrently with the Civil War, about 1860–1864. He advised boric acid as an antiseptic. He was at first greeted with skepticism, but when he proved that a disease of silkworms was caused by a microbe, saving the French silk industry in 1870, he became internationally celebrated.

3. Joseph Lister's 1867 study linked microbes with surgical infection and the benefit of sterile technique. *The Lancet* warned the medical profession against Lister's "radical" ideas of the transmission of infections and use of antiseptics such as phenol. His medallion now sits in Westminster Abbey alongside that of Darwin.

Answer #XII-2

The badly torn tissues where bullets or shells had injured the body virtually always became infected. The main cause of death and disability from these wounds were infections. The projectiles would break through the skin carrying with them infected material into the fractures. Erysipelas is a streptococcal infection that caused many deaths, as did staphylococcal infections.

Bone fractures provide perfect breeding grounds for bacteria and bone infections called osteomyelitis that would inevitably cause death if limbs were not amputated. Antibiotics given parenterally for many weeks, which Civil War surgeons did not have, remains the only curative treatment. When we look back on the Civil War surgeons, they did the right thing under the circumstances.

Further Reading

- Lively, M.W. "Early Onset Pneumonia Following Pulmonary Contusion: The Case of Stonewall Jackson." *Military Medicine*

177, no. 3 (March 2012): 315–317. https://pubmed.ncbi.nlm.nih.gov/22479920/
- http://medicine-during-the-civilwar.leadr.msu.edu/amputations/

Answer #XII-3

Goldsmith noticed that in hospital wards where bromine was used as an aerosolized deodorant, gangrene patients seemed to recover more often. He therefore placed volatile bromine in all patient wards with surprising success. Buoyed by this experience, he developed a method of applying bromine deep into muscular layers after wound debridement. This involved injecting bromine subcutaneously one time and applying it topically to exposed surfaces.

In 1863, he reported outstanding clinical results with this method. The report includes data, photographs, and case reports. Goldsmith's contribution to surgical antisepsis and his revolutionary bromine therapy weren't as well recognized as Pasteur and Lister but were made earlier. Bromine remains a frequently used antiseptic in modern medicine.

Further Reading

- https://library.uthscsa.edu/2014/08/middleton-goldsmith-and-hospital-gangrene/

Answer #XII-4

The Chisolm inhaler.

Dr. Chisolm solved the problem by designing a 2.5-inch inhaler, the first of its type. Chloroform solution was slowly dripped through the perforated circle on top onto a sponge in the interior. As the patient inhaled through the tubes placed in the nose, the vapor mixed with air. This method of administering anesthesia used only one-eighth of an ounce of chloroform compared with the usual two-ounce dose. Consequently, despite a similar number of operations (about 80,000), Confederate surgeons treated almost as many as Union surgeons with a fraction of the anesthetic.

Further Reading

- Bynum, B., and H. Bynum. "Chisholm Chloroform Inhaler." *The Lancet* 387, no. 10035 (2016): P2281.
- https://www.civilwarmed.org/chisolm/

Answer #XII-5

General Jackson's death was due to the effects of blood loss (hemorrhagic shock), a chest injury, and pneumonia. His death was not a direct result of his wounds. This was an all-too-common narrative of Civil War battle injuries.

Very likely, Jackson died of pneumonia not related to the wound infection itself but rather to rib fractures and pulmonary contusion sustained in being dropped in transportation. Such lung injuries are independently associated with pneumonia. Another possibility is pulmonary embolism, perhaps related to inadequate mobilization.

FURTHER READING

- Layton, T.R. "Stonewall Jackson's Wounds." *Journal of the American College of Surgeons* 183, no. 5 (1996): 514–524.
- Smith, A.D. "Stonewall Jackson and His Surgeon, Hunter McGuire." *Bulletin of the New York Academy of Medicine* 49, no. 7 (1973): 594–609.

Answer #XII-6

Major Jonathan Letterman.

General George McClellan ordered Dr. Letterman after Second Manassas to find a solution to the untimely medical transport and wound treatment the men received. It was recognized that men were dying and suffering who had sustained wounds that ought not to have been mortal.

Before Letterman, the wounded had to find ways to the hospital on their own.

Letterman conceived of an Ambulance Corps, with dedicated soldiers trained as stretcher bearers and to operate wagons with the sole purpose to pick up the wounded and bring them to field stations. He also instituted the concept of triage for treatment of the casualties, a concept that remains a first principle of medicine today.

Letterman also developed a system of care with increasing sophistication behind the lines. Field dressing stations were located on or next to the battlefield where medical personnel would apply initial dressings and tourniquets to wounds. If serious enough, the soldier would be transferred to the field hospital, which was located close to the battlefield, usually in homes or barns, where surgery could be performed immediately. Subsequently, those who had a chance to survive were transferred to a large hospital, located far away from the battlefield, to provide personnel for long-term treatment.

The success of this system was demonstrated at the Battle of Antietam. Despite over 23,000 casualties, all of the wounded were removed from the field in just 24 hours. Further successes at Fredericksburg and Gettysburg, each with 12,000–15,000 wounded, further proved the value of Letterman's system, saving thousands of soldiers' lives.

Further Reading

- https://www.battlefields.org/learn/biographies/jonathan-letterman
- https://www.civilwarmed.org/evacuation/
- https://www.warhistoryonline.com/american-civil-war/7-medical-advances-made-possible-american-civil-war.html

Answer #XII-7

He is considered the father of modern plastic surgery. He first conceived of taking photographs of the injury before reconstruction and after his procedures (before and after). Examples of his work are nothing short of amazing. https://www.warhistoryonline.com/american-civil-war/7-medical-advances-made-possible-american-civil-war.html.

Answer #XII-8

The French officer Claude-Etienne Minié invented the minié ball in 1849. The minié ball was a .58-caliber projectile made from soft lead. It flattened on impact and created a wound that grew larger as the bullet moved deeper into tissues.

The .58-caliber minié ball caused severe destruction to soft tissue and especially to bone. These bullets weighed 505 grains; when shot from a 32-inch barrel, the muzzle velocity was 725–1,395 ft/s, a huge force. When a bone fractured due to impact by these missiles, it shattered into many fragments that couldn't heal properly and were a nidus for infection. The force broke the bone above and below impact and usually did not exit but traveled internally, causing more damage in its path. Because of the relatively slow muzzle velocity, minié balls brought pieces of clothing and skin into the wound, introducing bacteria.

Gunshots were responsible for 94 percent of all wounds, artillery 5.5 percent, and saber or bayonet 0.4 percent. Surprisingly, artillery ballistics caused just 1 in 20 wounds. However, one must keep in mind that this was a count of wounds, not deaths; probably artillery caused death in a high percentage. If so, this figure undercounts artillery deaths and perhaps bayonet deaths. Saber wounds were typically more superficial and nonabdominal, and even though these wounds were painful, cavalry battles tended to have a lower death rate than other battles.

FURTHER READING

- Bollet, A.J. *Civil War Medicine: Challenges and Triumphs*. Galen, 2002. (See p. 84, table 3.1.)
- https://www.ncbi.nlm.nih.gov/pmc/articles/PMC4790547/#!po=1.61290

Answer #XII-9

The American Red Cross

After the war ended, she was given official approval to search for the bodies of "missing men" so their loved ones would know what happened to them. Working in the "Office of Missing Soldiers," she located more than 22,000 missing men and responded to almost 42,000 inquiries. She closed the office in 1868 and traveled to Switzerland, where she became involved in the International Red Cross and was asked to open an American branch. In 1870, she assisted the Grand Duchess of Baden in developing hospitals and received recognition from the Prussian and French governments.

FURTHER READING

- https://www.clarabartonmuseum.org/bio/
- Oates, Stephen B. *A Woman of Valor: Clara Barton and the Civil War*. Free Press, 1994. ISBN 0-02-923405-0 OCLC 29259364

Answer #XII-10

He had severe chest pain and breathing difficulty that was diagnosed in March 1863 as "rheumatism" and "pericardial inflammation." Lee probably suffered a heart attack then. He spent the first day at Chancellorsville conducting business from his tent due to chest pain. Although it has been thought that his illness could have had a major influence on his decisions at the Battle of Gettysburg, this is highly unlikely. No cognitive effects of a heart attack would appear four months later.

Further Reading

- Klein, L.W., and E. J. Wittenberg. "Did General Lee's Heart Attack Impact the Conduct of the Battle of Gettysburg?" *Gettysburg Magazine*, July 2022, 62–75.
- Mainwaring, R.D., and C.G. Tribble. "The Cardiac Illness of General Robert E. Lee." *Surgery, Gynecology & Obstetrics* 174, no. 3 (March 1992): 237–244.
- Reinhart, Richard A. "Robert E. Lee's Medical History in Context of Heart Disease, Medical Education and the Practice of Medicine in the Nineteenth Century." *Surgeon's Call* 21, no. 1. https://www.civilwarmed.org/surgeons-call/lee/

Answers #XII-11

#XII-11a

1. Stonewall Jackson, left arm, Chancellorsville
2. Richard Ewell, right leg, Battle of Groveton (or Brawner's Farm)
3. Isaac Trimble, left leg, Gettysburg

#XII-11b

Born to free black parents, he was not admitted to medical school in the United States. Dr. Thomas instead graduated from medical school in Toronto. He was appointed lieutenant colonel in the Seventh U.S. Colored Infantry and worked as a surgeon during the war despite racial bigotry.

Bonus: Dr. Thomas was also the first African American head of a hospital (Freedmen's Hospital) and the first black professor of medicine (Howard University). https://www.nps.gov/foth/learn/historyculture/alexander-augusta.htm.

#XII-11c

Mary Ann "Mother" Bickerdyke.

General Sherman thought so highly of her services that he specifically requested that Mother Bickerdyke ride at the head of the 15th Corps of the Army of Tennessee in the triumphant Grand Review of the Armies.

When threatened with dismissal by a hospital administrator, she proclaimed, "I will stay as long as the men need me—if you put me out of one door I will come in another; & if you bar all the doors against me, I will come in at the windows, & that the patients would help me in. When anybody leaves it will be you & not me!"

When a Union army surgeon came to Sherman to complain that he had been "dismissed," he asked who had done that. When the surgeon identified Mother Bickerdyke, Sherman proclaimed, "Oh, well, then, if it was she, I can't help you. She has more power than I—she ranks me."

FURTHER READING

- http://www.civilwarbummer.com/grants-chief-of-nursing-or-mother-bickerdyke-union-hero/?fbclid=IwAR0ruQ6QFdg7sGwKaeGr3jLCxyDyVhwb3KiCJUfUeHeK8N-HYOyezMvjgAw
- https://www.loc.gov/exhibits/civil-war-in-america/biographies/mary-ann-bickerdyke.html

#XII-11d

1. Dorothea Dix.
2. Volunteers were to be aged 35–50 and plain-looking; attractive women were rejected. Their dress was carefully chosen and described: only unhooped black or brown dresses were acceptable and no jewelry or cosmetics. Any nurse not following these orders was dismissed. Dix was trying to avoid sending vulnerable and attractive young women into hospitals where she feared they could be exploited (by doctors as well as patients). Dix famously fired volunteer nurses she hadn't personally trained or hired.

Dix routinely feuded with doctors over control of medical facilities and the hiring and firing of nurses which was resolved by Order No. 351 in October 1863. In this order, the War Department granted both Surgeon General Joseph K. Barnes and Superintendent of Army Nurses Dix the power to appoint nurses. She ultimately founded 32 U.S. hospitals and many others in Canada and Japan.

FURTHER READING

- https://www.womenshistory.org/education-resources/biographies/dorothea-dix

Answers #XII-12

Most modern physicians will recognize this as a brachial plexus injury. The brachial plexus is the network of nerves that sends signals from the spinal cord to the shoulder, arm, and hand. The trunks can be found within the posterior triangle of the neck, between the anterior and middle scalene muscles, which are in the upper back at the base of the neck. The brachial plexus, along with the axillary artery, can be considered as a large neurovascular bundle that travels in the axilla to supply the upper extremity. Hence, the main location of injury is the armpit or back by the shoulder blade.

The hoarseness will again be routinely recognized today as injury to the recurrent laryngeal nerve, a cervical structure that innervates the larynx.

Thus, the minié ball had to have severed two separate nerves. A scholarly medical presentation 20 years ago resolved the anatomy of this wound. The minié ball must have traversed from below with an upward trajectory ("kneeling or prone" men, remember!) and entered his upper back (not his shoulder) from behind (not in front) transecting both the brachial plexus and the right recurrent laryngeal nerve. That's why he was lifted up out of his saddle. This is the only way to explain his symptom complex. The bullet then traveled medially to his throat, tearing the trachea, then exited.

The reason why his surgeons, and Longstreet himself, were confused about all of this is that his neck wound was probably the exit wound, not the entry wound. They were fixated on the larger sized wound. He also thought he was riding toward his men, but in fact, they were on both sides.

FURTHER READING

- Longstreet, J. *From Manassas to Appomattox*. 2nd ed. Da Capo, 1992.
- Sorrel, G.M. *Recollections of a Confederate Staff Officer*. Konecky & Konecky, 1994.
- Stecker, R.M., and J.D. Blachley. "The Cervical Wound of General James Longstreet." *Archives of Otolaryngology—Head & Neck Surgery* 126, no. 3 (2000): 353–359. https://jamanetwork.com/journals/jamaotolaryngology/fullarticle/404442
- Steere, E. *The Wilderness Campaign*. Stackpole Books, 1960.

Answer #XII-13

He began to experiment with various painkillers that would serve as morphine-free and hence nonaddictive alternatives. His first recipe, developed in 1866, was "Dr. Tuggle's Compound Syrup of Globe Flower." The active ingredient of this concoction was the buttonbush (*Cephalanthus occidentalis*), a toxic plant.

He then began testing coca and coca wines and eventually created a formula containing extracts of kola nut and damiana, which he called "Pemberton's French Wine Coca." Coca leaves are recognized for being the source of the psychoactive alkaloid cocaine. Coca (*Erythroxylum coca*) is a tropical shrub. The cocaine alkaloid content of *E. coca* leaves ranges from 0.23 percent to 0.96 percent.

With public concern about drug addiction, depression, and alcoholism among war veterans and "neurasthenia" a common diagnosis, "wine" was not a smart consumer product. Atlanta and Fulton County enacted temperance legislation in 1886. Pemberton had to produce a nonalcoholic alternative.

This was the background to Pemberton's world-famous concoction. The idea originated in Columbus, Georgia, and brought to Atlanta. Atlanta drugstore owner-proprietor Willis E. Venable developed the recipe for the beverage, which was formulated by trial and error. He blended base syrup with carbonated water ("soda") to produce cola, a sweetened, carbonated soft drink flavored with vanilla, cinnamon, citrus oils, and other flavorings. The beverage contained caffeine, which was sourced originally from the kola nut. Pemberton decided to sell this as a fountain drink for 5 cents a glass rather than as a medicine. Frank Mason Robinson came up with the name "Coca-Cola" for the alliterative sound, but the name indicates the two main ingredients.

Thus, in May 1886, Pemberton developed the beverage that would later become Coca-Cola. He sold parts of his business to various partners and his interests in the drink shortly before his death to Asa G. Candler, who turned it into the business we know today. Because of controversy over its cocaine content, the Coca-Cola Company has stated that the name was "meaningless but fanciful," but this is yet another myth of the Old South. Coca-Cola contained coca leaf extract until 1903.

Further Reading

- https://www.coca-colacompany.com/company/history/the-birth-of-a-refreshing-idea

- https://www.georgiaencyclopedia.org/articles/business-economy/john-stith-pemberton-1831-1888/

Section XIII

1865: The End of the War and the Lincoln Assassination

Challenges

1. The End of the War

Challenge #XIII-1a,b

#XII-1a

The Hampton Roads Conference was held between the United States and representatives of the unrecognized Confederate States on February 3, 1865. The meeting took place aboard the steamboat *River Queen* in Hampton Roads, Virginia, to discuss possible terms to end the Civil War. President Abraham Lincoln and Secretary of State William H. Seward, representing the Union, met with three commissioners from the Confederacy. There are no official records of the conference, and all existing narratives originate from the subsequent commentary of involved parties. Within the first five minutes, it was clear that the conference wasn't going anywhere because the Confederate commissioners were intent on finding a path to independence.

Challenge: The three Southern commissioners were high officers of the Confederacy.

Who were they and why were these three men chosen for this task?

#XIII-1b

At the Hampton Roads Conference, Lincoln and Seward seemed to be open to discussion on when slavery would be abolished but were adamant that it must end. Lincoln and Seward reportedly offered some possibilities for compromise.

Challenge: What were the two concessions that were discussed?

Challenge #XIII-2

At the end of March 1865, Robert E. Lee knew that he could not hold out in the trenches around Petersburg much longer. The Battle of Petersburg had become a combination of steady slaughter mixed with trench boredom and a recognition that the days of the war were numbered. How much longer and how many more would die? He needed to find a way to break out.

Challenges: (1) Whom did he call to find a solution? (2) What was the outcome of that initiative?

Challenge #XIII-3

For 10 months, Lee had held off three Union armies entrenched around Richmond and Petersburg. On Sunday, April 2, 1865, Confederate president Jefferson Davis was sitting in his pew at Saint Paul's Episcopal Church in Richmond, Virginia. A messenger interrupted the Sunday service to deliver a telegram from General Lee. Lee was with his army, located 25 miles to the south defending Petersburg. "I advise that all preparation be made for leaving Richmond tonight," the telegram said.

Challenge: What had happened that convinced Lee that Richmond had to be abandoned?

Challenge #XIII-4

Faced with the decision to abandon Petersburg, Lee asked Lieutenant General John B. Gordon for his opinion as to the Confederate army's next steps. Gordon advised that the Confederate government should seek peace terms. If the terms were not acceptable, Gordon suggested that the army retreat south. If they could join General Johnston in the Carolinas, their combined forces could concentrate on defeating the Union army under General Sherman. By continuing the war, Lee was venturing that the Confederacy could survive the fall of its capital.

With the Confederate right flank turned, the defenders were exposed to attack from the rear. Grant realized Lee might withdraw his army from

Petersburg, abandon Richmond, attack Sheridan's force, and head south. This was a huge gamble for Lee, as it meant leaving strong defensive positions and hoping the enemy didn't catch on until it was too late.

Johnston was in North Carolina, which is south of Petersburg. Yet Lee went west toward Sailor's Creek, Farmville, and ultimately Appomattox.

Challenge: Why did Lee travel west if where he wanted to go was south?

Challenge #XIII-5

Considered a mathematical and engineering genius, he was Sherman's roommate at West Point, and they remained friends in postings to San Francisco and later in the western theater, where he rose to corps command. His most significant contribution came in a conversation with General Longstreet near the end of the war.

Challenges: (1) Who was he? (2) What was the conversation?

Challenge #XIII-6

The Appomattox Campaign is incorrectly viewed as a straightforward chase, but it was in fact a Grant masterpiece. Lee had a sizable force at the beginning with about 50,000–56,000 soldiers. Grant pursued with only 80,000 soldiers. It was a brilliantly executed set of maneuvers intended to prevent Lee from reaching a supply line. It was the only campaign of the war where an enemy army was captured on a battlefield due to being outmaneuvered. The victory was about much more than "lack of manpower."

Challenge: What body language after the surrender was signed did Lee betray?

Challenge #XIII-7

After Davis was informed at the Sunday morning church service, he immediately issued the first orders for the Confederate government's evacuation. Word spread across the city. It was reported, "quickly from mouth to mouth flew the sad tidings that in a few hours Richmond's long and gallant resistance would be over." The citizens of Richmond could not help but notice the fires in front of the government offices as official documents burned.

Official word of the Confederate government's departure was announced at 4:00 p.m. "The scene that followed baffles description. During the long afternoon and throughout the feverish night, on horseback, in every description of cart, carriage, and vehicle, in every hurried train that left the city, on canal barges, skiffs, and boats, the exodus of officials and prominent citizens was continual."

President Davis's train was scheduled to depart on Sunday, April 2 at 8:30 p.m. It was the second-to-last train out of Richmond. He had already ensured that his wife and family were safe and out of the city. He made sure to take one thing with him.

Challenge: What was on the very last train?

Challenge #XIII-8

The fall of Richmond was marked by a huge fire that destroyed most of the downtown area. A huge conflagration that began on the evening of April 2 and continued into April 3 gutted the center of the city.

The scene greeting the Union army on its arrival was apocalyptic. The fire in the city was out of control. Many buildings had been destroyed, and others were threatened. People of the town, blacks and whites, had no place to go with the belongings they had salvaged.

Challenge: Who started the fire?

2. Abraham Lincoln's Assassination

Challenge #XIII-9

Booth gained entrance to the president's box at Ford's Theater without any problem because the assigned bodyguard, a Metropolitan Washington, D.C., officer, was not where he was supposed to be located, seated just outside in a passageway by the door.

From where he sat, the bodyguard couldn't see the stage, so after Lincoln and his guests settled in, he moved to the first gallery to enjoy the play. Later, he committed an even greater folly: At intermission, he joined the footman and coachman of Lincoln's carriage for drinks in the Star Saloon next door to Ford's Theater.

Challenges: (1) Who was the bodyguard? (2) Who else was in the Star Saloon drinking at that time?

Challenge #XIII-10

Dr. Samuel Mudd, a physician in Bryantown, Maryland, set Booth's fractured leg after the assassination. Booth had fractured his left fibula on his escape from Ford's Theater. The photo shows Booth's boot, found in Mudd's home, cut by Dr. Mudd to minimize pain due to the fracture.

Booth had visited Bryantown in November and December 1864, allegedly to search for real estate investments. Bryantown is located 25 miles from Washington and about 5 miles from Mudd's farm. Of course, the real estate alibi was a cover; Booth's true purpose was to plan an escape route as part of a plan to kidnap Lincoln. Booth's original idea was that the federal government would ransom Lincoln by releasing a large number of Confederate prisoners of war. Booth's plot changed to murder after the fall of Richmond.

Booth met Mudd at Saint Mary's Catholic Church in Bryantown during his November trip and visited Mudd at his farm the next day. Booth stayed there overnight and purchased a horse from Mudd's neighbor to return to Washington the next day.

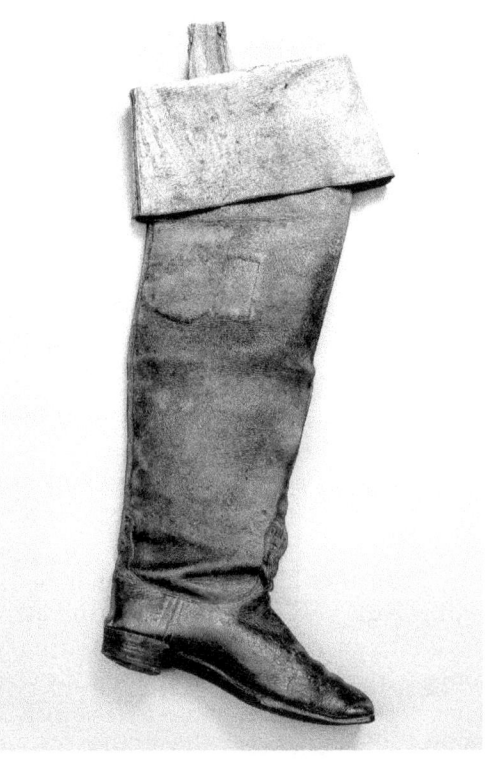

Boot worn by John Wilkes Booth. It was cut by Dr. Mudd to relieve the pain from the fractured leg (Carol Highsmith Archive, Library of Congress).

On December 23, 1864, Mudd traveled to Washington to meet with Booth again. These two men, along with John Surratt Jr., and Louis J. Weichmann, had a conversation and drinks. They met first at Booth's hotel and later at Mudd's hotel.

Mudd knew in advance about Booth's plans, according to written statement made by George Atzerodt while in federal custody on May 1, 1865. Atzerodt said he was sure Dr. Mudd knew Booth's plans because Booth had "sent (as he told me) liquors & provisions ... about two weeks before the murder to Dr. Mudd's."

Mudd was found guilty with the other conspirators. The testimony of Louis J. Weichmann was crucial in obtaining the convictions. Mudd escaped the death penalty by one vote and was instead sentenced to life imprisonment. He was later pardoned by President Andrew Johnson in 1869, in part for Mudd's outstanding service during a yellow fever epidemic at an offshore prison.

Challenge: What is the case that Dr. Mudd should be exonerated?

Challenge #XIII-11

The official investigation into the Lincoln assassination plot was a muddle of peculiar witnesses and unsubstantiated evidence. Without question, the trial had irregularities by today's standards, and the evidence presented was convoluted.

Mary Surratt ran the boarding house in Washington at which the Lincoln conspirators met frequently. She certainly was a Confederate sympathizer, and her tavern hosted many known spies. She may have moved into the city in 1862 after her husband's death precisely to enhance her son's espionage.

Soon after Lincoln was assassinated, a search for the members of the plot rapidly commenced. Mary Surratt was arrested within days of the assassination. She was tried by a military tribunal the following month, along with the other conspirators. She was convicted despite serious problems of evidence and witness reliability. After conviction, five of the nine judges at her trial asked that Surratt be granted clemency because of her age and gender, but it was not granted.

Her son, John Surratt, was a known Confederate spy but was found innocent despite the same evidence being presented at trial 18 months after his mother was hanged. Surratt was tried in a Maryland civilian court, not before a military commission, unlike the trials of his mother and the others. The difference occurred because a U.S. Supreme Court decision, *Ex parte Milligan*, had declared the trial of civilians before military tribunals was unconstitutional if civilian courts were open.

Judge David Carter presided in Surratt's trial, and Edwards Pierrepont conducted the federal government's case against him. Surratt's lead attorney, Joseph Habersham Bradley, admitted Surratt took part in a plot to kidnap Lincoln but denied any involvement in an assassination. John Surratt was released after two months at trial; eight jurors had voted not guilty, four voted guilty. The trial was declared a mistrial. The statute of limitations on any other charges had run out, and Surratt was released.

Challenge: No doubt the conspirators stayed at her home and plotted there. Undeniably, her son was a Confederate spy. Unquestionably, her son was part of Booth's kidnapping scheme. But what was the evidence that

Mary Surratt knew and participated in the assassination, leading to her capital punishment?

Challenge #XIII-12

There are many conspiracy theories concerning whether someone high in the Confederate government ordered Lincoln's assassination, and of course whether or not Booth was actually captured and killed, or if he in fact escaped. Most of these baseless theories lack plausibility because they are inconsistent with obscure details of the crime and the capture.

John Wilkes Booth and David E. Herold were sleeping in a tobacco barn owned by Richard H. Garrett, located about 60 miles south of Ford's Theater near Port Royal, Virginia, on the morning of Wednesday, April 26, 1865. Union cavalry commanded by Lieutenant Edward P. Doherty had caught up with them at around 2:00 a.m. The soldiers surrounded the barn. Lieutenant Luther Baker (a detective) yelled, "Surrender, or we'll fire the barn and smoke you out like rats! We'll give you five minutes more to make up your minds." Booth asked for time to decide and tried to carry on a conversation to stall for time. Finally, Booth said, "Well, my brave boys, you can prepare a stretcher for me! I will never surrender!"

Booth after a while then said, "Oh, Captain, there's a man in here who wants to surrender awful bad." The barn door rattled, and David Herold said he wanted to give up. Herold came out and was captured. He was tied up with rope to a nearby tree.

Booth would not surrender. Using straw and brush, Detective Everton J. Conger set the barn on fire. Booth was apparently visible to the soldiers because the barn was full of cracks and knotholes. They could see him moving inside the burning barn. Sergeant Boston Corbett shot Booth through the neck at this time. Booth was paralyzed and was mortally wounded. Booth was able to say only with difficulty, "Tell Mother I died for my country." A local doctor, Dr. Charles Urquhart Jr., arrived and confirmed that the wound that had pierced Booth's spinal cord was fatal. At around 7:00 a.m. Booth looked at his hands and moaned, "Useless! Useless!" which were the final reported words Booth spoke.

A search of his body turned up a pair of revolvers, a belt and holster, two knives, some cartridges, a file, a war map of the Southern states, a spur, a pipe, three Canadian bills of exchange, a compass with a leather case, a signal whistle, an almost-burned-up candle, pictures of five women—four actresses (Alice Grey, Helen Western, Effie Germon, and Fanny Brown) and his fiancée, Lucy Hale (the daughter of ex-senator John P. Hale from New Hampshire)—and an 1864 date book kept as a diary.

Challenge: Could the identification of his body have been phony and part of a conspiracy to hide his escape? There were reports for years after of the "real" Booth showing up in lots of strange places.

3. Capture of Jefferson Davis

Challenge #XIII-13

On April 3, 1865, Richmond lay in ashes as Federal troops occupied the city and were looking for stragglers. Over the subsequent weeks, Lee surrendered to Grant at Appomattox and Lincoln was assassinated. Davis and the other cabinet members fled deeper into the South, first to Danville, Virginia, then to Greensboro, North Carolina; Charlotte; Abbeville, South Carolina; and Washington, Georgia. Many Confederate officials and officers hoped to escape west beyond the Mississippi or overseas to Cuba or Britain. When Jefferson Davis was finally captured by members of the Fourth Michigan Calvary near Irwinville, Georgia, on May 10, he had only a few dollars in his possession.

Famously, the Northern papers suggested that Jefferson Davis had been caught wearing women's apparel. Secretary of the Navy Gideon Welles noted in his diary, "Intelligence was received this morning of the capture of Jefferson Davis in southern Georgia. I met Stanton this Sunday P.M. at Seward's, who says Davis was taken disguised in women's clothes. A tame and ignoble letting-down of the traitor."

The story of Jefferson Davis's capture became increasingly exaggerated by the Northern press, as one cartoonist after another used his imagination to depict the event in increasingly embarrassing ways. Over 20 lithographs were printed showing caricatures depicting Davis in bonnet and skirt. Some depict him in a dress clutching a knife and bags of gold. These cartoons were accompanied with mocking captions, many of them delighting in sexual puns and innuendoes.

Challenge: Was the story true?

Challenge #XIII-14

It's commonly said that the North won because of more men and more resources. This incomplete answer reflects inadequate reflection.

The final challenge: Give 20 reasons (military and nonmilitary) why the North won the war and the South lost.

Answers

Answers #XIII-1

#XIII-1a

Vice President Alexander H. Stephens, Senator Robert M.T. Hunter, and Assistant Secretary of War John A. Campbell. The two most lengthy accounts of the conference—written by Stephens and Campbell—concur on most of the details.

Stephens, who had given the Cornerstone Speech, had become an antiwar agitator and dissident against the Davis government. Campbell had been a U.S. Supreme Court justice and had opposed secession and the war. He declined many offers in the Confederate government but did accept the post of assistant secretary of war. Hunter had been a Confederate secretary of state and was a severe critic of President Davis.

Davis appointed them, but all three were political opponents of Davis and were openly opposed to the war. Some historians have suggested that Davis, who had no intention to surrender, had purposely allowed a conference that could not succeed to proceed to embarrass his opposition. The single condition Lincoln insisted on—reunion—was the single condition the commissioners couldn't agree to.

#XIII-1b

Lincoln would not compromise on Southern independence or emancipation. Lincoln was unwavering on the issue of emancipation but perhaps flexible in its application if the war would end immediately with reunion. He suggested that if the South rejoined, it would have a place in the debate as to how the 13th Amendment would be implemented. The two concessions that were discussed were the possibility to delay the 13th Amendment being approved or being enforced and the question of compensation for emancipation.

In February 1865, Lincoln had zero reason to compromise on these questions. The war was over except the final act. But the Confederate commissioners had no power to make these compromises and moreover, were not inclined to accept them, even with total defeat in clear sight.

Answers #XIII-2

1. Lee summoned Major General John B. Gordon to headquarters

and Lee instructed him, as Gordon wrote in his memoirs, to "deliver his last blow for the life of the Confederacy." Gordon recommended a surprise attack and chose to assault Fort Stedman.

2. The assault force consisted of three divisions of Gordon's Second Corps. Opposing them were the Union Ninth Corps commanded by Major General John G. Parke. Major General George G. Meade was away at City Point with Grant, so Parke was the acting commander of the Army of the Potomac. Interestingly, Parke did not realize that until after Gordon's attack started.

Gordon's attack started at 4:15 a.m. in darkness, detailed with skirmishers and engineers. Surprise and speed was the key—they carried unloaded muskets so that no one could accidentally fire. The movement achieved complete surprise.

General Napoleon B. McLaughlen, the officer in the Fort Stedman sector, heard sounds of the attack. McLaughlen ordered Battery XII to open fire on his own Battery XI and ordered a reserve infantry regiment, the 59th Massachusetts, to counterattack, which with fixed bayonets briefly recaptured Battery XI. He thought the small breach was sealed. Gordon saw the attack had so far exceeded his "most sanguine expectations." Fort Stedman was seized, opening a gap and initiated an enfilading fire on the entrenchments north and south of the fort. But the attack began to stumble when Union troops formed a battle line behind the fort. The successful Confederates were too confused by the maze of trenches to attack effectively.

Gordon turned his attention to the south, launching a division under General Clement Evans to flank attack the entrenchments. Federal artillery halted the assault. The Confederate artillery from Colquitt's salient began bombarding Fort Haskell and its field artillery answered round for round, along with the massive siege guns in the rear.

Gordon sent a message back to Lee that the attack was going well, but trouble was brewing. The Confederate cavalry had not found an avenue to advance into the rear. Pickett's reinforcement division was behind schedule and the main Union defense force was hardening.

Union forces worked furiously to limit the Confederate penetration and to eliminate the pocket. Federal forces had ringed the Confederate penetration by 7:30 a.m. Further advance had been stopped short of the military railroad depot that was Gordon's objective. Union artillery, aware that Confederates possessed the batteries in Fort Stedman, dropped a punishing fire into them.

Gordon, who was in the fort at the time, realized the plan had reached its zenith and further effort would fail. With permission from Lee, who had arrived to watch the battle, Gordon withdrew. By 7:45 a.m.,

4,000 Union troops positioned in a semicircle attacked. The withdrawing Confederates came under Union cross fire, suffering heavy casualties.

There were 1,044 Union casualties. Confederate casualties were probably much higher, possibly 4,000, but no report was ever filed. The last chance to break out had failed. The war ended a little over two weeks later at Appomattox.

Answer #XIII-3

When General Philip Sheridan's troops overran Confederate defenses at Five Forks on Saturday, April 1, Lee made the decision to abandon the Petersburg defenses and, in doing so, to abandon Richmond. Union troops threatened his main line of supply and retreat. Lee had to abandon Petersburg and Richmond, or he would be forced to surrender.

When the Union army took Five Forks, a vital supply line and evacuation route, they were able to reach the South Side Railroad and the Richmond and Danville Railroad, cutting the major supply routes to and retreat routes from Petersburg and Richmond. They were also in position to cut the wagon roads to the west and circle around Hatcher's Run and attack the Confederate right flank.

Major General Philip Sheridan had defeated a Confederate force from the Army of Northern Virginia commanded by Major General George Pickett. The Union force inflicted over 1,000 casualties on the Confederates and took 4,000 prisoners.

After the Battle of Dinwiddie Court House (March 31), Fifth Corps infantry began to arrive near the battlefield to reinforce Sheridan's cavalry. Pickett's orders from Lee were to defend Five Forks "at all hazards" because of its strategic importance.

At about 1:00 p.m., Sheridan had isolated Pickett on the right flank and front of the Confederate line, while the massed Fifth Corps, commanded by Major General Gouverneur K. Warren, attacked the left flank. Pickett and cavalry commander Major General Fitzhugh Lee did not hear the opening stage of the battle due to an "acoustic shadow" caused by the surrounding woods. Further, their subordinates could not find them; they were at a shad bake several miles behind the lines.

Despite the Union infantry being unable to take advantage of their excellent position because of an absence of reconnaissance, they were able to defeat the Confederate line. After the battle, Sheridan controversially relieved Warren of command of Fifth Corps for attacking too slowly. He incorrectly blamed him for a missed opportunity.

Warren's military career never recuperated. He served as an army engineer for the rest of his life. A court-martial at his request was finally convened by President Hayes, which fully exonerated him. Still, the hero of Little Round Top never received the military advancement he deserved due to Sheridan's action that day.

FURTHER READING

- Holloway, Don. "Chasing Jefferson Davis." Warfare History Network, Winter 2017. https://warfarehistorynetwork.com/2018/12/11/chasing-jefferson-davis/#:~:text=When%20the%20end%20came%2C%20on,to%20the%20south%20defending%20Petersburg

Answer #XIII-4

He needed supplies and hoped to find them in Farmville. The train never arrived, as the Union army stopped it. He needed an open road and maybe a train: the Union army was all over the southern routes.

So, out of necessity, Lee went to plan B: To get far enough west to outrun Grant, then turn south. Grant immediately ordered a general assault to begin in the early morning of April 2, intending to pin Lee's forces in their trenches while Sheridan began to roll them up from the west. But Lee had already left and was on his way west. The Appomattox Campaign therefore was a race for Lee to get sufficient supplies for his men and horses.

The final scene occurred when, at 4:00 a.m. on April 9, Major General Edward Ord, commander of the Army of the James, arrived with the 24th Corps west of Lee. Major General John Gibbon's corps of Ord's army played the critical final role. On April 9, Ord led a forced overnight march to Appomattox Court House to relieve Sheridan's cavalry and force Lee's surrender.

Lee wrote to Grant and asked to meet to discuss terms of surrender.

FURTHER READING

- Reaction to the Fall of Richmond. https://www.battlefields.org/learn/articles/reaction-fall-richmond#:~:text=Gordon%20for%20his%20opinion%20as,retreat%20south%20to%20join%20Gen.
- Sass, Erik. "Fall of the South: Breakthrough and the Burning of Richmond." https://www.mentalfloss.com/article/62799/fall-south-breakthrough-and-burning-richmond

Answers #XIII-5

(1) Major General Edward Ord. (2) The conversation occurred in March 1865 during a prisoner exchange. He suggested that peace talks might be initiated if Lee and Grant had a meeting. That overture ultimately led to Appomattox.

Answer #XIII-6

After Robert E. Lee surrendered the Army of Northern Virginia in the Wilmer McLean house in the town of Appomattox, Virginia, he was described as stoic and reserved. On leaving the home, Lee walked down the steps of the house and threw his fist into his hand three times while waiting for Traveler and rode back to his army.

Answer #XIII-7

Shortly after midnight, a second train departed the Richmond station. The cargo included the hard currency reserves of the Confederate States of America, guarded by a group of young midshipmen from the Confederate navy. Some claimed there were hundreds of crates and barrels containing gold and silver coins, bullion, and a substantial amount of fine jewelry donated by women across the South. In addition, there was more than $450,000 in gold from Richmond bank reserves, taken to keep it from falling into the hands of the invading Yankees.

Further Reading
- "The Lost Confederate Treasure." https://southernsentinel.wordpress.com/the-lost-confederate-treasure/

Answer #XIII-8

The Confederate army; this is not controversial, despite popular history to the contrary. Confederate commanders ordered their soldiers to set fire to bridges, warehouses, and weapons caches before retreating in order to deny them to the enemy. These fires quickly blazed out of control and burned the entire downtown district to the ground. It is unlikely that there was intent to torch the whole town.

FURTHER READING

- https://www.usa-civil-war.com/Opinions/burning_richmond.shtml

Answers #XIII-9

1. John Parker
2. John Wilkes Booth entered the theater around 10:00 p.m. Ironically, he'd also been in the Star Saloon, drinking quite heavily.

When Booth crept up to the door to Lincoln's box, John Parker's chair stood empty. It is believed that Booth knew there was no one on duty because he saw Parker drinking in the saloon.

Answer #XIII-10

There is no definitive evidence to conclude that Mudd knew that Lincoln was assassinated when he set Booth's leg or that Booth had committed a crime. Despite the evidence that Mudd was involved in the kidnapping plot, Atzerodt's statement about Mudd's involvement didn't identify knowledge of murder.

The key points were that Mudd lied about knowing Booth, how much he knew about the kidnapping plot, and his delay to report Booth's presence. That was sufficient to find him guilty but saved him from the death penalty. Interestingly, there were others who knew about the kidnapping plot who weren't convicted in the murder.

A lack of planned involvement in the assassination plot mitigates any participation after the fact. Then there is his Hippocratic oath, which obligated him to treat Booth's leg. The best legal defense was given in *American Brutus* by Michael Kauffman on page 348. Although Weichmann tied Booth to Mudd as cited above, he did not know what they said, resulting in a lack of specificity in the evidence. The fact that Mudd underwent a military trial is important in this regard because the rules of evidence differed significantly from a trial by jury.

FURTHER READING

- http://www.annandalechamber.com/doctormuddhouseandmuseum.rhtml
- https://circulatingnow.nlm.nih.gov/2014/04/14/dr-samuel-mudd-prisoner-and-physician/#:~:text=My%20great-grandfather%2C%20Dr.%20Samuel%20A.%20Mudd%2C%20was%20convicted,epidemi-

c%20at%20his%20military%20prison%2C%20Fort%20Jefferson%2C%20Florida.
- https://columbialawreview.org/.../the-law-of-the-lincoln.../

Answer #XIII-11

Federal soldiers arrested Mrs. Surratt as being a key person within the conspiracy following the Lincoln assassination. Mary Surratt was charged with "abetting, aiding, concealing, counseling, and harboring" her codefendants. She was convicted primarily due to the testimonies of John Lloyd and Louis Weichmann and to a coincidental circumstance. Lloyd was arrested as a co-conspirator and placed in solitary confinement until he testified against Mrs. Surratt.

John Minchin Lloyd was a Washington, D.C., policeman in the 1850s but resigned in 1862. In 1864, he moved to rural Surrattsville, located in Prince George's County, Maryland. He rented a local tavern from Mary Surratt for $500 a year. He served as its innkeeper as well as farmed her land. He was arrested and charged in the conspiracy, and his testimony convinced the government and the military tribunal of the guilt of Mary Surratt, who became the first woman executed by the U.S. government.

Booth spoke with Surratt on the afternoon of the assassination. He handed her a package containing binoculars for Lloyd, who was one of her tenants. Surratt allegedly told Lloyd to have the "shooting irons" ready for pickup and handed him the wrapped package. Booth and David Herold later retrieved the rifles and binoculars as they escaped from Washington after Lincoln's assassination.

Lloyd testified that conspirators John Surratt, George Atzerodt, and David Herold had visited the tavern and asked him to hide "a pair of carbines, ammunition, some rope, and a monkey wrench" on the premises on March 13. These items were hidden in the ceiling joists above the tavern's main dining room. Lloyd later implicated Mrs. Surratt as having knowledge of the weapons. She was convicted and hanged primarily on his testimony, while Lloyd was freed.

Louis J. Weichmann testified about Surratt's associations with Confederate sympathizers. Weichmann drove Surratt to the tavern on April 14 and confirmed that Surratt and Lloyd had spent much time in conversation. He also testified that he saw Booth give her the package of binoculars and attested that she had turned the package over to Lloyd. He confirmed that Mary Surratt had met with Booth no fewer than three times the day of the assassination.

Lewis Powell had returned to the Surratt house seeking Surratt on

April 17. He was suspected of the Seward attack from the start. Military investigators arrived at Surratt's home at about 11:00 p.m. on Monday, April 17 to bring her and others in for questioning. Powell arrived at the house just as they were about leave. He had blood on his clothing and no hat (it had been found at the scene of the Seward crime). She denied knowing who he was. This denial of knowing his identity was later considered prima facie proof of her guilt and led to her conviction. A modern lawyer would have moved to keep this event out of evidence.

Further Reading
- Kauffman, Michael W. *American Brutus: John Wilkes Booth and the Lincoln Conspiracies.* Random House, 2004.
- https://famous-trials.com/lincoln/2163-home
- https://www.history.com/topics/american-civil-war/abraham-lincoln-assassination
- https://lincolnconspirators.com/the-trial/

Answer #XIII-12

We know exactly who identified his body and when; contrary conspiracy claims are bogus. The items found on his person still exist, owned by the National Park Service and held at the Ford's Theater Museum. Only Booth could have owned these effects. They have a long history in themselves. *https://www.fords.org/visit/historic-site/museum/*

Booth's body was sewn up in a horse blanket and placed on a wide plank which served as a stretcher. The body was placed in an old market wagon and returned to Washington. At 1:45 a.m., Thursday, April 27, Booth's body arrived at the Washington Navy Yard and was transferred to the deck of the ironclad *Montauk*.

Several people who knew Booth personally are known to have identified the body. One was Dr. John Frederick May, a surgeon who had removed a large fibroid tumor from Booth's neck. Dr. May found a scar from his operation on the corpse's neck exactly where it should have been.

Charles Dawson, the clerk at the National Hotel where Booth was staying, identified the initials "J.W.B." pricked in India ink on the corpse's hand. As a boy, Booth had his initials indelibly tattooed on the back of his left hand between his thumb and forefinger.

Alexander Gardner, the photographer, was among those who positively identified the remains of John Wilkes Booth, as was his assistant, Timothy O'Sullivan. Seaton Munroe, a prominent Washington attorney, did as well.

The corpse was again positively identified in February 1869 when Booth's remains were exhumed and released by the government to the Booth family. At that time, an inquest was held at Harvey and Marr's Parlor in Washington. Booth's corpse was taken to Baltimore for burial and was positively identified by many people, including John T. Ford, Henry Clay Ford, and Joseph Booth (John's brother).

FURTHER READING

- Kauffman, Michael W. *American Brutus: John Wilkes Booth and the Lincoln Conspiracies.* Random House, 2004.
- https://rogerjnorton.com/Lincoln40.html

Answer #XIII-13

On May 7, the Fourth Michigan received orders to move down the Ocmulgee River and scout on both sides in order to find and capture Jefferson Davis. At about noon on May 8, the Fourth Michigan were informed of a train of ambulances and wagons that were reported to contain Davis's family near Abbeville, Georgia. Near Irwinville, a small village of a half dozen houses, they were informed of a column of horses and wagons that had passed by. A camp was identified, and the army pursued.

Witnesses claimed that three people dressed in women's garb were seen moving toward the road. It is disputed as to whether this was true; no one knows for sure whether Davis was wearing women's clothes or simply a cloak. These three people were Mr. and Mrs. Davis and Mrs. Davis's maid.

The Davises' version diverges in some details. Varina asked Davis to wear a raglan overcoat, also known as a "waterproof." She hoped the raglan might camouflage his fine suit of clothes, which resembled a Confederate officer's uniform. "Knowing he would be recognized," Varina later explained, "I pleaded with him to let me throw over him a large waterproof which had often served him in sickness during the summer as a dressing gown, and which I hoped might so cover his person that in the grey of the morning he would not be recognized. As he strode off I threw over his head a little black shawl which was round my own shoulders, seeing that he could not find his hat and after he started sent the colored woman after him with a bucket for water, hoping he would pass unobserved."

"I had gone perhaps between fifteen or twenty yards," Davis recalled, "when a trooper galloped up and ordered me to halt and surrender."

Davis was captured by a detachment of Union general James H. Wilson's cavalry. He was then imprisoned for two years at Fort Monroe, Virginia, and was indicted for treason, He was never tried because the federal government feared that a Virginia jury might find the Southern secession was legal. His wife, Varina, worked determinedly to secure his freedom, and in May 1867, Jefferson Davis was released on bail, with several wealthy Northerners helping him pay for his freedom.

FURTHER READING

- https://www.americanheritage.com/was-jefferson-davis-captured-dress
- https://www.realclearhistory.com/2021/05/10/was_jefferson_davis_captured_in_a_dress_776296.html
- https://warfarehistorynetwork.com/2018/12/11/chasing-jefferson-davis/

Answers #XIII-14

1. The Union had the advantages of an established government and military with all the foundations and resources of a functional country; the Confederacy had to build these starting with no treasury in the midst of a war.

2. Population Discrepancy: The North had a much larger population and hence a larger manpower pool from which to build an army. North population 1860: 22 million; South population: 9 million (4.5 million whites), 4.5 million blacks of whom 4.2 million were slaves. So the recruitable male population in the North was roughly 11 million and in the South 2.2 million.

3. Economic/Banking/Financial: The North had four times the deposits as the South at the start of the war. The Confederate States of America's economy was built "on the fly": quickly starting from scratch. Much of the economic strength of the South was based on the value of slaves.

4. Industry/Manufacturing: The North had a huge advantage in manufacturing, engineering, and building armaments. The North produced 94 percent of all cloth, 93 percent pig iron, boats and ships, shoes, and so forth. The South had little industrial capacity or know-how. Sherman had this right.

5. Transportation: The North had 80 percent of the railroad miles, all of the same gauge. This allowed rapid transportation of men and supplies among the various cities and battle areas. In contrast, the

Southern railroads were of different gauges, and all led to ports, not interconnecting the cities of the South.

6. Logistics: The North had better plans and more options as to how to bring supplies to their armies. Adjutants Montgomery Meigs in the east and Lewis Parsons in the west used railroads and rivers in innovative ways. Samuel Cooper and Josiah Gorgas for the Confederacy were highly effective as well, but they had limited resources to work with.

7. Political: The North had an established, working two-party government. Lincoln was elected in a fair, free, and universal election. The minority party could build a coalition and channel opposition. The South suppressed any overt opposition, recognizing only one center of political power. The South had to create a government from a culture rooted in states' rights and localism. There was no party system: how do you organize power, patronage, loyalty; can you disagree without being disloyal?

8. Better Military Strategy: Lincoln, Scott, and Grant recognized that the war was about supplies, transportation, and defeating the other army, not the Napoleonic strategy of campaign to capture cities and capitals. The Anaconda Plan, the use of the Tennessee and Mississippi Rivers, and the use of the railroads were critical to victory. In contradistinction, Davis never had a general-in-chief to coordinate strategy. His strategy involved defending wide swaths of territory, which could not be accomplished.

9. Legislative: The North produced a revolutionary set of legislation: the Homestead Act in the west, the Transcontinental Railroad, the Morrill Act of 1862, and the Land Grant College Act, which created agricultural colleges across the country with federal money. In comparison, the South was unable to deal effectively with inflation, lack of gold reserves, or trade/commerce.

10. Superior Political Leadership: The single best answer to this question is Abraham Lincoln. The advantage of leadership he provided over Davis is incalculable.

11. Diplomacy: Britain did not take sides or join the war. Charles Francis Adams performed superbly as diplomat to Britain.

12. Military Leadership: In the end, better military leaders (Grant, Sherman, Sheridan, Thomas). Ulysses Grant found the strategy that won the war and the emotional stamina to see it through.

13. A Moral Goal: Emancipation of the slaves, while not at the outset a universally agreed-on goal, became the central ideological purpose. A new meaning of liberty and freedom.

14. Geographical Advantage: Despite a 1,500-mile coastline,

the ports of the South were blockaded by a huge naval force—the Anaconda Plan. The rivers ran north-south, allowing them to be used as a transportation and supply road—an observation for which General Grant should receive great credit.

15. Squandered Military Advantage: The South had an advantage as a revolutionary insurgency; it didn't have to win, just outlast the North. The South had better officers and better soldiers at the start, but they could not be replaced. In a short war, this might have been decisive, but Davis selected a wide defense and Lee a fighting strategy that paradoxically played to its disadvantages. Lee's strategy of attack was inconsistent with a strategy of protecting scarce resources.

16. Communications: The use of the telegraph as means of instantaneous communications between military commanders in the field strategically with their civilian leadership in Washington changed warfare. The 19th-century "information highway," the telegraph enhanced the concept of military "command and control." The Lincoln administration had the advantage of being able to receive from and deliver information to commanders in the field instantly. Grant was able to communicate with his subordinates in other theaters while campaigning in Virginia in 1864.

17. Psychological Advantage: The South at the start had an advantage of a clear purpose—independence. Did the South lose the Civil War because it ultimately lost its will to sustain the fight? Where was its sense of nationalism? See #18–20.

18. Class Distinctions and Power: Less than 1 percent of property was held by approximately 50 percent of free adult males in both sections. The richest 1 percent held 27 percent of all the wealth. Despite this structural similarity, the economic foundations, and hence its aspirations, were distinct. The Southern planters composed an oligarchy, controlling elections and media, and they perceived that Lincoln's election was a threat to their prosperity. The origin of the war was in the perceived threat to the prosperity of the planter class.

19. Infrastructure: As the war continued, able-bodied men could not return to their farms to produce the supplies needed, resulting in a stagnating economy. What about the farms whose male owner had been killed in the war? Who was going to protect against a slave rebellion? Who was going to watch over the slaves when everyone was at the front?

20. Desertion: Confederate desertions were much higher than the Union, especially during 1864 and 1865, as the war effort seemed to be failing and when the Confederate States of America was bankrupt and Confederate soldiers were told there would be a reduction of pay or no

pay at all. A lot of Confederate soldiers also eventually came to realize they were fighting a rich man's war and their death wouldn't benefit anyone besides wealthy slave owners, so they deserted. This led to notable criminal behavior that stressed the home front even further.

Essential Reading

Catton, Bruce. *The Centennial History of the Civil War*. Doubleday, 1965.
Coddington, Edwin B. *The Gettysburg Campaign: A Study in Command*. Scribner, 1968.
Davis, William C. *Look Away!* Free Press, 2002.
Dew, Charles B. *Apostles of Disunion: Southern Secession Commissioners and the Causes of the Civil War*. 15th anniv. ed. University of Virginia Press, 2017.
Donald, David Herbert. *Lincoln*. Simon & Schuster, 1995.
Foner, Eric. *The Fiery Trial: Abraham Lincoln and American Slavery*. Norton, 2010.
Foote, Shelby. *The Civil War: A Narrative*. 3 vols. Random House, 1963.
Freeman, Douglas Southall. *Lee's Lieutenants: A Study in Command*. 3 vols. Scribner, 1942–1944.
Goodwin, Doris Kearns. *Team of Rivals*. Simon & Schuster, 2005.
Gordon, John B. *Reminiscences of the Civil War*. Louisiana State University Press, 1993.
Grant, Ulysses S. *The Autobiography of General Ulysses S Grant: Memoirs of the Civil War*. https://www.gutenberg.org/files/4367/4367-h/4367-h.htm
Longstreet, James. *From Manassas to Appomattox: Memoirs of the Civil War in America*. 2nd ed. Lippincott, 1912. http://www.wtj.com/archives/longstreet/
McCurry, Stephanie. *Confederate Reckoning*. Harvard University Press, 2010.
McPherson, James M. *Battle Cry of Freedom*. Oxford University Press, 1988.
Pfanz, Harry W. *Gettysburg—Culp's Hill & Cemetery Hill*. University of North Carolina Press, 2001
Pfanz, Harry W. *Gettysburg—The First Day*. University of North Carolina Press, 2010.
Pfanz, Harry W. *Gettysburg—The Second Day*. University of North Carolina Press, 1987.
Potter, David M. *The Impending Crisis: 1848–1861*. Harper & Row, 1976.
Royster, Charles. *The Destructive War: William Tecumseh Sherman, Stonewall Jackson, and the Americans*. Vintage, 1991.
Sherman, William T. *Memoirs of General William T. Sherman*. https://www.gutenberg.org/files/4361/4361-h/4361-h.htm
Tucker, Glenn. *High Tide at Gettysburg*. Bobbs-Merrill, 1958.
Tucker, Glenn. *Lee and Longstreet at Gettysburg*. Macmillan, 1968.

Index

Numbers in ***bold italics*** indicate pages with illustrations

abolition 44–46
acoustic shadow 106, 113, 154–155, 301
Alexander, Edward 92
amputations 272–273
Anaconda *see* blockade
Antietam 131–134, 146–149

Barton, Clara 277–278, 286
Beauregard, PGT 90, 107, 116–117, ***117***
Best Farm ***147***
Bickerdyke, Mary Ann "Mother" 279, 287–288
"Bleeding" Kansas 9–10, 24–25
blockade 38, 69–70, 117–118, 121, 259, 271
Booth, John Wilkes 265, 294–298, ***295***, 304–307
border states 14–15, ***15***, 31–32
Boyd, Belle 251–252, ***252***, 263–264
Brady, Mathew 133–134, 149–150
Bragg, Braxton 94–95, 137, 138–139, 154, 164–165
Bristoe Station 158–159, 168
Brown, John 10, 25
Buford, John 45, 180–181, ***181***, 199–200
Bureau of Military Intelligence (BMI) *see* Sharpe, George
Burns, John ***178***, 179, 198
Burnside, Ambrose 132, 134–135, 150–151, 229–230, 2235, 241–243, 246

Cabinet, Confederate 37–39, 49–50
Cabinet, US 42–44, 53
Chamberlain, Joshua 186–187, ***187***, 205
Chancellorsville 157–158, 166–168
Chesnut, Mary 87
Chickamauga 85, 91, 113, 163–164, 171–173
Chisolm Inhaler 273–274, ***274***, 283
Clay, Henry 5, 7, 20, 22–23, 63
Cleburne, Patrick 95, 111–112
Cold Harbor 221–222, 239–240
Constitution, Confederate 49
Constitution, US 4, 5–6, 18, 32–34

Cooper, Samuel 95–96, 112–113
Corwin Amendment 14, 31
cotton 5, 6, 8, 17, 20, 21, 38, 40, 69, 77–78
Coville, William J. 206
Crittenden, John 13–14, 30
Cushing, Alonzo ***193***, 214–215
Cushman, Pauline 257–258, 269–270

Davis, Jefferson 35–36, ***36***, 47–48, 68–70, 292–294, 298, 307–308
Doubleday, Abner 120, 181, 200
Douglas, Stephen 7–9, ***9***, 23–27; *see also* Lincoln-Douglas Debates
Dred Scott v Sandford 12–13, 28–29

Fire Eaters 38–41, 51–52
First Manassas (Bull Run) 116–117, 120–121
Forrest, Nathan Bedford 93, 109–111, 231–232, 248
Fort Sumter 115–116, 119–120
Franklin 232–235, ***233***, 248–249
Fredericksburg 134–135, 150–151
Fugitive Slave Act of 1850 8, 23–24

Gadsden, James 10–11, 27
Gaines's Mill 142–144, ***143***
Gordon, John B. 292, 295–301
Grant, Ulysses S 83, ***84***, 97, 99, 135–137, 138, 151–152, 217–224, 239–242
Greenhow, Rose O'Neal 250–251, 261–262, ***262***

Habeas Corpus 15
Hampton, Wade 93, 110–111
Hancock, Winfield S. 141, 206, 207, 218, 220, 236, 240, 241, 280
Heth, Henry ***179***, 179–180
Hill, Ambrose Powell (AP) 89, 105–106
Hill, Daniel Harvey (DH) 91, 108
Hood, John Bell 228–229, 232–234
Hunt, Henry 84–85, 100

Iuka 137–138, 154–155

313

Index

Jackson, Thomas J "Stonewall" 89, 105–106, 124–125, *125*, 140, 272–275, 284
James River, Crossing of 222–225, *223*
Johnson, Andrew 42, 52–53, 100, 296
Johnston, Albert Sidney 47, 83, 90, 100, 104, 135–136, 152, 153
Johnston, Joseph E. 88, 91, 104, 107, 120–121, 126, 127, 141–142, 226–227, 243–244, 292
Johnston, Samuel 202

Kansas-Nebraska Act 9, 24
Kernstown 141
Knights of the Golden Circle 253, 264–265
Knoxville 229–230, *230*, 245–246

Lee, Robert E. *87*, 87–88, 101–103, 125–129, 131–134, 146–149, 157–158, 166–168, 176–177, 196–197, 209–211, 237–238, 278, 292
Lee, Stephen D. 120, 161, 245, 249
Letterman, Jonathan 275–276, 284–285
Lincoln, Abraham 4, 14–16, 29–31, 32, 35, 42–44, 45, 47–48, 52–54, 56–65, *57*, 66–68, 71, 75–76, 81, 97, 116, 118–120, 149, 152, 162–163, 169–170, 195, 221–222, 227, 242, 243, 247, 254–255, 265, 267, 291–292, 294–299, 304–305, 309, 310
Lincoln-Douglas Debates 13, 29–30
Longstreet, James 88, 89, 92, 104–107, 127, 130, 142, 144–145, 151, 163, 166, 172, 177, 191, 202–203, 211, 212, 226, 229–230, 235, 238, 244, 245–246, 266, 268, 280–281, 289

March to the Sea 230–231, 246–248
McClellan, George 125–129, 131–132, 141–145, 148–149, 151, 222, 254–255, 267
McPherson, James B. 228, 244–245
Meigs, Montgomery 86, 101
Mexican War 4–5
minie ball 277, 285–286
Missionary Ridge/Lookout Mountain 164–165, 173–175
Missouri Compromise 7–9, 12–13

North Anna 219–220, *237*, 237–238
nullification 5–6, 19–21

O'Rorke, Patrick 203–204
Ostend Manifesto 26–27
Overland Campaign 217–225, 235–245; *see also* individual battles

paper currency 72–74, *73*, 258, 270
Pemberton, John Clifford 102, 104, 161, 169
Pemberton, John Stith 281, 289–290
Peninsula Campaign 125–129, *126*, 141–144; *see also* Gaines's Mill
Perryville 137, 154
Pickett, George 90, 106–107, 190–193, *192*, 211–215, *213*
Pickett's Charge *see* Pickett, George

Pinkerton, Allan 254–255, 267
Prioleau, Charles K. 271

railroads 27, 32, 110, 118, 121, 122, 137, 153, 163, 167, 177–178, 196, 197–198, 221, 226–227, 228, 231, 241, 243, 245, 257, 267, 269, 300, 301, 308–309
Rosecrans, William 85, 138–139, 154–156, 162–164, 170–173, 229, 257

salt 70–71, 79–80
secession 3, 5, 6, 14, 15-16, 20, 27, 30,-31, 33–34, 36, 38–42, 47–48, 51, 68, 71, 75–77
Second Manassas (Bull Run) 130, 145
Seven Days *see* Peninsula Campaign
Seward, William 14, 30, 42–44, 53–54, 63, 291–292, 298, 306
Sharpe, George (& BMI) 255–257, 260–261, 267–269
Shenandoah Campaign 1862 124–125, 140
Sheridan, Philip 220–221, 238–239, 301–302
Sherman, William T. 83–84, 98–99, 113, 136, 153, 164–165, 174, 226–228, *227*, 230–231, *231*, 232, 243–244, 246–248, 292, 308–309
Shiloh 83, 113, 114, 136, 137, 152–153, 155
Sickles, Daniel 42, 43, 52, 85–86, 158, 167, 183–184, *184*, 202–203, 268
slavery 3–19, 21, 22, 23–31, 40–42, 44–45, 48–49, 57–58, 60, 62–65, 67–68, 71, 75–77, 81–82, 291
Special Order #191 131, 146–148
Spotsylvania 217–219, 235–237
Stanton, Edward 43, 54, 85, 162, 171, 178, 195, 263, 270
Stephens, Alexander 36–37, 48
Stones River 138, 162
Stuart, James Ewell Brown (JEB) 92–94, *93*, 109, 158, 167, 177, 188, 195, 196–197, 215, 220–221, 228, 239, 252, 264
Sumner, Charles 10–11, 25–26

tariffs 5, 6, 20, 72
Thomas, George 47, 85, 100, 102, 172–173, 233, 243, 247
Trenholm, George A. 37–39, 50, 259, 271
Tubman, Harriet 22
Tullahoma Campaign 162–163, 170–171, 257

Underground Railroad 6–7, 22, 24

Valley Campaign 1864 225–226
Van Lew, Elizabeth 250, *251*, 260–261
Vicksburg 104, 155–161, 168–170
Vincent, Strong *186*, 203–205

Warren, Gouverneur *185*, 204
Waud, Alfred 193–194, *194*, 215
Webster, Daniel 5–6, 19–21
Wilderness 217–218
Wilmot, David 19

www.ingramcontent.com/pod-product-compliance
Ingram Content Group UK Ltd.
Pitfield, Milton Keynes, MK11 3LW, UK
UKHW041924140426
5217IPUK00014B/299